CW00918314

The

CELTS

Origins, Myths
&Inventions

Thus in the groves of academe do the blind often trustingly follow the purblind.

Ferguson 1998, 268

The
CELTS

Origins, Myths
& Inventions

JOHN COLLIS

TEMPUS

First published 2003
Reprinted 2006

Tempus Publishing Limited
The Mill, Brimscombe Port,
Stroud, Gloucestershire, GL5 2QG
www.tempus-publishing.com

© John Collis, 2003

The right of John Collis to be identified as the Author
of this work has been asserted in accordance with the
Copyrights, Designs and Patents Act 1988.

All rights reserved. No part of this book may be reprinted
or reproduced or utilised in any form or by any electronic,
mechanical or other means, now known or hereafter invented,
including photocopying and recording, or in any information
storage or retrieval system, without the permission in writing
from the Publishers.

British Library Cataloguing in Publication Data.
A catalogue record for this book is available from the British Library.

ISBN 0 7524 2913 2

Typesetting and origination by Tempus Publishing Limited.
Printed in Great Britain.

CONTENTS

PREFACE TO THE SECOND IMPRESSION

I take this opportunity to make a number of minor corrections both to the text (especially names!) and to some of the drawings. Gilbert Kaenel has located the origin of the map of Celtic expansion, published first in A. Aymard and J. Auboyer (eds), *Histoire Générale des Civilisations, Vol. II, Rome et son Empire* (Paris, Presses Universitaires de France, 1954: 51-75), so I have replaced this for the later version published in Moreau's book (Fig. 41). As an addendum I have also added two maps showing my own ideas on the location of the Ancient and Modern Celts (p.232). The two most important publications to appear since I wrote my book are Mike Morse's *How the Celts Came to Britain: Druids, Ancient Skulls and the Birth of Archaeology* (Stroud, Tempus Publishing, 2005), and the papers in the five volumes marking the retirement of Christian Goudineau from the College de France in July 2006, *Celtes et Gaulois: l'Archéologie face à l'Histoire* (Collection Bibracte 12). The conference was a useful indicator of the impact of the new ideas about the Celts – an important group of scholars who largely accept the critique; a small minority implacably opposed; and a majority who have still not realised what is happening! The first panel in the exhibition at Lyon on Celtic religion which accompanied the conference stated confidently that the Ancient Celts were defined by their language; it takes time to eradicate ingrained misconceptions!

One other topic not covered properly in this book is the reason why the Celts became so popular in Britain in the eighteenth and nineteenth century. The idea of being a Celt cuts across the concept of Britishness described by Sarah Colley in her book *Britons: forging the nation 1707-1837*, and there is still little consensus as to why this should be. I have discussed the various possibilities in an article entitled 'Die Entwicklung des Kelten-Konzepts in Britannien während des 18. Jahrhunderts' to be published in the *Viertes Symposium Deutschsprachiger Keltologinnen und Keltologen* held in Linz in 2005, and hope to find a context to publish an English version in the near future. Mike Morse covers this period in greater detail in his book *How the Celts came to Britain.*

ACKNOWLEDGEMENTS

I owe much to my many colleagues who have discussed, criticised, attacked and added to my ideas over the years, in the Hillfort Study Group (dinner after wandering up and down hillforts all day is a great stimulus to conversation!), the Association française pour l'Étude de l'Âge du Fer (in whose conferences and proceedings many of my ideas have been floated), and at the International Conferences of Celtic Studies. I have lectured to receptive but critical audiences in Cardiff and Cork (both more than once), in Edinburgh, and Lampeter, suggesting that my views, rather than being something 'anti-Celtic', are of considerable interest to modern Celts; in Spain and Germany and the former Czechoslovakia; as well as at numerous venues in England; and I have discussed Celts on chat shows in Britain and Australia. The Celts are indeed of worldwide interest!

I must especially thank Mike Morse who continually visited me and discussed Celts while he was writing his doctorate, to the point where we were not sure whose ideas were whose; I certainly owe to him the introduction to James Cowles Prichard and craniology, which solved one problem for me of why in the late nineteenth century the arrival of the Celts was placed in the Bronze Age. I have, of course, discussed the subject often with other 'sceptics', though they may not necessarily share my 'extreme' views: Tim Champion, Margarita Díaz-Andreu, Simon James, Barry Raftery, Ian Ralston, Patrick Sims-Williams, Alex Woolf, and also with Vincent Megaw (despite our public abuse of one another, we still exchange information, and even have dinner together!). In France, Vincent Guichard has helped in many ways including obtaining illustrations, as has Laurent Olivier. In Germany, Jörg Biel at Hochdorf and Sabine Rieckhoff at Leipzig have given me platforms on which to rehearse my ideas; and especially I must thank my Spanish colleagues Gonzalo Ruiz Zapatero, Martin Almagro-Gorbea, Jesús Alvarez-Sanchís, Alfredo Jimenez and Jesús Arenas Esteban, who have regularly invited me to lecture, tour and work in Spain.

However, many of my ideas go back to my student, even school, days, indeed I have had to revisit my sixth-form struggles with Greek and Latin, when I first had to read sections of Caesar and Herodotus. As a schoolboy I dug with Christopher and Sonia Hawkes at Longbridge Deverill, and thus began my training in Iron Age matters (though I found my first piece of Iron Age pottery in Winchester as an eleven-year-old!). I studied in the 1960s in Cambridge where a scepticism of the culture-historical paradigm in Iron Age studies was given birth by Grahame Clark, and David Clarke was giving stimulating tutorials; Roy Hodson and Terence Powell were External Examiners during my time there. I had the opportunity to study in Prague in 1967 when Jan Filip was still Director of the Archaeological Institute, and I remember having coffee with him on my first day there, a stimulus to learn enough Czech to plough through his books with a dictionary! Eva Soudská was my supervisor, and she arranged my visits to Brno and Nitra, forging friendships there which have continued to this day; Natalie Venclová, Karol Pieta and Jiří Waldhauser have helped me on Iron Age matters. At Tübingen I had the fortune to study under Wolfgang Kimmig, and to meet those scholars who have done so much for Iron Age studies in southern Germany, especially Ludwig Pauli, Egon Gersbach and Jörg Biel. France was a later and less formal experience, starting in 1973 with an invitation to dig with Robert Périchon at Aulnat in the heart of the territory of the Arverni, continuing with the inception of the Association française pour l'Étude de l'Âge du Fer in the 1980s under its dynamic secretary Alain Duval, and from the late 1990s an increasing involvement with the Aedui of Burgundy, through the Centre européen du Mont Beuvray and the chairmen of its Scientific Advisory Committee, Christian Goudineau and Gilbert Kaenel. This too was when relationships with Spain developed, and I started fieldwork around Ávila in the territory of the ancient Vettones with Gonzalo Ruiz Zapatero; I was also invited to give courses on the Celts at Vienna by Otto Urban. At various times I have had chances to visit Switzerland, Hungary (where I first met Miklós Szabó), southern Poland, and Denmark, and meet colleagues whose home territory I have yet to visit, Mitja Guštin from Slovenia and Daniele Vitali from Bologna.

To all these, and many more friends to whom I am indebted, I extend my thanks.

INTRODUCTION

This is a book about European ethnicity. This had not been my original interest when I began my work on the Celts, but in recent years for various reasons, questions of identity have become more strong, indeed racism has started to hit the headlines again, and archaeologists forced to consider how their material is used, and abused, for political ends. Though I hope this book will be of interest to a wider public, it is mainly aimed at archaeologists, to demonstrate how we ourselves fall into the trap of illogicality and false interpretation, simply because we do not know where our ideas come from, whether they are right or wrong, and how they fit in with the historical development of our subject.

When I was a student of archaeology in the 1960s, there seemed to be much more interesting and important things to study than the traditional 'culture-historical' paradigm to which the concept of the Celts belonged. It was a time when we were rejecting interpretations of the British Iron Age which saw it in terms of a series of invasions, of 'Hallstatt warriors', of 'Marnians' and Belgae, or which tried to define 'cultural groups' by plotting types of pottery, metalwork, burials rites and settlements in terms of time and space. My own interest was in 'economic' or rather 'socio-economic' interpretations (in prehistory it was becoming clear that economy was not something which could be divorced from its social context). So, in the 1960s, I directed the large-scale excavations at Owslebury in Hampshire specifically to reconstruct the changing economy of an Iron Age and Roman farming settlement, and so better understand the 'everyday story of country folk'. The wider questions I tackled in my doctoral thesis: matters such as the origin and impact of urbanisation in the Iron Age, the function of Iron Age coinage, and the role of trade and exchange (my Owslebury farmers were consuming wine from Italy a century or more before the Roman conquest).

Two events in the mid-1980s brought me back to the question of the Celts. The first was when I was asked to review the first of Barry Cunliffe's reports on his excavation of the Iron Age hillfort at Danebury in Hampshire. The interpretation which Cunliffe imposed on the hillfort, that of a hierarchical 'Celtic' society with a king or chief living in the fort with his warrior nobles and craftsmen, seemed to bear no relationship to the archaeological evidence that had been excavated; indeed wealth and industrial production seemed more characteristic of the smaller settlements such as Owslebury or Gussage All Saints. Cunliffe quoted descriptions of supposedly 'Celtic' societies in Gaul and Ireland to support his interpretation; neither case seemed particularly relevant. However, this interpretation was disseminated to a wide public through popular books, through television, and in the Museum of the Iron Age at Andover where the Danebury finds were displayed.

The second occurrence originated from my involvement in French archaeology, with excavation and fieldwork in the territory of the Arverni around Clermont-Ferrand. Various of my French colleagues were publishing articles about the 'Celticisation' of central and western France, meaning the adoption of 'La Tène' material culture which they believed emanated out from the Champagne area of northern France (the 'Marnians' again!). This seemed to me to be a travesty of interpretation, and it certainly bore no relationship to what I was excavating in central France. One or two of my French colleagues initially refused to accept my chronologies, even though they were based on good stratigraphical observation, in part because they did not fit in with the 'arrival' of the Celts, though subsequent work has confirmed what I was then writing. So why did the Celts have to arrive sometime in the Iron Age? Part of this was due to the concept of Iron Age 'cultures', especially the significance of the so-called Hallstatt and La Tène cultures, and in 1986 I brought together examples in my paper 'Adieu Hallstatt! Adieu La Tène' showing how at various times and places the archaeological record had been grossly misinterpreted to fit the preconceived interpretation. It was a paper which passed virtually unnoticed in Britain and France, but surprisingly had a great resonance in Spain.

The late 1980s–90s I have called a second period of Celtomania with a rash of books on Celtic religion, Celtic art, and the Celts themselves, both ancient and modern; several major exhibitions such as those at Venice and Rosenheim, which attracted thousands of visitors; and the opening of the research centre and museum at Mont Beuvray in France. As we enter the 2000s, this interest has not diminished, with a very successful exhibition on *Celtas y Vettones* at Ávila in Spain in 2001, and a continued outpouring of books (to which I can add this one!). The Celts, at the same time, have become a symbol of European unity as well as of regional identity. However, criticism and scepticism were also growing; an article by Nick Merriman on 'Celtic spirit', and Timothy Taylor's review of Vincent and Ruth Megaw's book on Celtic art, as well as my own offerings in Britain, France and Spain. The younger generation of Iron Age scholars in Britain such as J.D. Hill, Jane Webster and Mike Morse have consistently criticised interpretations based on Celtic formulations; and Malcolm Chapman has openly challenged the modern concept of the Celts from the point of view of a sociologist. Finally, some like Simon James have admitted that they have been swayed by the arguments, and have changed their viewpoints. In Ireland, Spain and France opinion is more divided, though it is generally shifting in favour of the new interpretations; however, there has been a strong backlash from certain quarters about the 'New Celts', particularly from Ruth and Vincent Megaw, and from Barry Cunliffe, and also from historians such as William Ferguson (1998, 176–7).

Yet in all these writings, both for and against, there are repeated misunderstandings and misconceptions, and it is some of these that I wish to lay to rest.

Ferguson, for instance, is confused about Edward Lhuyd's usage of the term 'Celtic', claiming that he never used it (1998, 177). Chapman has stated that the term 'Celt' is something which was always imposed by outsiders on groups of people seen as peripheral, and some have gone so far as to say that they never existed, at least as an entity recognised by the people themselves. This might have surprised some of the ancient authors such as Martial who considered themselves, at least in part, to have Celtic ancestry, and the modern concept of the Celts was something which was developed internally, by a Scotsman, a Breton, and a Welshman: George Buchanan, Paul-Yves Pezron and Edward Lhuyd. Maps are published in many of the archaeological books showing Celts migrating from and to places where we have no evidence there ever were any Celts, or even, in some cases, going in the opposite direction from what the ancient sources tell us!

As I delved deeper into the literature to find out what authors ancient and modern actually said, a whole series of questions was raised which clearly needed answering:

What do the ancient sources actually tells us about how the ancient Celts were defined and where they lived?

Why are Celtic languages called Celtic?

Why do archaeologists often tell us that the ancient sources never said the inhabitants of Britain and Ireland were Celts, and then proceed to tell us about the Insular Celts?

Why do most books talk about the Celts coming from the east, when most ancient sources talk about them expanding from the west?

Why is Celtic art so called when it may not have even been invented by the Celts?

When did the modern definition of the Celts come into existence, that is, as a people who speak, or whose recent ancestors spoke, a 'Celtic' language?

Does it really matter if the modern Celts have little or nothing to do with the ancient Celts?

These are some of the questions which I hope to tackle in this book.

As we shall see, one major problem is the ambiguity of the classical texts on which the whole existence of the Celts is based. There is a lack of geographical precision, especially in the early authors; different definitions of the Celts appear, from a general term covering all the people in the west of Europe to a very specific usage with well-defined geographical limits. Then there is a confusion of terminology, how different authors employed the interrelated terms of *Keltoi*, *Celtae*, *Galatai* and *Galli*.

Some of the questions can be answered, at least in part, by a study of the historiography of the Celts. I shall be arguing that there has been a series of misinterpretations, one heaped upon another, which have been accepted by subsequent generations of scholars without questioning the academic reasoning behind their predecessors' conclusions. Thus, the first person to assume that the Celts were a people who speak, or spoke, a language called Celtic was the Abbé Pezron in 1705; but this was based on the wrong assumption that Breton was the last survival of the language spoken by the ancient Celts of Gaul, whereas it is now generally accepted that it was introduced from Britain in the fifth century AD. Pezron's definition of a Celt was taken over by Edward Lhuyd, meaning that the Welsh, Scots and Irish could be labelled as Celtic too. So, when an art style came to be recognised in Britain and Ireland in the mid-nineteenth century by John Kemble and Augustus Franks which was neither Roman, nor Saxon, nor Viking, it was labelled (Late) Keltic, a terminology subsequently adopted on the continent. The origin of this art style was later claimed to lie in northern France and southern Germany. Its spread was linked in with the nineteenth-century interpretations of the spread of the Celts, developed by Henri d'Arbois de Jubainville on the basis of linguistic theories. Since then, archaeologists have used the spread of this so-called Celtic La Tène culture to document the spread of the Celts. On the back of these supposed migrations, geneticists are now attempting to explain the Celts via genetic variation in modern populations, using DNA.

Thus, anyone dealing with the Celts has to range over a number of different disciplines: classical texts and historical criticism; linguistics; archaeology; art history; genetics; anthropology; and inevitably no one is the master of all of them. There is a danger that we will take as proven, or given, the interpretations of other disciplines, when in fact these interpretations may be highly contentious if not rejected by the majority of specialists in that field. So, geneticists assume that archaeologists can identify evidence for migrations, and archaeologists assume that historical records can be taken at face value to define where the ancient Celts lived. There is a danger of a continuous circular argument, in which we all assume other disciplines have clear answers to questions which we then try to address using our own data sets, such as archaeologists trying to identify linguistically-defined Indo-European- or Celtic-speaking groups. However, there are problems which we all share in common, such as the statistical methods linguists, archaeologists and geneticists use in defining their groups, usually employing only partially preserved data.

This book, though written from the viewpoint of an archaeologist, will try to cut through the Celtic knot of these inter-related disciplines, mainly by looking at the historical context in which they have contributed to the modern concept of the Celts. I will also consider the way in which these concepts were used in the past and in our own societies for political and social ends. I make no claim that this is a definitive statement; as I edit the final version of this text I am becoming aware of sources which I should have read, of interesting byways that I hope to wander along in the future, and also I hope there will be reactions from scholars in those specialist areas such as history which are not my own and whose views I may have misrepresented. The 'origin of the Celts' is a fascinating story which has considerable repercussions well outside its western European context, and here I offer my thoughts.

1

CLASSICAL SOURCES

If it were not for the classical texts written mainly by Greek and Italian authors, we would never have heard of the Celts. The earliest contemporary mention dates to the end of the sixth century BC, the latest to the fifth century AD, after which they virtually disappear until the Renaissance when they are only referred to in the past tense; the idea of being a Celt seems to have died in the generation of Sidonius Apollinaris. There are, however, many problems with these texts, some of which will be mentioned briefly here. There is at present no single collection where all the relevant texts can easily be consulted; information on the various authors was gathered together by Henri d'Arbois de Jubainville, the first professor of Celtic Studies in the Sorbonne, for a series of lectures which he published as French summaries in 1902. W. Dinan had the ambitious aim of publishing parallel Greek/Latin texts alongside English translations, but only one volume was published, and this also includes many references to Britain and Ireland, on the assumption that their inhabitants too were Celts, but which we may not consider relevant.

There are, of course, many problems with the manuscripts themselves; we do not exactly possess first editions! Most are in fact of medieval date, and had been copied, recopied, and copied again, by scribes who often did not fully understand what they were copying, not helped by the common practice of running words together to form a continuous text without breaks. The texts are therefore almost universally corrupt. Not until the sixteenth century did scholars such as Joseph Scaliger start the arduous task of editing and trying to clean up the texts, and prepare them for wider dissemination through the printing press. This tradition reached its highest point in the nineteenth century, when most of the edited texts we now use as standard were first published. However, in some cases, especially where we are using standard translations, we may not be aware of alterations which have been made because they seem to make no sense, but which may be important for our interpretations; one such key alteration, for instance, concerns the routes Livy says were taken by the Gallic invaders over the Alps.

Many major sources do not survive directly or have been completely lost, such as half of the books of Livy's *Histories*. The major loss from the point of view of studying the Celts is the *Ethnography* written by Poseidonius in the early first century BC, though parts of it can be reconstructed, as plagiarism or quoting was extensive in the ancient world; Athenaeus, Diodorus Siculus, Strabo, and even Julius Caesar made heavy use of it in their descriptions of the Celts. For other authors such as Hecataeus of Miletos we have only the briefest snippets of information; Trogus Pompeius only survives in an abridged version written by Justinus in the second century AD; and the full *Periplus* of Himilco exists merely in a poetic rendering by Avienus Festus, the *Ora Maritima*, dating to the fourth century AD, almost a millennium after the original was written.

All the texts are written in Latin or Greek, though, contrary to what is often claimed, the writers include some who had Celtic connections, if not ancestry. The poet Martial several times claims that, as a Celtiberian from *Bilbilis*, his ancestry was half Celtic and half Iberian; Sidonius Apollinaris seems to admit some sort of Celtic ancestry both for himself (from near Lyon) and for the nobility of the Arverni; Trogus Pompeius, from the southern Gaulish tribe of the Vocontii, too, might have labelled himself as a Celt in origin, while the late fourth-century Gaulish poet Ausonius states that two of his colleagues in Bordeaux claimed descent from the Druids. Other authors such as Pliny and Tacitus came from areas which were historically settled by Celts (**1**).

All authors wrote for a purpose, and often this was political or philosophical. Caesar's *De bello gallico* was a justification of his wars in Gaul and to promote his political interests in Rome. Despite his laconic matter-of-fact style and the use of the third person, certain statements must be treated with a certain scepticism, such as his emphasis on the importance of the Rhine as a frontier between Celts and Germans. Tacitus, too, has a strong political agenda, in promoting the activities of his father-in-law Julius Agricola, a former governor of Britain, and in contrasting the degenerate morals of imperial Rome with the noble savages depicted in his *Germania*. Plato and Aristotle, in contrast, wrote disparagingly of the morals of the Celts, most notably of their alleged drunkenness.

Naturally the authors generally have ethnic biases, writing from the attitude of civilised upper-class Greeks and Romans about uncivilised barbarians. The tendency towards ethnic stereotyping is fairly universal, and to describe that which is peculiar or shocking. There is also a general trend through time towards greater geographical accuracy and ethnographic detail, from the vague Hyperboreans of Hesiod, or the brief sentences of Herodotus, to the more informed statements of authors who travelled among the peoples they were describing (Polybius, Poseidonius, and Caesar) or who came from areas occupied by them. Even so, it is often better to produce maps of how these ancient authors might have pictured the geography rather than trying immediately to impose their statements on to a modern map.

As with geographical 'mind maps' we must be careful not to impose our own modern preconceptions on to the ancient authors. We do not know, for instance, how a Celt was defined in the ancient world, and it is clear that there were differences from one author to another. We can, however, be certain that the ancient definition was not ours, and that speaking a Celtic language was not necessarily a

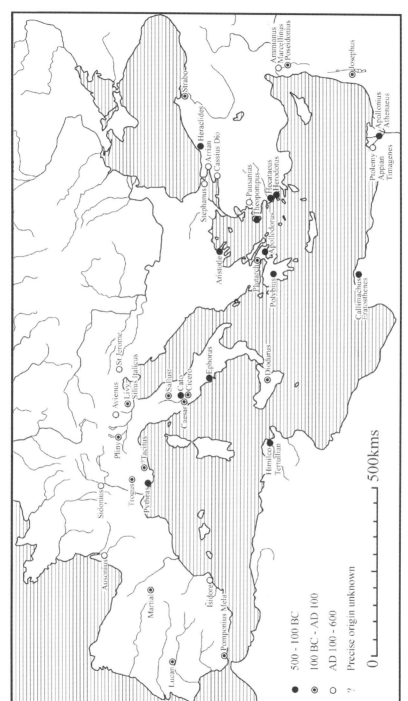

1 *Home town of the key classical authors dealing with the Celts. Author*

500 - 100 BC ●

100 BC - AD 100 ◉

AD 100 - 600 ○

Precise origin unknown ?

500kms

Strabo

Heraclides

Arrian
Cassius Dio

Stephanus

Pausanias
Theopompus
Hecataeus
Herodotus

Apollodorus

Aristotle

Plutarch
Polybius

Callimachus
Eratosthenes

Ammianus
Marcellinus
Poseidonius

Iosephus

Apollonius
Athenaeus

Ptolemy
Appian
Timagenes

St Jerome

Avienus
Silius Italicus
Livy

Salust
Cato
Cicero

Ephorus

Diodorus

Pliny

Tacitus

Himilco
Tertullian

Trogus

Pytheas

Sidonius

Ausonius

Martial

Isidore

Pomponius Mela

Lucan

0

criterion that was used; indeed, even the concept of a group of related languages that could be labelled Celtic was a much later discovery.

I will now give a list of the more important authors who wrote on, or mention, the Celts, in their strict chronological order. Many of the general books on the Celts treat all sources as of equal validity, even though the authors may be chronologically and geographically far removed from the events or places they are describing, and many of the stories we hear, for instance surrounding the capture of Rome, were invented, or first appear, several centuries later. This list is more for quick consultation than for easy reading!

Early sources (700–100 BC)

Homer (eighth century BC) makes no mention either of Celts or other peoples of the north or west of Europe, but he is sometimes quoted for using the word *kassiteros* (tin) which is assumed to be a Celtic word and to imply that Celts in Britain were already producing the metal. In the early sources the term Hyperboreans, as the people who live in northern Europe, the people beyond the north wind, first appears in the poems of **Hesiod**. However, it is sometimes used for the Celts; **Aeschylus** in his lost play *Prometheus Unbound* written *c*.460 BC says the Danube rises in the territory of the Hyperboreans, and as late as the fourth century BC, Heraclides of Pontus uses the name to describe the Gauls who attacked the 'Greek' town of Rome which lay near the great Ocean (an indication of the poor knowledge among the Greeks at this time of the geography of western Europe). However, the Greeks were putting together the first maps of the world, the earliest recorded being that of Anaximander in the late sixth century. At the same time, we are told, in a quotation by a later author, Stephanus of Byzantium, that **Hecataeus** (*c*.540–475) stated that the Celts lived inland from *Massalia*, thus placing them in southern or central France.

The other early source is more problematic, coming from a poem written by the fourth-century AD poet Avienus Festus, the *Ora Maritima*. Part of his highly poetic description of the western Mediterranean contains quotes from the account of a voyage up the Atlantic coast to Britain and beyond in the late sixth century by the Carthaginian **Himilco**, and he refers to the Celts somewhere on the adjacent coast, perhaps as far north as the mouth of the Rhine (Himilco is also discussed by Eratosthenes, Pliny and Strabo). However, the geography is unclear, and many of the peoples he mentions are not known elsewhere, and this has been used to demonstrate the late arrival of the Celts on the coast of Iberia and France. Avienus also uses a description of the coast (*Periplus*) sailing west from *Massalia*, dated by some scholars to pre-600 as it does not mention the Greek colony of *Emporiai* (Ampurias), but others suggest it may be disguised under the name of *Pyrene*. This name only appears in one other author, **Herodotus** (*c*.490/480–424), who says it lies near the source of the Danube, in the territory of the Celts; he also talks about Celts living outside the Pillars of Hercules, on the Atlantic coast. Also possibly belonging to the fifth century (it is summarised by Pindar c.466 BC) is the *Argonautica*, though it is only preserved in the third-century BC version of **Apollonius of Rhodes**. In it the Argonauts starting in the Adriatic sail up a river which has three mouths (generally interpreted as the Po, the Rhône and the Rhine), and they enter the territory of the Celts where there are large lakes, though it is not clear if this appeared in the early versions; they finally exit via the Rhône.

This geographic confusion continues with the next major author to talk about the Celts, the philosopher **Aristotle** (384–322 BC), as he claims that the source of the Danube lies in the Pyrenees, but he knows of the Rhipaean and Hercynian mountains, that is the Black Forest and the German Mittelgebirge (*Meteorologica* I, 13, 19, 20). He is one of the first to start stereotyping the Celts as barbarians: homosexual relationships, fearlessness and crazed mentality; **Plato** refers to their drunkenness. According to Plutarch, Aristotle knew of the Gallic attack on Rome, which, along with the already cited mention by **Heraclides of Pontus**, and one by **Theopompus** (375–306 BC), are the earliest references to the event; there are no contemporary Latin sources. The other major early fourth-century source is the *Histories* of **Ephorus** (405–330 BC), now lost, but used by later authors such as Strabo. He is best known for his division of the barbarian world into four, with the Celts occupying the west, the Scythians the north, the Indians the east and the Ethiopians the south; he mentions Celts in Iberia as far south as Cadiz; he also says that the Celts carry weapons, and suffer penalties for being overweight! **Pytheas** who voyaged up the Atlantic coast around 310–306 BC is the first to describe the 'Pretannic Isles', locating them just north of the land of the Celts. In contrast, the so-called **'Pseudo-Scylax' Periplus** (mid-fourth century) describing the south coast of Gaul does not mention Celts, only Iberians west of the Rhône and Ligurians to the east. We also have the first mention of Celtic mercenaries by **Xenophon** (*fl.* 362 BC) in the *Hellenica* (VII, 1, 20; VII, 1, 31); in 369 Dionysus of Syracuse took a fleet to Sparta including Celts and Iberians, and in 368 there were Celts in a second army under Cissidas which defeated the Boeotians.

The major event of the third century was the attack on Greece in 279 and invasions of Asia Minor starting in 278 which saw the establishment of the Galatians around Ankara. Several contemporary inscriptions are preserved or described by Pausanias (the dedication of the shield of Cydias, the three maidens from Miletus), and there are descriptions of the defence of Delphi by the poet **Callimachus** (*fl.* 285–247? BC); in a gloss on one of his poems Brennus is mentioned as the leader, and he also describes a revolt by Celtic mercenaries in Egypt. Callimachus was the librarian at Alexandria and he was succeeded by the geographer **Eratosthenes** (c.275–195 BC) who followed Pytheas in locating Galatai on the west coast of the Iberian Peninsula. There is a papyrus from Egypt which mentions 'wild Celts', and Celtic mercenaries were also employed in the army of

Antigonos Gonatos king of Macedon; in 274 he was defeated by Pyrrhus king of Epirus who dedicated some shields belonging to Galatai to Athena of Itona in Thessaly which were recorded by Pausanias.

There are four third-century Greek authors whose writings deal with the Celts, all of them lost, and only known from later quotes: **Ptolemy son of Lagos** (d. 283 BC), **Hieronymus of Cardia** (*fl.* 270–260 BC), **Timaeus** (352–256 BC), and **Phylarchus of Naucratis** (*c.*360–270). Ptolemy wrote a history of Alexander; he was a general of Alexander, and mentions two embassies of the Celts, the first in 335 of Celts from the Adriatic who met Alexander on the Danube, when they famously claimed the only thing they feared was that the sky would fall on their heads; the second was at Babylon in 323. Hieronymus came from Thrace and was in the service of the kings of Macedon; he wrote a history of Alexander's successors around 272 BC. Only Pausanias mentions him by name, but he was a probable source for Diodorus Siculus. He is the first author to use the term Galatai (though it appears on the Cydias and Pyrrhus inscriptions), and he says they lived on the edge of the Ocean, and sacrificed humans to the gods. He is also the possible source of Pausanias' description of the Celtic invasions of Greece, and the first to mention Brennos. Timaeus was born in Sicily, but lived 40 years in Athens; he wrote a two-part history on Sicily, Italy and Greece, and importantly he gives the foundation date of 600 for the Greek colony at *Massalia*. He describes the Celts as living by the Ocean into which the rivers of *Keltike* flow. He also has a version of the story of the Argonauts in which they sailed up the Tanaïs (River Don) from the Black Sea and sailed down another river to the Ocean, arriving at Cadiz from the north. Phylarchus is the source of Athenaeus' stories of the eating habits of the Galatians, especially the feasts set up by Ariamnes.

To the end of the third century and the early second century belong the first Latin writings, those of **Q. Fabius Pictor** (b. 254 BC) and **M. Porcius Cato** (243–149 BC); though they are only known from brief quotes, both must have been used by later historians. Pictor was the first Roman historian, and wrote a history from the origins of Rome to the Second Punic War (219–202). He personally served in the Roman army which fought Gauls from north of the Alps, but there is little on the Gauls in the surviving fragments. He names the Volcae in southern France in the context of Hannibal's crossing of the Pyrenees, the earliest mention of them in southern Gaul. Cato also locates them in southern France, around *Massalia*, and is the first to name the tribes of northern Italy, the Salassi, the Lepontii and the Cenomani in the context of the events of 225 BC.

Roman chronologies were based on the *Commentarii pontificum*, the annual records made by the *Pontifex Maximus*, though those before the Gallic attack on Rome had all been destroyed. These sources were correlated by **P. Mucius Scaevola** (consul in 133 BC) and published as the *Annales Maximi*, which gave a basic chronology 'from the foundation of the city'. However, we know that the lists used by Cicero recorded an eclipse of the moon in 351 BC but whose real date was 354 BC, implying some inaccuracy in the early dates. Thus, we find the Roman records date the capture of Rome by the Gauls to 390 BC, whereas Polybius, who related it to historical events such as the battle of Aegospotami, dated it to 387 BC.

This brings us to the first of the major extant works on the Celts, the histories of **Polybius** (*c*.205–123 BC) in which he narrates the historical rise of Rome (five of the forty books survive, and extensive fragments of many of the others). A native of Megalopolis in Arcadia, Polybius was involved from an early age in the politics of the Achaean League which came into conflict with the Roman state. Polybius was one of a thousand hostages taken by the Romans, and he was lodged in Rome as an honoured guest of two of the leading political families, those of the Aemilii Paulli and the Cornelii Scipiones, and he was adopted into the *gens* of the latter. In his sixteen years as a hostage (166–150) he was able to travel extensively, and he continued these travels even after he returned to his home where he acted as the main mediator between the defeated Achaeans and the Romans. We thus know that he visited north Africa (he was at the siege of Carthage in 146 BC), and sailed along the Atlantic coast; he visited Spain (he may have been at the siege of *Numantia*), Gaul, the Alps, and later we hear of him at Sardis and Alexandria. He thus had access to the written sources of Rome and the Greek world, and he went out of his way to interview interesting informants, such as Massinissa king of Numidia, and in Sardis Chiomara, wife of Ortiagon king of the Galatian Tolistobogi, whose story he relates. He also talks of Scipio Aemilianus questioning merchants from *Corbilo* on the lower Loire who were in *Massalia*, which led him to doubt the information given by Pytheas; he was a bit confused about the geography of the northern part of the Alps, believing that the Rhône had its source just north of the Adriatic, a misconception which led to problems in the nineteenth century in identifying the origins of the Gauls who invaded northern Italy. However, his direct knowledge of the sources, the geography of the Mediterranean, and some of the personalities involved in the events he was describing, makes him a prime source on the Celts and the historical events in northern Italy, Spain and Asia Minor, and it is interesting to contrast his narration with later sources such as Livy (e.g. he mentions no conflicts between the Romans and the north Italian Gauls between 390–299 BC, suggesting that some of Livy's wars were fictitious). For our purposes he is important in listing the tribes who made up the Celtiberians in Spain, locating the Gallic tribes of northern Italy, and mentioning the Celts of southern France. The only other Greek authors worth noting for this period are **Sotion of Alexandria** (*c*.200 BC) and **Alexander Polyhistor** (late second century BC) both of whom discuss the Druids, and **Apollodorus Athenaeus** (to 144 BC) who mentions alliances between the Romans and the Arverni and the Aedui of central Gaul.

The apogee of the Celts: first century BC to first century AD

The first century BC is the zenith of writing on the Celts, dominated by the Celtic 'ethnography' of **Poseidonius of Apameia** (135–51 BC), the leading scholar and teacher of his day. Though based in Rhodes, he travelled extensively in western Europe, and his comments on the Celts was based on personal observation in Gaul. The work does not survive, but it was extensively quoted or plagiarised by Diodorus Siculus, Strabo, Athenaeus and even Caesar, so that considerable parts of it can be reconstructed. It is the source of many of the standard stories of the Celts, of the display of human heads, or the role of the Druids in human sacrifice, the power of the Arverni and the story of their king Luernios, the identification of Cimbri with the Cimmerians, and techniques of fighting. Our main source for this is **Diodorus Siculus** (*fl.* 58 BC), who was a compiler of information rather than an original writer, but whose work has fortunately survived.

It has been claimed that Poseidonius recognised the Germani as a separate group, but he seems rather to have made a distinction between Celtae and Galatai on either side of the Rhine, and the name Germani does not appear until the middle of the century, in the description by **Sallust** (86–34 BC) of the revolt of Spartacus in 73 in which Germani and Celtae took part; it was written in 67 BC. This distinction was further developed by **Caesar** (100–44 BC) in his *De bello gallico*, in part to justify his intervention in the domination of the state of the Sequani by the Germanic Suebi under Ariovistus. For him there was a contrast between the Germans east of the Rhine and Gauls to the west; indeed, it has been suggested that in this he invented the concept of 'Gaul', though he did recognise Germans settled west of the Rhine (see **55**), and Gauls (the Volcae) east of the Rhine, though he is vague about their location. Some of Caesar's description of the Gauls is clearly derived from Poseidonius, and though his information may be exaggerated for political ends or personal aggrandisement, and also some is anecdotal, nonetheless his narrative gives us greater detail of the course of the conquest and of his opponents than we have for any other phase of Roman expansion. It helps us locate the Gallic states with considerable precision when linked with later sources such as Ptolemy and place-name evidence.

Cicero (106–43 BC) too is a major independent source of information even though he personally never travelled in Gaul, but as governor of Cilicia he had contacts with some of the Galatians in Asia Minor. His brother was one of Caesar's generals, and he was involved in a major legal case defending M. Fonteius accused of corruption during his governorship of Gaul (*c.*74–72 BC), and in the *Pro Fonteio*, the published version of his text, he is quite scathing of the qualities of the complaining Gauls, mainly Volcae and Allobroges, but he gives interesting information, for instance, on the wine trade. He is equally uncomplimentary about the introduction of Cisalpine

Gauls into the Senate, and the Gallic origins of one or two of his political enemies. On the other hand he successfully defended the Galatian Deiotarus who had been accused of plotting against Caesar, held long philosophical discussions with the druid Diviciacus when he was in Rome with an embassy from the Aedui, and, in what he considered the climax of his career, the unmasking of the Cataline conspiracy, a group of ambassadors from the Allobroges were his main informants.

In the early first century BC it became the custom to deliver grandiloquent funerary speeches for members of the major families in Rome (*laudatio funebris*), and it was in this context that mythical stories appeared to explain the cognomens of some of their ancestors, including some in the context of the conflicts with the Gauls, especially where it was claimed they had engaged in single combat. Thus it was said that a crow had perched on the head of the Gaulish adversary of M. Valerius Corvus, or Manlius Torquatus acquired a torc in his fight. Stories appeared of the involvement of M. Furius Camillus and Pontius Cominius in the events of the Gallic attack on Rome, or of M. Manlius Capitolinus and the sacred geese (though the name Capitolinus was already found in the family as early as 439 BC, and was shared with other major families, perhaps merely indicating that that was where they lived). These invented stories were related in the lost history of **Quintus Claudius Quadrigarius** (*fl.* 80–70 BC), as well as by **Dionysius of Halicarnassus** (*fl.* 8 BC), who also says that *Keltike* extends as far as the Scythians and Thracians, and was divided in two by the Rhine, with the Danube as its southern limit. The mythical stories become common tales, and appear in the work of poets such as **Vergil** (70–19 BC), who talks of the 'glory of Manlius Capitolinus driving off golden-haired Gauls from the Capitoline Hill'. In the works of **Cornelius Sisenna** (d. 67 BC) we find the first mention of Brennus in the story of the attack on Rome. **M. Terrentius Varro** (116–27 BC) gives a small amount of information, such as his statement that Spain was controlled in succession by the Iberians, the Persians, the Phoenicians, the Celts and the Carthaginians.

For the end of the century the major source is the historian **Livy** (64/59 BC – AD 17). Though from northern Italy, his hometown of *Patavium* (Padua) belonged to the Veneti, so was not in the area settled by the Gauls. Of his history of Rome *ab urbe condita* only 35 of the 142 volumes survive, but these are mainly the early ones and so deal with the invasion of northern Italy, the attack on Rome, and the wars with the Gauls in northern Italy, but only small extracts survive on other areas such as Asia Minor. Writing between 27 and 9 BC, he mainly relied on Roman records and traditions, and he is the main source for many of the well-known myths which were prevalent in the first century; his fame lies mainly in his style rather than his critical judgement of his information, and he can be contradicted by other more reliable sources such as Polybius, for example his dating of the Gallic invasion of northern Italy to the reign of Tarquinus Priscus around 600 BC, and linking it to the foundation of *Massalia*. What his source was for the names of the various tribes which took part in the invasion, and especially the prominent role played by Ambigatus king of the Bituriges and his nephews Segovesus and Bellovesus, is unclear. The comparison of his version of events with that of Polybius suggests there was considerable invention in the events in northern Italy which led up to the final defeat of the Gauls and the annexation of Cisalpine Gaul. Some of the same stories were to be found in the lost work of **Timagenes** (80/75 – *c*.10 BC), a Greek born in Alexandria, captured and enslaved at Rome where he was freed by the younger Sulla, and founded a school; he became a specialist on the Celts.

Other authors possibly or certainly came from Gallic backgrounds. **Cornelius Nepos** (90–24 BC) was born in the territory of the Insubres and, according to the poet Catullus, he attempted to make a study of the history of the Gallic tribes. He fixed the date of the capture of the Etruscan town of *Melpum* (possibly *Mediolanum*, Milan) as 396 BC, the same year the Romans captured Veii. Certainly of Gallic origin was **Pompeius Trogus** (late first century BC), who states that he was a member of the Vocontii from southern Gaul. His grandfather had served in Spain with Pompey, and his father Gnaeus Pompeius was Caesar's interpreter, and is mentioned in the negotiations with Ambiorix (*De bello gallico* 6, 36). Unfortunately, his main intention was to write a 'universal history' rather than one on the Celts, and this only survives in the abridgement written by Justinus in the second century AD. However, he does give some information about the Galatians of Asia Minor, and, nearer to home, on the relationships between *Massalia*, the neighbouring tribes and Rome, and the story of the capture of the treasure of Toulouse by the Roman general Caepio.

The major surviving text from the early first century AD is the *Geographica* of **Strabo** (d. AD 19). Though not a primary source (he seems not to have travelled out of the east Mediterranean), he is one of our major informants on the Celts as he gathered together extensive information from many sources that are no longer extant in his systematic descriptions of the geography and customs of each Roman province. He quotes extensively from Poseidonius, and gives us information on the writings of many other authors such as Himilco, Eratosthenes, Ptolemy son of Lagos, Dikaiarchos, Polybius, Dionysus of Harlicarnassus, Ephorus and Asclepiades (who wrote a lost history of the Spanish peoples). The geographical information was becoming more accurate, and we have the earliest cartographic representation which has come down to us, a copy of the map painted for Augustus' colleague **M. Vipsanius Agrippa**, and completed just after his death in AD 12; it was copied with additions in the fourth century and then further copied in the thirteenth century in a form known as the *Peutinger Table*; it unfortunately lacks Iberia, Ireland and much of Britain.

In the epic poem on Hannibal written by **Silius Italicus** (AD 25–101) we are told of the Celtiberians' belief that the souls of those killed in battle go straight to heaven if they are eaten by vultures; he uses Celtae and Galli as synonymous. *Plutarch* (AD 40–120) in his *The Lives of the Caesars* draws extensively on the earlier authors Aristotle, Timaeus and Timagenes, and has a detailed description of Vercingetorix surrendering to Caesar. *Josephus* (AD 37–101) is the latest author to give us information of the use of Galatian mercenaries in the east Mediterranean (Cleopatra had Gallic soldiers in her army and she gave 400 to King Herod Phillip; Galatian soldiers were also present at the funeral of Herod the Great in 4 BC). More important for later writings in the seventeenth and eighteenth century, he is the first to try to correlate biblical and classical sources, and to suggest that the Gauls were descended from Gomer, son of Japhet.

Increasingly, the most informative writers come from the provinces, either ones which had been colonised by Celts, or close to their territories. The epigrammist *Martial* (*c*.AD 40–102) describes his home town of *Bilbilis* (near Calatayud in central Spain), and several times states that, as a Celtiberian, he was half Celt and half Iberian. Another Spanish poet *Lucan* (AD 39–65) is best known for his evocative description of a Gallic temple site in a grove, destroyed at the siege of *Massalia* in 49 BC. He mentions the Gallic gods Teutates, Esus and Taranis, and the Trojan origin of the Aedui. *Pomponius Mela* (*fl.* AD 40–41), also from southern Spain, states that human sacrifice among the Gauls was a thing of the past in his time. Burial of grave goods by Gauls he interpreted as a sign of their belief in immortality of the soul, a belief promoted by the Druids to induce lack of fear in battle. He also mentions Pytheas and the Cassiterides. *Pliny the Elder* (AD 23–79) came from Como in Cisalpine Gaul, though his ethnic origins are unknown. His *Natural History* is full of comments on the Celts, their location, the ethnicity of many of the tribes and Celtic religious beliefs, such as the rituals of the Druids. *Tacitus* (*c*.AD 55–120) was also from Gaul, probably Transalpine Gaul, and his father-in-law, Agricola, came from *Forum Iuliae* (Fréjus). He was mainly writing about the first century AD, so already the Celts had become a thing of the past, though he gives some information on the ethnicity of some of the Gallic tribes such as the Treveri and of more recent events in Gaul in the *Historiae* and the *Annales*. The biography of his father-in-law, the *Agricola*, gives the most detailed account of early Roman Britain and its conquest; the *Germania* provides some interesting comments on the language and ethnicity of German tribes such as the Aestiones, the Cotini and the Cimbri.

The Celts in retrospect: late Roman sources

The writers of the second and third century mainly rely on earlier sources for their information. In the case of *Julius Florus* (*fl.* 98–117), his history of Rome was mainly an abridgement of Livy, and *Justinus* (second/third century AD) in his *Historiae philippicae* does the same for Trogus Pompeius, important as the original no longer exists. More commonly we have information repeated from the original sources. ***Appian*** (*fl.* AD 117–161), born in Alexandria, but who spent much of his life in Rome and wrote about the relationship between the Celts and Rome, repeats many of the myths of Camillus, Manlius Torquatus, and Valerius Corvus. Moreover, he is a major source on the Celtiberians, and follows Lucan in saying that the Celtiberians migrated to avoid famine from Gaul. He also gives some information about central Europe (e.g. on the Scordisci) and the Galatians in Asia Minor. ***Cassius Dio*** (AD 150–235), part of whose 80-book history survives, talks of the surrender of Vercingetorix, the sexual promiscuity of Celts and of polyandry among the Britons and Caledonians; he is one of the sources for the invasion of Britain.

Athenaeus in his *Deipnosophistai* written some time after AD 193 contains many stories from Theopompos, Polybius, Poseidonius, and others, including that of Ariamnes who set up an annual feast for the Galatians, and of how the Arvernian Luernios son of Bityes attained the kingship. Other writers either only give us snippets of information such as ***Arrian*** (AD 95–175) who uses Ptolemy son of Lagos in his lost *Life* of Alexander, and repeats the stories of the Celtic embassies on the Danube and in Babylon. ***Aulus Gellius*** (*fl.* AD 160) used Claudius Quadrigarius in his description of the siege of Rome, but does inform us that *Gallice* was still spoken in Gaul in the second century AD. ***Dionysus Perigetes*** (*fl.* AD 97–117) quotes Himilco and repeats the information on the Kempsi in Spain, and on the Cassiterides and the British Isles.

Diogenes Laertes (*c.*AD 200) made a brief mention of the Druids. ***C. Julius Solinus*** (*fl.* AD 258–268) in his *Collectanea rerum memorabilium* says that the sea near the Cimbri was called *Morimarusa*, Celtic for 'The Dead Sea', a piece of evidence also to be found in Pliny, and taken by Renaissance authors to mean that the Cimbri may have spoken a Celtic language. He also quotes M. Antonius Gnipho in claiming that the Umbrians of central Italy were Gauls, though all other sources consider them to be Italic speaking. ***Tertullian*** (*fl.* AD 199–208), in his discussion of the introduction of Christianity into Spain, Gaul and Britain, says that the Gauls had sacrificed humans to Teutates and Esus, but this had long since ended.

Two second-century authors provide primary and original information. One is the geographer ***Ptolemy*** (*fl.* AD 125–151); his *Geographike huphegesis* is a major source for locating urban sites and geographical features both within and outside the Roman Empire, and he also assigns many towns to specific tribes, including many mentioned by earlier authors, but otherwise not located precisely. The other is ***Pausanias*** (*fl.* AD 173). He is a major source on events in 279 BC, probably using the History of Alexander written by Hieronymos of Cardia. However, in his travels around Greece recording the monuments, he includes ones recalling the Celts and the Galatai, and the attack on Delphi (e.g. the dedication of Celtic shields by Pyrrhus, and the Shield of Cydias).

As late as the fourth century one or two authors were still quoting from the earlier sources. **Ammianus Marcellinus** (AD 330–400) mainly using Timagenes, stated that some of the inhabitants of Gaul were indigenous, but others had come from distant islands or from beyond the Rhine which they had left because of floods and the frequency of war; he also repeats that the Aedui were descended from Trojans. **Rufus Festus Avienus** (*fl*. AD 366) was using several sources in his *Ora maritima*, including Himilco and a lost *Periplus* written in *Massalia*, but as will be discussed in a later chapter, this work presents many problems of interpretation. One fourth-century source, the **Antonine Itinerary** (AD 333), is a major key to the identification of some Roman (and pre-Roman towns). Otherwise we either find authors looking back to the past like **D. Magnus Ausonius** (AD 310–395) who came from *Burdigala* (Bordeaux) and mentions the druidic ancestry of some of his colleagues. Or they give us information about the survival of the Gallic or Celtic language which was gradually disappearing. Thus **Lampridius** quotes the *Historia Augusta* about a warning of defeat received by the emperor Alexander Severus (222–235) from a female druid *in Gallico sermone*; **St Jerome** (AD 331–420) compared the language of the Galatians of Asia Minor with that spoken around Trier (he had lived in both places), and also repeats that the Gauls are descended from Gomer, son of Japhet; **Sulpicius Severus** (*c*.AD 365–425) relates how a visitor from central Gaul was asked by the Aquitanians to 'speak either *Celtice* or *Gallice*, but speak of Martin'. Finally **Sidonius Apollinaris** (AD 430–479), who came from Lyon, but became bishop of Clermont-Ferrand, apologises for the local Arvernians who suffered from the scurf of the Celtic tongue. But this marks the end of the classical sources talking in anything like contemporary terms of anything Celtic. **Stephanus of Byzantium** (*c*.AD 480–500) discusses the peoples he lists in the past tense, as does **Isidore of Seville** (AD 560–636) for the Celtiberians, but after them the word 'Celt' virtually disappears from the literature, though the term 'Gaul' (*Gallus*) gradually becomes the standard term for the inhabitants of Gaul, and eventually the French, and so their symbol became the cock (*gallus* in Latin).

Conclusions

This rapid survey of the sources underlines several major points:

1. Our information on the Celts is derived essentially from three main sources who had direct contact with the Celts, and travelled in the territory of the Celts: Polybius, Poseidonius and Julius Caesar.

2. Much of the information we have has been recycled, repeated and plagiarised from a small number of sources.

3. Much of the writing is retrospective, even that written in the first century BC which is the major period for works on the Celts.

4. Most of the sources are written by Greeks and Romans, and there are no authors from the northern parts of the Roman Empire (northern Gaul, the Germanies, Britain), but, contrary to what is often claimed, there are some who certainly have a Celtic background, and several others who come from territories occupied by the Celts, or close by.

2

THE PEOPLING OF THE WEST

With Sidonius Apollinaris in the fifth century AD the Celts, at least as a contemporary ethnic group, disappear from the literature; Isidore of Seville (AD 560–636) already seems to be talking of the Celtiberians in the past tense, and other authors such as Stephanus of Byzantium (*c*.AD 480–500) in his compendium of peoples even more obviously so. But where the inhabitants of Gaul are discussed, the term *Galli* is the favoured expression to refer initially to the indigenous subjects of the newly established Germanic kingdoms, and later as the expression for the French in general used by authors writing in Latin. Sometimes hybrid names such as *Celtigalli* appear, but where authors wish to be more explicit they refer to the individual tribes as named by Caesar (Latham 1965, 1981). Thus Bede refers to the Gauls, or to the Belgic Gauls, but also to the Morini or the towns where individuals come from (e.g. Germanus of Auxerre); much later we find Geoffrey of Monmouth mentioning the Allobroges.

As previously mentioned, no extant authors speak of Celts in Britain. The closest we have is Hipparchus, quoted in Strabo:

> But this phenomenon [the height of the sun at the winter solstice] is more marked among the people who are six thousand three hundred stadia distant from *Massalia* (people who live two thousand five hundred stadia north of *Keltike* whom Hipparchus assumes are still Celts, but I think they are Britons).
>
> Strabo 2.1.18.

Strabo himself certainly distinguished Britons from Celts (see **50**).

For the origin of the inhabitants of Britain, Caesar states:

> The inland part of Britain is occupied by people who claim that, according to their own tradition, they are indigenous to the island, but the coastal part by peoples who had crossed from *Belgium* with the aim of capturing booty and waging war. Almost all of them bear the name of the states from which they originated. At the conclusion of the war they remained there and began to cultivate the fields.
>
> *De bello gallico* 5.12.

However, he places no timescale on these events.

Tacitus (*Agricola* 11) speaks more generally on the possible origins of the Britons:

> However, who the peoples were who inhabited Britain originally, native or immigrants, as usual among barbarians, has been too little investigated. Their physical shape is varied from which inferences can be drawn. The reddish hair of the people inhabiting Caledonia and the size of their limbs point to a Germanic origin; the swarthy faces of the Silures, their generally curly hair, and their location facing Spain, suggest ancient Iberians came across and settled these areas. Those closest to the Gauls are similar to them, either due to continuing effects of heredity or, where lands jut out opposite one another, the climatic conditions give shape to the inhabitants' bodies. However, in general, it seems likely that the Gauls colonised the neighbouring island.
>
> *Agricola* 11.

In the late classical and early medieval world, authors who conjectured on the origins of peoples largely made recourse to Greek and Latin mythology, as the other major source on the past, the Bible, had little to say on the spread of peoples to the west after Noah's Flood and the Tower of Babel:

> The sons of Japheth; Gomer, and Magog, and Madai, and Javan, and Tubal, and Meschech, and Tiras. And the sons of Gomer; Ashkenaz, and Riphath, and Togarmah. And the sons of Javan; Elishah, and Tarshish, Kittim, and Dodanim. By these were the isles of the Gentiles divided in their lands; every one after his tongue, after their families, in their nations.
>
> *Genesis* 10.2–5.

Attempts had been made by a number of authors to reconcile the classical and biblical sources, starting with Josephus (AD 37–101) in his *History of the Jews*, by Orosius (*fl.* AD 414–417), and by Isidore of Seville, and, while the biblical story was accepted for the origin of the world, many of the Greek and Latin myths could be fitted in with later events. The earliest classical literature available was that of Homer, and like the Romans, many other peoples in the west looked to the dispersal of the Trojans for their origins. Caesar (*De bello gallico* I.33) refers to the Aedui as *fratres consanguineique* ('brothers of the same blood' as the Romans) in a treaty which seems to date back to the mid-second century BC. Ammianus Marcelinus in the fourth century AD makes a more general statement about Trojans settling in Gaul (XV.9.5). More specifically Lucan (*Pharsalia* I 427–8) says the Arverni claimed (falsely) a common Trojan origin as the Latins, and in his

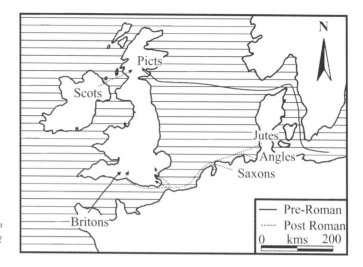

2 *The colonisation of Britain according to Bede.* Author

appeals to Rome for assistance against the Visigothic attacks which the Arverni had hitherto successfully withstood, Sidonius Apollinaris makes a similar claim (*Carmina* VII, p.139). In the seventh century even the Franks were being given a Trojan ancestry (Asher 1993).

One exception to this classical mythology-based conjecture was Bede. In the introductory chapter to his *Ecclesiastical History of the English Speaking People* there is a laconic discussion of the origin of the pre-Roman inhabitants of Britain (**2**). The Britons, he says, came from Brittany, while the Picts came from 'Scythia', that is, Scandinavia, and he contrasts them with the rest of the Britons in terms of their language, and also in their customs (e.g. the use of matrilineal descent), though he does relate that the Scots assisted the Picts to settle when the latter first arrived in Ireland. His description of the post-Roman population movements in Britain still forms the basis for the origin myths of the modern British Isles: the invasions of the Angles, Saxons and Jutes from north-western continental Europe, and the colonisation of western Scotland by the Scoti from Ireland. He talks of the five languages spoken in Britain: Anglian (English), Scottish, British and Pictish, with the fifth, Latin, being that of the educated religious elite. He also sets up the dichotomy between the English and the indigenous Britons, blaming the latter especially for not educating his Anglian pagan ancestors in the ways of Christianity, and for their failure to conform to the norms of Christian practice, for instance in the form of the monks' tonsure and the date for the celebration of Easter, agreed by the Vatican in 532, when also the AD system of dates was adopted, based on the calculations of Dionysus Exiguus. Bede was the first to adopt it in Britain (the idea of counting backwards from the birth of Christ was not introduced by the Vatican until 1627).

However, in the medieval period the predominant view of the peopling of Ireland and the British Isles followed continental fashions in employing the classical mythology of the Greeks and Trojans. The earliest written Irish traditions are those in the *Lebor Gabála Érenn*, the *Book of Invasions of Ireland*, in which the history of Ireland is explained in terms of a series of colonisations and invasions. The story as related in the version in the *Book of Leinster* dating to the eleventh century is heavily influenced by biblical stories, and all the groups ultimately can be traced back to Noah and his son Japhet, as are all the other major nations of Europe. Six invasions are listed:

1. Just before the flood Ireland is occupied by Cesair, daughter of Bith, son of Noah, but this group died out.

2. Three hundred years later it was occupied by Pathelón from Greece, nine generations after Noah. He is claimed to descend from Japhet via his son Magog. The people die out from plague.

3. One hundred and twenty years later another descendant of Magog, Nemed, and his followers arrived. After his death one of his grandsons, Semul or Sémión went to Greece, where his descendants multiplied, but were enslaved. Another, Britan Mael, colonised Britain, giving rise to the Britons, who subsequently the 'Old Saxons drove . . . to the edges of the islands' (52).

4. The *Fir Domnan*, *Fir Galeóin* and the *Fir Bolg* all of whom traced their ancestry back to Sémión. They escaped from servitude in Greece. The last king of the *Fir Bolg*, Eochu, was killed by the *Tuath Dé Donnan*.

5. The *Tuath Dé Donnan* also descend from Magog and Nemed, but came from the north, whence they introduced the arts and magic to Ireland. They include the gods of the Irish such as Nuadu Argatlam, the Dagda, and Lug.

6. The final invasion was by the Sons of Míl, the Gaels. These were descended from Gomer, whose grandson Fénius Farsaid, king of Scythia, was one of the 72 kings present at the building of the Tower of Babel. His younger son Nél went to Egypt where he married the Pharoah's daughter Scota. Their son was Gáedal Glas, eponymous ancestor of the Gaels, who constructed the Gaelic language from the 72 languages of Babel. His successor returned to Scythia, and subsequently voyaged around Europe until they reached Spain. There Bregon constructed a tower and the city of *Brigantia* from which his son Íth espied Ireland. His brother Bile had a son called Míl whose seven sons invaded Ireland, and originated the major dynasties of Ireland.

The story of Míl does in fact have a longer history going back to the eighth century, though Byrne rightly says that 'it is more than doubtful if the *Lebor Gabála* preserves any genuine traditions of invasions, Celtic or otherwise'. Nonetheless various scholars in the nineteenth and twentieth centuries have attempted to link in the linguistic and archaeological evidence with the literary tradition. Also, as we shall see, these legends had a major influence on later writers such as John of Fordun and George Buchanan.

The story of Scota appears in the *Historia Britonum* of the Welsh tradition ascribed to Nennius, written somewhere around 806, but with little elaboration other than that she arrived from Iberia. A second myth also appears concerning the population of the British Isles. Britto, the eponymous ancestor of the Britons, and a grandson of Aeneas travelled from Italy through Syria, Mauritania, past the Pillars of Hercules, and arrived in Britain.

The fully expanded version of the Britto/Brutus story appears in the *Historia Regum Britonum* of Geoffrey of Monmouth, written around 1133. Geoffrey claimed that the historical sources for his stories lay in an 'ancient book' given to him by one of his Oxford colleagues, but subsequently lost. Though other anonymous versions dating to the twelfth century are also known, and it could have been one of these, he is usually credited with having invented much of it himself. In his version we find many of the familiar characters of the national mythologies of England, from King Ceolh to King Lear, and, of course, the story of King Arthur and his conquest of Gaul and expedition to Rome. The Britons too, under another Brutus, were the Gauls who attacked and captured Rome.

The story of Brutus and of the colonisation of Britain is also considerably expanded. Brutus, grandson of Aeneas, was born in Italy, but forced to flee after an accidental homicide (**3**). After travelling in Greece and Mauritania, and passing though the Pillars of Hercules, he came to Aquitaine where he fought a battle on the lower Loire. He and his companions then sailed to Britain, landing at Totnes, expelling or killing the giants who were the only occupants of the islands. He and his Trojans occupied the whole of Britain, and he left part of it to each of his sons on his death: to Locrinus, the eldest, Loegria (England); to his second son, Kamber, Cambria (Wales); and to his youngest, Albanactus, Albany (Scotland).

This myth of the common origin of the kingdoms of England, Scotland and Wales was an important factor in the subsequent relationships between the three kingdoms, especially between England and Scotland, with the English kings using it as the basis for their claims that Scottish kings owed them allegiance. Thus, with the death in a horse-riding accident of Alexander III in 1286, and subsequently of his heir, Margaret, the 'Maid of Norway' in 1290, Edward I employed the myth in his various submissions to the Pope who had been appointed as adjudicator of the competing claims, which were not resolved until 1328 with the recognition by the English of Robert Bruce as legitimate king of Scotland. Brutus appears again in the claims of Henry IV to the Scottish throne in 1401, and the propagandist of Henry V and Henry VI, John Harding, used

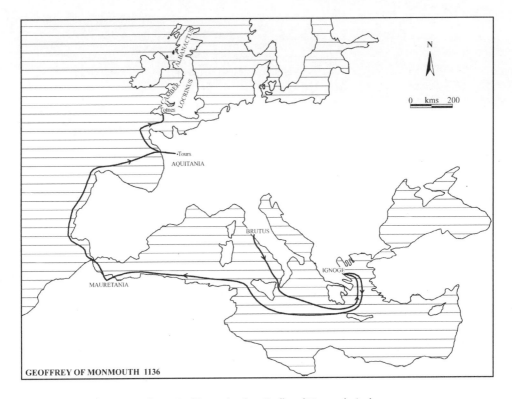

3 *The travels of Brutus, based on Geoffrey of Monmouth.* Author

him between 1420 and 1427. As late as 1547–8, the Scottish propagandist for
the union of the two kingdoms, James Henrissoun, invoked Brutus to support
the cause of the Earl of Somerset, who had invaded Scotland to force a marriage
between Mary Queen of Scots and Edward VI, the unsuccessful 'rough wooing'.
The Tudors considered themselves to be descendants of Brutus, and so to attack
the myth was to undermine the authority of the English Crown, and also to
deny the past glories of England.

The Scottish counter-claims were naturally based on the myth of Scota; this
had already been invoked by Baldred Bisset, the lawyer employed to refute Edward
I's claims to the Scottish throne in the submission to the Pope in 1301, and this
was further formalised in the Declaration of Arbroath in 1320. The story was
further elaborated by John of Fordun (*c*.1300–1385) in his *Chronicle of the Scottish
Nation*, written around 1380, and based on his literary researches in Scotland and
Ireland. In his version a Greek prince, Gaythelos (Gáedal Glas), was forced,
through an accidental homicide, to flee from Greece to Egypt, where he met and
married the Egyptian princess Scota (**4**). They travelled first to Numidia, and then
on to north-west Spain, where they founded the town of *Brigantia* (A Coruña).

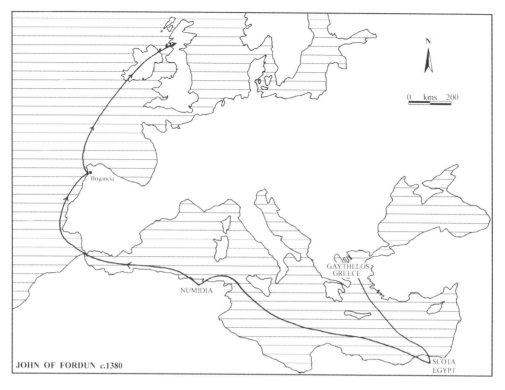

4 *The travels of Gaythelos and Scota, according to John of Fordun.* Author

Later their sons set sail to colonise a fertile green island they had heard about (Ireland), whence later their descendants, the Scoti, set out to colonise Scotland. Under this version, the Scots owed no allegiance to England!

The story was further bolstered by the genealogical claims of the Scottish kings. The kingdoms of the Scots and Picts had been united under Kenneth MacAlpine in the ninth century, under circumstances unknown (one suggestion is that he inherited the Pictish throne through his mother, through matrilineal descent, and that of the Scots from his father through patrilineal descent). The genealogy of the Scottish kings was based on a series of Irish sources, especially the *Irish Annals* and the compilations of Flan Maistreach. On the Pictish side, the succession of the Pictish kings was recorded in the *Pictish Annals* which were compiled between 970 and 1090. There were thus two parallel genealogies to both of which Kenneth MacAlpine might have been able to lay claim, but by the twelfth century they had been conflated into one long genealogy, and from the time of William the Lion this was recited at all Scottish coronations between 1165 and 1317. The truth of what happened was not finally unravelled until the eighteenth century when the pre-twelfth-century sources were rediscovered and published.

By the sixteenth century, historians were falling into two camps: those who continued to recite the foundation myths, and those, like Polydore Vergil, who ridiculed the logic of them, though not providing an alternative version. The Scottish historian, Henry Boece or Boethius (*c.*1465–1536) embellished the rather bald information of the genealogies with sketch histories of each of the kings' names, stories which were further repeated by later historians such as George Buchanan and Raphael Holinshed, the latter being the immediate source for Shakespeare's *Macbeth*. Like Geoffrey of Monmouth before him, Boece claimed access to an old book which was subsequently lost. However, as Ferguson (1998) has pointed out, the model for these Scottish historians was Livy, who had himself incorporated many myths of dubious origin, and it is style rather than critical acumen which was the major attribute of a good historian. The other major history of this time was John Mair's (or Major's) *Historia Majoris Britanniae*, a title which contains a deliberate pun on his name and his theme (the need for the unification of Scotland and England), either *Major's History of Britain*, or the *History of a Greater Britain*.

Before turning to the next major development, brief mention needs to be made of another falsification which became popular in the sixteenth century, and which, for a while, influenced thinking on the colonisation of western Europe, the forgeries of Annius of Viterbo, published in 1498. Annius claimed to have found a manuscript written by a Chaldaean philosopher, Berosus, and an Egyptian historian, Manetho, in the fourth century BC, which stated that the first king of the Celts and Britons was Samothes (d. 2014 BC), son of Japhet, who numbered amongst his descendants individuals such as Magus, Druys, Bardus and Celtes, and who inhabited Britain before the arrival of the Trojans under Brutus. Despite the obvious sources of these spurious names, the story was picked up by John Bale in 1548, and subsequently by John Caius in his history of Cambridge University (*De Antiquitate Cantebrigiensis Academiae*), published in 1568, and claiming that the early inhabitants of Britain were Celts.

George Buchanan (1506–1582)

This, then, was something of the political and intellectual backdrop to the first of the major figures who developed the concept of the Celts, assigning them a major role in the peopling of Ireland and Britain. George Buchanan (**5**) was a classical scholar of international reputation, a poet and playwright (in Latin), as well as author of the history of Scotland which concerns us here, the *Rerum Scoticarum Historia*, published in the year of his death, 1582. He was also deeply involved in the religious and secular politics of his day, and it is important to try to understand his motivation in writing his history.

Between 1520 and 1522 he was studying in Paris, before returning to Scotland to serve in the army of the Scottish Regent, Jean Stuart, Duke of Albany, Comte

5 *Supposed portrait of George Buchanan, after Arnold van Bronkhurst.* Reproduced courtesy of the University of St Andrews, University Museum Collections

d'Auvergne, and uncle of Catherine de Medici. In 1524 and 1525 he studied at St Andrews, where one of the teachers was John Mair, but there seems to be considerable antipathy on the part of Buchanan towards Mair, despite their common sceptical approach towards the medieval historical sources. Mair is not mentioned by name in Buchanan's *Historia*, but he is certainly to be included among the 'Scottish historians' scathingly dismissed by Buchanan; Boece, on the other hand, despite his gullibility and probable falsification, is treated kindly by Buchanan, and was extensively used by him.

Buchanan then returned to teach in Paris, coming back to Scotland in 1536. Here he was moving in court circles, acting as tutor to the illegitimate son of James V, James Stewart, the future Earl of Moray. He was increasingly involved in church politics on the reforming side, and on the king's instigation wrote a poem attacking the Franciscan friars. This placed him in a difficult position with the rise to power of the Guise family, both in Scotland (Mary of Guise married James in 1538 and became regent in 1554) and in France. St Andrews was the scene of considerable conflict between Protestants and Catholics, with the murder of the Catholic Cardinal David Beaton, and the public burning at the stake of several Protestants. Buchanan himself was imprisoned in St Andrews' Castle, but, as he relates in his history, he escaped by climbing out of a window, and fleeing to Paris in 1539. He remained in exile for nearly 20 years, including the period of war with England. He taught in Paris, before moving to Bordeaux, visiting Agen where he had hoped to meet the Latin scholar Julius Scaliger, father of Joseph. He then moved on to teach in Portugal where he was imprisoned by the Inquisition for four years. He was released in 1552 and returned to Paris.

His return to Paris was auspicious as in 1556 Mary Queen of Scots married the Dauphin, subsequently Francis I, one of the sons of Catherine de Medici. Buchanan ingratiated himself with Mary by writing an *Epithalamion* to celebrate the marriage. On the death of Francis, he returned with Mary to Scotland in 1561 as her Latin tutor. With the Protestants' faction now in ascendancy, Buchanan achieved high office, becoming at one point Moderator of the Assembly of the Presbyterian Church, the only layperson ever to hold the office. However, the murder of Mary's second husband, Lord Darnley, placed him in opposition to Mary, and when she fled to England, Buchanan was in the deputation led by the Earl of Moray which handed over to the English the 'casket of letters' which implicated Mary in her husband's death; some have even claimed that Buchanan forged the letters. With the imprisonment of Mary in England, her son by Darnley ascended the throne as James VI, and Buchanan was appointed as his tutor, not a happy experience, at least on James' side. This may have been one of the motivations for Buchanan writing the *De Iure Regni apud Scotos* a treatise attacking the concept of the Divine Right of Kings, and arguing that ultimately kings are responsible to their people who have the right to oppose tyranny; this was one of the works quoted in the condemnation to death of James' son, Charles I.

In Church affairs Buchanan had Protestant sympathies as his brushes with the Guise family and the Inquisition demonstrate. In state affairs his long association with France would naturally have made him pro-French, so not particularly pro-English, though he was abroad during the 'rough wooing'. He would not, then, have been particularly worried about attacking the Brutus myth. However, events in his later life must have shifted his allegiances. The St Bartholomew's massacre of 1572 which confirmed Catholic ascendancy in France, and the swing to Protestantism in England with the ascent of Elizabeth to the throne in 1558 and the conflict with Spain might explain his willingness to help Elizabeth over the matter of Mary's imprisonment. Towards the end of his life he would have realised that he was tutoring the future king of England. The *Historia* dedicated to James therefore had a double role, firstly reminding the young king of the antiquity of the Scottish throne, and so how the two kingdoms should be seen as equals rather than as a kingdom united under English domination; and secondly giving advice to the king by relating the histories of 'good' and 'bad' Scottish kings and their fates.

Much of Buchanan's *Historia* was a regurgitation of the stories to be found in Boece, and it is the first book which concerns us here, dealing with the peopling of Britain and Ireland. Firstly he rejected the myths based on Greek and Roman stories. He argued mainly in terms of logic, that, for instance, it was unreasonable to suggest a small band of Trojans could have multiplied so quickly that they could populate the whole of the British Isles in one generation. Having thus, as various of his predecessors had done, effectively rejected the myths, he uniquely went on to propose his own solution to the question. For his methodology he returned to Pliny, who had argued that there were three ways in which the origin of a people might be identified:

1. By studying their language.

2. By identifying which deities they worshipped.

3. By scrutinising place-names, especially the 'eternal' names such as those of cities and rivers.

Buchanan dismissed the first as he had no direct evidence of the languages spoken by early peoples, and such information as was available was ambiguous, for instance in the statements of Caesar, Strabo, Tacitus, Bede, etc. For the religious aspects he noted the names of certain deities such as Teutates which occurred in Gaul, Spain and Britain, as well as a shared nomenclature for the priestly caste, druids and bards.

His primary evidence, however, came from place-names, especially the names of towns ending in words which could be translated using Gaelic or Irish: -*briga* (hill); -*dunum* (fort); -*magus* (market). He then trawled through all the sources available to him systematically listing their occurrences, utilising, for instance, Caesar, Strabo, Ptolemy and the Antonine Itinerary, in all some 40 or more Biblical, Classical and Late Antique writers (**6**). He noted that these names were common throughout much of western and south-western Europe, especially Gaul and Iberia (**58**, **59**), concluding that the population of Britain must therefore derive from the adjacent parts of the continental mainland, and that all the peoples there had spoken a related group of languages which had given rise to modern Welsh, Irish and Scots Gaelic. He also argued that, contrary to what Bede had written, the Picts too must have spoken a similar language, as there was evidence that Picts, Scots and Britons had been able to communicate with one another.

He thus recognised a group of related languages which he termed 'Gallic' (**7**). His terminology is not particularly precise, but within it he recognised three dialects:

1. *Belgice*, which was spoken in northern France and south-eastern England.

2. *Celtice*, spoken in Spain, Ireland and Scotland, and presumably, though he does not state it, in southern and central Gaul; it was the origin of Irish and Scots Gaelic.

3. *Britannice*, an insular dialect, the ancestor of Welsh.

In contrast he recognised two other major language groups spoken in western Europe, the first derived from Latin, which included Italian, Spanish and contemporary French (*lingua gallica adhuc*); the second was the *lingua germanica*, including German, Frisian, English, etc., and which, following Bede, he accepted as a post-Roman introduction into Britain.

```
          Rerum Scoticarum
omnibus è Gallia esse vel hinc apparet, quòd Galli antiquitus in Thraciam &,His-
paniam,non autem illi in Galliam colonos misisse dicantur. Igitur apud scriptores
idoneos hæc fere huius generis leguntur.
¶Abobrica Plinio in conuentu Bracarensi.                                    50
¶Amalobrica in Itinerario Antonini.
¶Arabrica Plin. conuen. Braca.
¶Atabrica altera Ptolemæo in Lusitania.
¶Arcobrica Ptol. in Celtiberis .
¶Arcobrica alt. Ptol. in Celticis Lusitanis.
¶Arcobrica tertia Plin. in conuent. Cesaraugustano.
¶Artobrica Ptol. in Vindelicis.
¶Augustobrica Pli, & Ptol. in Lusitania.
¶Augustobrica alia Ptol. in Vectonibus.
¶Augustobrica 3. Ptol.in Pelendonibus.
¶Axabrica Plin. in Lusit.                                                   60
¶Bodobrica It. Ant. &lib. de noticia imperij Romani in Germania prima.
¶Brige It. Ant.in Britannia.
¶Brige vicus Straboni ad Cottias alpes.
¶Brutobrica Stephano inter Betim,& Turdulos.
¶Cæliobrica Ptol.Celerinorum.
¶Cæsarobrica Pli. in Lusitania.
¶Carobrica in Turdulis It. Ant.
¶Corimbrica Pli. in Lusi. sed nisi fallor corrupte pro Conimbrica,cuius meminit
   It. Ant. & quæ suum vetus nomen adhuc seruatad Mundam amnem.          70
¶Cotteobrica Ptol. in Vectonib.
¶Deobrica Ptol.in Vecton.
¶Deobrica alt. Ptol. in Autrigonib.
¶Deobricula Ptol.Morbogorum.
¶Dessobrica non longe à Lacobrica It. Ant.
¶Flauiobrica Pli. ad Amanum portum. Ptol,in Autrigonib.Magnum vocat: ac ne-
   scio an apud Plin.Magnum scribi debeat.
¶Gerabrica in conuent. Scalabitano,quæ in eodem Ierabrica.
¶Iuliobrica Pli.& It. Ant.in Cantabris,olim Brigantia.
¶Lacobrica in Vaccæis Pli.& Ptol. & Festo Pompeio.
¶Lacobrica in sacro promontorio Mele.                                      80
¶Lancobrica in Celticis Lusit. Ptol.
¶Latobrigi vicini Heluetijs Cæsari.
¶Medubrica cognomento Plumbaria Pli. in Lus.Hæc ni fallor in Itinerario Ant.vo
   catur Mundobrica .
¶Merobrica cognomento Celtica in Lusita. Pli. & Ptol.
¶Mirobrica in Oretanis Ptol.
¶Mirobrica alt.in Beturia,siue Turdetanis Beticis Pli. & Ptol.
¶Nemetobrica in Celticis Lus. Ptol.
¶Nertobrica in Turdulis Beticæ Ptol.
¶Nertobrica alt. in Celtibe.Ptol. in It. Ant.Nitobrica.                   90
¶Segobrica in Celtiberis. Plin. Ptol.vero Celtiberiæ caput.
                                                         Talabrica
```

6 *Page from Buchanan's* Historia rerum Scoticarum *showing listing of names in* –briga/brica. Buchanan 1582

To establish when and why the pre-Roman colonisation had happened, he turned again to the classical authors, especially Livy and Caesar. From Livy he took the story of Ambigatus and the Bituriges Cubi, and the problems of overpopulation in Gaul. Livy talked of two migrations, one into northern Italy, but the other through the Hercynian Forest into central Europe. Buchanan conjectured that there may have been similar migrations to the south-west into Iberia, to account for the historically documented Celts there, and an undocumented series of migrations to the north and north-west colonising the still-unoccupied Ireland and British Isles (**8**). The only migration mentioned by an ancient source was the Belgae who, according to Caesar, had settled in south-eastern England. His thinking was also probably influenced by Tacitus who mentioned the possible Iberian origin of the Silures and other tribes in western Britain (*Agricola* 11); he thus argued for an Iberian origin for the Irish and the Scots. To support this he noted the name of *Brigantia* (A Coruña) in Spain, and the *Brigantes* of south-eastern Ireland and of northern England mentioned by Ptolemy. He may, however,

7 *Location of 'Gallic' languages according to Buchanan. Collis 1999*

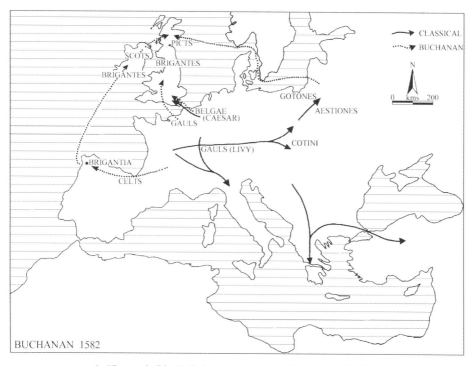

8 *The spread of the Gallic languages according to Buchanan. Collis 1999*

have also been influenced by the long medieval tradition for the links with the Iberian peninsula. As the inhabitants of Spain were called Celts, he suggested a Celtic origin for the Irish and Scots. For southern Britain he suggested colonisation from northern Gaul, especially by the Belgae.

For the origin of the Picts, he followed Bede in looking for an origin in 'Scythia', that is the Baltic or eastern Europe. Here he seized on the statement by Tacitus that one of the tribes mentioned in the *Germania* (ch. 45), the Aestiones, spoke a similar language to the British; Tacitus says also that the Cotini (who Buchanan renders as 'Gothuni') spoke 'Gallic'. According to Pliny (IV.13) the fourth-century BC author Philemon stated that the Cimbri referred to the adjacent sea as *Morimarusa*, a Gallic word meaning the 'dead sea', from which Buchanan concluded they also spoke a Gallic language. The term *Picti* he interpreted literally as meaning painted or tattooed, a practice found commonly, according to Herodotus, among the Scythians. As the Gothuni (Cotini) and Aestiones occupied territory fairly close to the Scythians, he suggested these tribes were the ancestors of the Picts, and had taken over tattooing from the Scythians. For the chronology of these events, he linked them in part with the historical evidence of Livy, so dating them somewhere around 600 BC. Allowing for a period of establishment in Britain, this accorded well with the long Scottish royal genealogy (i.e. that which joins the Scottish and Pictish chronologies end to end) which extended back to somewhere in the fourth century BC.

Buchanan's legacy

In his *Historia* Buchanan is the first author to suggest that the origin of some of the population of Ireland and the British Isles was Celtic (**9**). Only the Irish and Scots were strictly speaking Celtic, while the Britons and their successors, the Welsh, were Gallic or Belgic, and the Picts, though of Gallic origin and Gallic speaking, came from *Germania*. He also rejected the medieval origin myths, though the Brutus story at least was to live on into the early eighteenth century, but the fabricated genealogies for the Scottish crown were perpetuated (**10**). However, Buchanan's theories were only one of a number of competing ideas about early British history. Though his book went through some twenty reprints, most of these were in continental Europe, indeed after the two original editions in 1582 it was not republished in Edinburgh until 1700, and never in England. The reasons for this were several. Firstly his books were almost immediately recalled in Scotland because James objected to the depiction of his mother, Mary, Queen of Scots. Secondly, in England his attitudes towards kingship, and especially rule by females, upset Elizabeth and subsequent rulers; indeed, along with Milton, his books were picked out for public burning in Oxford as late as 1683. As a Protestant he was naturally no longer accepted in Catholic countries, so the only re-publications were in German- and Dutch-speaking Protestant areas, and these often included the inflammatory *De Iure*

IN G. BVCHANANI HISTORIAM, IOANNIS
LINDESII EPIGRAMMA.

PARNASSO nuper ducete (Buchanane) relicto
    Venit ad extremos musa Caledonios.
Nunc addis laudem historiæ: rediuiuaque per te
    Gesta patrum, & patriæ splendet origo tuæ.
Quamque olim mendax ausa est miscere vetustas,
    Ægypti,& Scotæ fabula tota ruit.
Dum generi antiquo nos reddis, origine Celtas,
    Qua fœcunda virûm Gallia terra patet.
Iure igitur patrięque parens,& conditor alter,
    Fergufijs magnis par tibi furgit honos.

9 (Left) *Dedicatory poem prefacing Buchanan's* Historia rerum Scoticarum, *noting the demolition of the Scota myth, and the restoration of the Scots to their Celtic ancestry.* Buchanan 1582

10 (Below) *Historical sources and genealogies leading up to Buchanan's* Historia rerum Scoticarum. Author

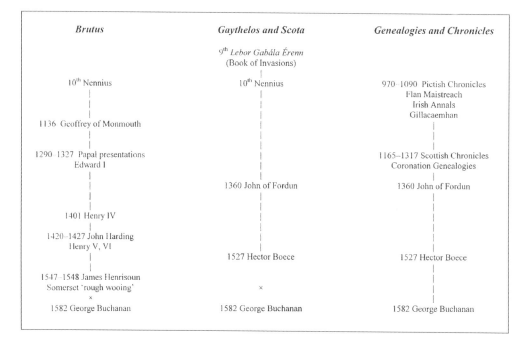

Brutus	Gaythelos and Scota	Genealogies and Chronicles
	9th *Lebor Gabála Érenn* (Book of Invasions)	
10th Nennius	10th Nennius	970–1090 Pictish Chronicles Flan Maistreach Irish Annals Gillacaemhan
1136 Geoffrey of Monmouth		
1290–1327 Papal presentations Edward I		1165–1317 Scottish Chronicles Coronation Genealogies
	1360 John of Fordun	1360 John of Fordun
1401 Henry IV		
1420–1427 John Harding Henry V, VI		
	1527 Hector Boece	1527 Hector Boece
1547–1548 James Henrisoun Somerset 'rough wooing' ×	×	
1582 George Buchanan	1582 George Buchanan	1582 George Buchanan

11 *Portrait of William Camden from the 1789 edition of* Britannia

Regni. However, it was clear that people like Samuel Johnson were reading him (see p.73), and this must have influenced the romantic writers such as Sir Walter Scott, and, as Ferguson discusses, Buchanan was an influential source in many of the religious and political debates in Scotland in the eighteenth century, but for political reasons he was still rarely mentioned by name. The renewed interest in the Celts in the early eighteenth and early nineteenth century may explain the appearance of the first English version in 1827. However, one of the dedicatory poems in the front of the *Historia* says 'so you restore us to our ancient race, Celts in origin, which the land of Gaul, abounding in men, manifests' (**9**).

In contrast, the most influential book on the early history of Britain, William Camden's *Britannia*, first published in 1586, went though eight reprints before the author's death in 1623, and an English translation by Philemon Holland was published in 1610 (**11**). The book was substantially revised on a number of occasions, the last major one in 1695; it has also been reprinted in facsimile in the twentieth century.

In the *Britannia* Camden quotes Buchanan's theories on the Gallic origin of the British, but he nowhere uses the term 'Celtic', preferring rather 'Ancient British', a term which was to remain the normal usage well into the nineteenth century, and which still appears in the archaeological literature today. Camden relates three alternative theories without committing himself to any, a judicious move by an Englishman given the sensitive nature of the Brutus myth to the standing of the English Crown (a recent exhibition of Elizabeth's private possessions included her personal volume of Camden). He thus simply quotes Buchanan's theories alongside the Brutus story. The third theory he advances concerns the origin of the Welsh. This follows the link between the Cimbri and the Cimmeroi made by Pliny (it first appears in Poseidonius and Diodorus Siculus), but makes a further link with the information in the Bible with the sons of Gomer, first suggested by

Josephus in the first century AD, a theme taken up by the early Irish traditions. Thus the three sons of Noah are seen to be the colonisers of the world, each taking over a continent. Ham and his descendents colonised Africa, giving rise to the Hamitic languages (e.g. Egyptian), and Shem colonised Asia, with its Semitic languages. Japhet was responsible for Europe and its 'Japhetic' languages. One of Japhet's sons, Gomer, and his descendants, the 'Gomerians', were commonly equated with the Cimmerians. Camden takes it one stage further by adding a link with the Cymry. The same Gomerian-Cimmerian-Cimbri-Cymry version was more graphically illustrated by Aylett Sammes in his book *Britannia Antiqua Illustrata*, published in 1676, showing a procession of settlers migrating from the east (**12**), and variations on it appear until the beginning of the nineteenth century.

The great difference between Buchanan and these other authors was that Buchanan's theories were not just based upon myth and conjecture, or assumed similarity of names, but from an extensive and systematic assembling of the data, with theory made explicit, and interpretation logically based on the observations, the sort of scientific breakthrough we associate with Francis Bacon and the major scientists of the seventeenth and eighteenth centuries. Sadly, it was not until recent years that Buchanan's brilliance has started to be recognised. His use of place-name evidence was not repeated until the late nineteenth century, and then apparently independently by Holder in his *Alt-Celtischer Sprachschatze* (1896), while his role in the history of linguistic classification is equally unrecognised (to be discussed in the next chapter).

To what extent Buchanan influenced thought in the following century or two is unclear. Certainly he is not generally acknowledged, but we must remember his acquaintance with Julius Scaliger, and his son Joseph whose role in linguistic studies is generally recognised, and some of his ideas may have originated in the discussions with Buchanan (Buchanan and the younger Scaliger certainly met in Paris after the former had returned from Portugal). Equally, Camden did acknowledge him, and Edward Lhuyd must surely have read him in the process of helping to revise for the 1695 version of the *Britannia*, and he remarks in his preface to the *Archaeologia Britannica* (1707) that 'A Third Means [of retrieving the language of the Ancient Gauls] . . . is a comparing of the Proper Names of Persons and Places amongst the Gauls with those of *Britain* and *Ireland*', something which Buchanan had done, and which Camden also mentions. Was he simply ignored, were his works read but not referenced, or did he lay down a climate of thought on which others were to build? Or was he, as Ferguson argues, read, but not mentioned because politically he was *persona non grata*? By the late eighteenth century, however, Boswell's mentions of him suggest his work was well known in the Hebrides.

The final important area of enquiry which we should note in the late sixteenth and seventeenth centuries was the various attempts to devise a biblical chronology, such as Joseph Scaliger's *Eusebii Thesaurus Annalium* (1606). From 1627 the Vatican officially recognised a method of counting backwards from the birth of Christ to give dates 'before Christ'. The traditional Byzantine

12 *Migration of the Cimmerians according to Aylet Sammes 1676.* Copyright Society of Antiquaries of London

chronology envisaged the creation of the Earth in 5009 BC, but in the west James Ussher's (1581–1656) calculations in the *Annalium* (1650 and 1654) and *Annales Veteris Testamenti* in 1659 became the official explicit chronology for the origin of the world and its peopling and appeared in the margin of the Authorised Version of the Bible. Thus the creation of the world was placed at 4004 BC, and Noah's Flood at 2350 BC. The colonisation of the world took place after the collapse of the Tower of Babel, at the same time as the languages of the world came into existence.

3

PEOPLE AND LANGUAGES

In the ancient world there is no evidence of any attempts at classifying languages or understanding their relationships. Though language was clearly considered to be one of the defining characteristics of ethnicity, it was not used as the deciding factor as it can be in the modern world. Greeks may speak Greek, Gauls Gallic and Romans Latin, but we also encounter cases where language is ignored. Thus Caesar contrasts Aquitani, Celtae and Belgae, stating that they all spoke different languages, but it is clear from both Caesar himself and other sources that the Belgae and Celtae, and indeed the Britanni, spoke dialects of the same language, or closely related languages, what we nowadays label as Celtic languages. Some of the Aquitani may also have been Celtic speaking, but others were not, speaking languages related to Iberian, or even the ancestor of modern Basque. In the *Agricola*, Tacitus also mentions the similarity between the languages spoken in Gaul and Britain.

But as we have seen, Tacitus refers to Germanic tribes who spoke *Britannice*. What actually does he mean by this? He certainly would have had no direct experience himself, but someone seems to have decided that these languages were not dialects of the languages normally spoken by Germani. In the case of the Aestiones in the *Germania* (ch. 45) whose language he describes as *lingua Britannicae proprior* ('their language closer to British'), we might conjecture it was a Baltic language (possibly Prussian, *Prutenicus*, which might be confused with *Britannicus*). On the other hand, in the case of the Cotini, who inhabited roughly northern Slovakia, he says their language indicates they are Gauls rather than Germans, so in this case the language was decisive (*Germania* 43). It is also interesting to note that Tacitus says the Treveri considered themselves to be Germani (*Germania* 28), though we know that they spoke a Celtic dialect. We must extend similar scepticism to Bede's statement that the Picts spoke a different language from the Britons and Scots.

References to what we assume to be Celtic languages occur a number of times in the ancient texts. We have already mentioned the views of Tacitus about *Britannice* being spoken by certain Germanic tribes, and it is strange that he should use this term rather than *Gallice*. The latter is the normal term for languages spoken by the Gauls, but just occasionally there are references to *Celtice*. Sulpicius Severus writing around AD 400 relates how a northern Gaul asks his more refined colleagues from Aquitaine if he should speak Latin when describing the life of Martin of Tours. The reply is:

> *Vel celtice, aut, si mavis, gallice loquere, dummodo iam Martinum loquaris.*
> Speak Celtic, or, if you prefer, Gallic, as long as you talk of Martin.
>
> *Dialogia* 3.

Here the two terms are either being used to contrast the two languages as being different, or rather it may have been a way of underlining the fact that Latin was not being used. Sidonius Apollinaris is likewise ambiguous:

> Due to you personally our nobility, in sloughing off the scurf of Celtic speech, now is imbued with a rhetorical style, now even with the measures of the Muses.
>
> *Letters*, Book III.3, to Ecdicius.

Did he mean by *sermonis Celtici* that the Arvernian elite in the fifth century AD still spoke a Celtic language, or did they merely speak Latin with a strong regional accent and vocabulary, the predecessor of Arvernian, a dialect of southern French, the *langue d'Oc*? Whatever, the comment is contrived, as Sidonius himself was not Arvernian in origin, but came from near Lyon, and he was writing to his brother-in-law, Ecdicius, son of the emperor Avitus, both of them Arvernian (Avitus' name is probably preserved in the name of the modern village and lake of Aydat, which Sidonius describes in his letters).

Early language classifications

The earliest attempt we know of to classify languages systematically was by the poet **Dante Alighieri** (1265–1321). He argued in *De vulgari eloquentia* that the original language of Adam was Hebrew, and that other languages derived from the time of the Tower of Babel. He recognised three groups of languages in Europe, Greek, northern and southern. The northern, 'Slavonians, Hungarians, Teutons, Saxons, English and many other nations', were distinguished by the word *jo* for the word *yes*. East of Hungary, other languages predominated. In the south there was a common language, but that also divided into three variants, Spanish, Italian and French, likewise distinguished by the word *yes*: *oc* (west of Genoa), *si* (east and south of Genoa) and *oil* (north of the other two). He argued that they had a common origin, as evidenced by words such as *deus, coelum, terram, vivit, moritur* and *amat*. These similarities and differences were due to the natural evolution of the spoken word which could be found in all languages, and suggested that the modern inhabitants of each region or town would have difficulty in understanding their ancestors. He took the example of Italy with its many regional dialects, and even variation within individual cities such as Bologna. He contrasted the 'vulgar tongue' with 'grammar', a set of agreed conventions which prevent too much variation. His main aim was to define the best version of Italian for writing poetry, but he is clearly defining what we now call the Romance languages, recognising a common origin, and explaining the mechanisms for change. His knowledge of the languages of northern Europe was clearly limited.

The next chronologically is **George Buchanan** (1582), whose ideas we have already discussed. He recognised three groups:

linguae latinae (Italian, French: the Romance languages)

linguae germanicae (English, German, Frisian: Germanic languages)

linguae gallicae (Belgic, Britannic and Celtic: Celtic languages)

Nowhere does he discuss his criteria, and he only deals with his Gallic group in any detail. In the case of Gallic it seems to have been largely on the basis of vocabulary.

The next classification is that of **Joseph Scaliger** (1540–1609), published posthumously in 1610. I have noted earlier the personal contact that had existed between the Scaligers, father and son, and George Buchanan. He introduced the concept of 'mother languages' (*matrices linguae*), by which an original language could give birth to later languages, as Latin had done for Italian, French and Spanish, e.g. the use of the word *gener* (Latin), *genero* (Italian), *yerno* (Spanish) and *gendre* (French). He identified eleven mother language groups in Europe, of which four were important, distinguished on the basis of their word for 'God':

Deus (Latin, Italian, French, etc.: Romance languages)

Theos (Greek)

Godt (German, English: Germanic languages)

Boge (Russian: Slavic languages)

The other seven languages (using modern terms) were: Albanian, Tartar, Hungarian, Finnish (with Lappish), Irish (with Scots Gaelic), Welsh (with Breton), and Basque. Unlike Buchanan, he did not recognise the links between Irish and Welsh.

Finally we should note the contribution of **Gottfried Wilhelm von Leibnitz** (1646–1716). He further developed the idea of Scaliger that Hebrew was not the mother language, and so argued that the other original 'mother' languages must have occurred at the time of the Tower of Babel, which were then transmitted throughout the world by the descendants of the sons of Noah; of these 'Original Languages', 'Japhetic', or 'Kelto-Skythian' dominated in northern Europe, and 'Aramaic' the south. Similarities between languages, such as shared vocabulary, could be explained by cross influence, and one language adopting words from another.

13 *The Abbé Paul-Yves Pezron.* Pezron 1809

Paul–Yves Pezron (1639–1706)

This Breton monk (**13**) was arguably the most influential figure in the development of the modern concept of the Celts (there are notes on his life in Pezron
1809). The abbot of La Charmoie Monastery in Paris, he published his major
work *L'Antiquité de la Nation et de la Langue Celtique* in 1703, and it was quickly
translated by D. Jones into English as *The Antiquities of Nations, more particularly of
the Celtae or Gauls, taken to be originally the same as our Ancient Britains*, and published
in 1706. His theoretical basis was very close to that of von Lebnitz, but in addition
he used the theories of Euhemerus, which claim that events in classical mythology
are based ultimately on real events, and that behind the names of the gods were
real historical characters.

His basic premise, false as we now know it to be, was that Breton was the last
surviving remnant of the pre-Roman languages of Gaul. As the Armorican tribes
had been classified by Caesar as 'Celtae', by definition Breton must be the descendant of the Celtic language mentioned by the ancient authors. He further claimed
that this Celtic language was one of the 'Original Languages' spoken at the time
of the Tower of Babel. He noted that in Greek, German and Latin there were
many words similar to those in Breton, and thus betrayed periods when Celtic had
been in close contact with those languages, and in his appendices he listed the
similar words in these languages. According to Pezron, nations were defined by
their languages, so Greeks were defined by the Greek language, Romans by Latin,
Germans by German, and therefore Celts by the Celtic language.

His major aim was to trace the Celts and their ancestors from the time of the
Tower of Babel to the ancient Celts. Like many of his contemporaries he saw their

origin in the Gomerians, who then developed into the Cimmerians and Cimbri, and finally the Celtae. The similarities, which he could see with other languages such as Greek and Latin, he interpreted as traces of periods when the Celts were overlords of these other nations, in the period when they were gradually moving westwards. So the Titans of Greek mythology were simply a mythological memory of the Celtic-speaking kings, while Saturn and Neptune, Celtic kings of the Italians, later became part of the Roman pantheon.

Fanciful though this historical reconstruction may seem, it did not seem outrageous to Pezron's contemporaries; indeed, it was in the main stream of thought about the origins of nations and languages until the end of the eighteenth century. The English translation had an enormous impact, on Edward Lhuyd and Henry Rowlands; Pezron had recognised the similarities between Welsh and Breton, and so claimed that the Ancient British population had reached Britain via Celtic Gaul. Thus the Welsh too were Celts. He makes no mention of the Irish or of Scots Gaelic, but from this time onwards the Welsh were considered to be of Celtic descent, and Celts were defined by the language they spoke.

Edward Lhuyd (1660–1709)

Lhuyd (**14**) was a Welshman who became the second curator of the Ashmolean Museum in Oxford, successor to Dr Plot. He was also a friend of the naturalist John Ray, and it was from him that Lhuyd's interests in fossils, plants, languages, and their classification, largely derived. Lhuyd was originally requested to provide the contribution on antiquities in the revised version of Camden's *Britannia* which appeared under the editorship of Edmund Gibson in 1695. For his contribution, Lhuyd had developed the novel idea of sending questionnaires to educated landowners and clergymen around the country asking for information on antiquities and monuments, and he soon decided to write his own book, the *Archaeologia Britannica*, which would include sections on monuments and languages. To supplement the information gained from his correspondents, he himself undertook a number of not uneventful journeys in Britain and Ireland. In Ireland he was briefly held captive by Tory brigands, but his trip to Brittany to meet the Abbé Pezron was even more disastrous. Not only did he never meet Pezron, or receive any reply to his letters, but immediately on his arrival in France, he was arrested as a spy, imprisoned in Brest, and, after a few days, deported.

In the event, only one of his volumes was ever published before his untimely death, *The Glossography*, which is a comparative compilation of vocabulary in Welsh, Irish, Gaelic, Cornish and Breton, with comparable Latin and Greek words, a list which goes far beyond those compiled by Pezron and other early authors such as Boxhorn (1654). His *Glossography* is described as 'Celtic', but it is clear from his preface that he felt the term Celtic should properly only be used on the continent for the ancient inhabitants of Gaul, and his use of it in an insular context is doubtless a

14 *Edward Lhuyd.* Copyright Ashmolean Museum, Oxford

tacit acceptance of the nomenclature of Pezron. In this introduction he also recognises the major contrast in the use of the letters P and C in Welsh and Irish/Gaelic. Thus 'son of . . .' in Welsh is *(M)ap*, and in Irish and Gaelic *Mac*. He further conjectures that this difference might be chronological, with new arrivals in Britain pushing the former inhabitants westward as the English were to do with the Welsh in post-Roman times. The 'C' Celts he labelled as 'Goidels', and, like Buchanan, assumed an Iberian origin, while the 'P' Celts or 'Brythons' came from Gaul. This division between P and Q Celtic and his nomenclature was picked up again in the nineteenth century when the full importance of his pioneering work was finally recognised.

A couple of interesting points emerge from his letters. In one dated to Dr Martin Lister dated August 1698 he surprisingly states that the major differences between Welsh and Irish were because Irish was derived from Greek, and Welsh from Latin, presumably a reflection of the stories of Brutus and Gaythelos. Brutus still appears in the 1696 version of Camden's *Britannia*, and Lhuyd mentions the arrival of John Toland in Oxford who had come to study Brutus.

> You have done me, I doubt not, an unexpressible kindness by procuring a correspondence with Mr Pezron; I am yet so much a stranger to his Works, that I have never heard of his name. His notion of the Greek, Roman and Celtic Languages being of one common origin, agrees exactly with my observations. But I have not advanced so far as to discover the Celtic to be the mother tongue, tho' perhaps he may not want good grounds, at least plausible arguments, for such an assertion. The Irish comes in with us, and is a dialect of the Old Latin, as the British is of the Greek, but the Gothick or Teutonick, tho' it has also much affinity with us, must needs make a Band apart. I shall speedily write to him, and trouble him with a few enquiries about their Armorican antiquities, etc.
>
> Gunther 1945, 400.

Archæologia Britannica,

GIVING SOME ACCOUNT

Additional to what has been hitherto Publiſh'd,

OF THE

LANGUAGES, HISTORIES and CUSTOMS

Of the Original Inhabitants

OF

GREAT BRITAIN:

From Collections and Obſervations in Travels through
Wales, Cornwal, Bas-Bretagne, Ireland and *Scotland.*

By EDWARD LHUYD M.A. of *Jeſus College,*
Keeper of the ASHMOLEAN MUSEUM in OXFORD.

V O L. I.
GLOSSOGRAPHY.

O X F O R D,
Printed at the THEATER for the Author, MDCCVII
And Sold by Mr. *Bateman* in *Pater-Noſter-Row, London* : and *Jeremiah Pepyat*
Bookſeller at *Dublin.*

15 *Frontispiece of Edward Lhuyd's Celtic glossography (1707)*

In a letter to Mr John Lloyd, dated Michaelmas 1703, he comments on Pezron after finally obtaining a copy of his book:

> One Abbot Pezron, an Armorique Britan, has lately published his *Antiquité de la Nation et de la langue Gauloise* (*sic*) wherein he had infinitely outdone all our Countreymen as to national zeal. He proves that they and we are the onely nations in the world that have the honour to have preserv'd the language of Jupiter and Saturn, whom he shews to have been Princes of the Titans, the progenitors of the Gauls, and to have had an Empire from the Euphrates to Cape Finister in ye time of Abraham.
>
> Gunther 1945, 489.

Contrary to Simon James (1999, 49–50) who takes this as evidence that Lhuyd's statement was reflecting Welsh nationalism, I would read it as the reverse, and that Lhuyd simply considered himself as an educated Oxford scholar, a role in which one's nationality was of little importance, and was rather making an ironic statement about nationalism.

James Parsons (1705–70)

In 1767 Parsons published his *Remains of Japhet*. Having learnt both Irish and Welsh, he was struck by their close affinity, and investigated their origins. His basic premise was that they represented the language spoken by the descendants of Japhet, specifically Magog and Gomer, and he used the terms 'Magogian' for Irish and 'Gomerian' for Welsh. He laid great emphasis on the Irish written tradition as found in the *Book of Invasions* and other Irish sources, which he considered the tradition introduced by the first inhabitants of Ireland, and independent of the Bible and the classical sources. He thus sought a Scythian, and ultimately Armenian, origin for the European languages. In this he specifically rejected Buchanan's theories (p.177), though he seems only to have encountered these second hand through Jeremy Collier. He was a supporter of the authenticity of Macpherson's *Ossian* (p.157). He also used Lhuyd's *Archaeologia Britannica*, Pezron and Sir Isaac Newton's *Chronology* (1728).

His opinion was that, as Irish showed considerable conservatism in its written texts, unlike other languages such as Latin which had been transformed into many different dialects and languages, Irish and Welsh must be closest to the original language of Japhet spoken after the Flood, and which contrasted with those of Shem and Ham. His innovation was to compare Irish and Welsh not only with Latin and Geek, but with various other languages in Europe (including Hungarian) and also Asiatic languages. After a detailed discussion of how words change (changes of consonants, metathesis, etc.), he goes on to a detailed examination of the numerals, and noted that, for instance, Persian and Bengali were close to the other European languages, whereas Turkish, Hebrew, Malay and Chinese were totally different. He also suggested that the Americas were colonised from Kamchatka, and thus the native languages could be related to the European. Caribbean, he noted, was totally distinct, but he found some similarities in the numerals with some of the languages spoken in North America, which could be by chance, but he opted for some common ancestry with the European. He thus envisaged a colonisation, as outlined by the Irish records, originating in Scythia, and carried onwards by the Pelasgians into Italy, and then on to Ireland, but as part of a process introducing a common language over much of Europe and parts of Asia if not America. Pelasgian, he thought, was the language later known as Celtic.

The Indo-Europeans

The views of Pezron and Lhuyd form the essential backdrop to the Druidomania and Celtomania which swept Britain and France in the eighteenth century. Though Lhuyd has some claims to be the founder of comparative linguistics, it was not until more than a century later that his work was properly recognised for its originality, and it became a point of reference for languages which had either disappeared (Cornish) or were under pressure. This recognition came with the realisation that the features which the many languages in Europe shared in common was due not to 'original' languages influencing one another, but rather that they shared a common origin.

Symbolically it is a speech given by Sir William Jones (1746–96) to the Asiatic Society of London, and published a year after his death, that is taken to mark the new paradigm with the recognition of the common features of a large number of languages in Europe and western Asia. Jones drew heavily on Sanskrit which he had studied in India, and for which there was already a long history of academic study by Indian grammarians. He compared its grammar with that of Greek and Latin, and further suggested that Gothic (Old German), Celtic, and possibly Old Persian were also related. He postulated an origin for this language group in Iran, and suggested that it had been spread by the sons of Noah. In fact similar claims had been made by A. Jäger over a century before. In his *De Lingua Vetustissima Europae* published in 1686 he suggested that Persian, Greek, Gothic, Slavic, Celtic and the Romance languages were all descended from an original ancient language that had disappeared, and, as we have seen, Parsons made a similar claim.

It was, however, with the rise of the Germanic school of comparative linguistics that Indo-European or Indo-Germanic studies took off. Rasmus Rusk (1787–1832) had recognised the similarity of declensions and forms of words, and these were formalised first by Franz Bopp (1791–1867) in his comparison of sentence construction between Sanskrit and related languages, and by Jakob Grimm (1785–1863) with his formalisation of the principle of 'sound shifts' (*Lauterverschiebung*) from one language to another. This worked especially with consonants, the labials, dentals and gutturals (**16**). Thus *pater* in Latin becomes

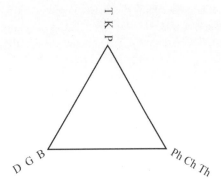

16 Lauterverschiebung *(sound shifts) according to Grimm's Law.* Author

father in English and *vater* in German; *tres* in Latin became *drei* in German and *three* in English; and *phegos* in Greek becomes *beech* in English.

The first book on the Celtic languages was, however, written by a Welshman, John Cowles Prichard (1781–1848), whose work as a physical anthropologist will be discussed in the next chapter. He had decided that language was the best indicator of the origins of racial groups, and as a Welsh speaker, he applied Grimm's principles to the Welsh language (the book, published in 1831 is dedicated to Jakob Grimm). From his work it was clear that Welsh belonged to the Indo-European group (the Celtic languages had been dismissed or ignored by the mainstream of Indo-Germanic studies), and Prichard concluded that the Celtic languages (and the Celts) had originated in eastern or central Europe, spreading westwards. In 1837 Bopp produced his own study of the Celtic languages, dealing with grammatical structure. This work culminated in the definitive comparative study of the Celtic languages published in 1853 by J.C. Zeuss, and Alfred Holder's glossary of early Celtic words (1896–1907).

The question that these studies of the Indo-European languages posed was how and why this large group of languages spoken from Ireland to the Indian sub-continent could be related to one another. The main theory was developed by August Schleicher (1821–64) in his *Compendium of the Comparative Grammar of the Indo-European Languages* published in 1861, and especially in the posthumously published *Darwinian Theory and Linguistics* which appeared in 1886. He built on Scaliger's concept of the 'mother language', suggesting that languages could be related to one another like a genealogical tree. When a population speaking a language became too great for the speakers to communicate adequately, or the distance became too great, for instance if one group migrated, then two different languages would evolve from the original single language. He thus postulated a three level division for Indo-European languages:

Ursprache ⟶ Grundsprache ⟶ Sprache

The resulting concept is like a tree (hence, in German, the *Stammbaumtheorie*), in which the original Indo-European language is the trunk of the tree, the language groups form the branches (Slavic, Baltic, Germanic, Romance, Celtic, etc.), and the individual languages the twigs (**17**).

This also gives a chronological structure, with Latin, for instance, preceding its offspring (Italian, French, Provençal, Catalan, Castilian, Portuguese, Romanian, Romance). In that case we know the pedigree as the mother language is well recorded, but where the mother language has not survived, for instance for Celtic, it can be reconstructed to a certain extent using evidence of systematic shifts in sounds and grammar, based on the similarities in its successor languages.

Schleicher's theory in fact was merely a systematisation of what previous writers from Rask onwards had conjectured. It did, however, allow a hypothetical reconstruction of the original 'Indo-European' language by working back from the various descendant languages and their sound and grammar shifts, and also to study what words they shared in common. This in turn allowed an area of origin to be postulated (one in which the trees and animals lived whose names are shared in common by the majority of the languages), and also use developments in archaeological dating to date the various splits (the word for copper shares a common ancestry, but not iron, and so it was suggested, the 'Indo-Europeans' knew about copper, but not iron, so the split did not start until the Chalcolithic). Rask had suggested Thrace as the point of origin, Jones, Persia, but this more systematic study seemed to point to an area north of the Black Sea.

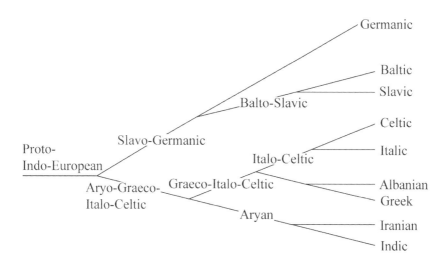

17 *The Stammbaumtheorie (tree stem theory) of the relationship between Indo-European languages.*
After Mallory 1989

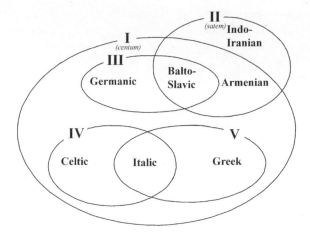

18 *The wave model in Indo-European languages.* After Mallory 1989

An alternative, but not mutually exclusive, theory of language change was put forward by Johannes Schmidt (1843–1901) in a book published in 1872. The 'wave' theory saw linguistic innovations happening in a specific area and radiating out from there like the waves caused by a pebble thrown into a pond. The importance of this theory is that changes are not seen as flowing in a simple linear direction, and different changes could be seen as radiating out from different areas, producing a complex multi-dimensional matrix of features (**18**). This fits the reality of dialect and language differences much better than the *Stammbaumtheorie*. However, it does not explain why Indo-European (and other) languages appear in a specific area. We have seen in Pezron and others how language and race had been linked together in eighteenth- and nineteenth-century thought. The spread of languages was thus seen in terms of movements of people, even if preceding populations were not necessarily wiped out, but absorbed. This concept was extended back into the past, so that it became normal to speak of 'Indo-Europeans' as a definable racial group who spoke the reconstructed Indo-European language, and had a distinctive social structure.

Language theory was thus beginning to distance itself from the 'Tower of Babel' and biblical paradigm which had dominated seventeenth- and eighteenth-century theories. Though it might still be argued that the lost 'Indo-European' language was one of the 'original' languages, the distribution of Indo-European languages did not fit the 'sons of Noah' theory. Nor did the postulated points of origin coincide with the biblical texts. Language and race were thus becoming interlinked, so in the next chapter we need to consider eighteenth- and nineteenth-century concepts of race.

4

RACE AND TIME

Two major trends in the seventeenth and eighteenth century have not yet been discussed: the rise of the nation state in Europe and the impact of the voyages of discovery. The nation state will be dealt with mainly in a later chapter, but here it is important to note that understanding the origin of the peoples who made up the nation was an important part of the origin mythology of the state; and so scholarly work on the state intensified in the nineteenth and early twentieth centuries, with dire political consequences. The European exploration of the world was showing the enormous variety of the ways of life of the human race, the great variability of social organisation, technology and cultural behaviour, and especially the great range of physical characteristics, such as skin, hair colour and stature. How had this variability originated?

Two basic theories developed in the eighteenth century within the biblical paradigm. The 'Monogenesists' took the biblical story of a single creation literally, and therefore mankind had to be seen and treated as a unity. Higher levels of technology and social organisation had to be explained, either in terms of more intelligent groups who developed to a higher level from a universally shared standard at the time of the Creation, or of groups who had degenerated, technologically, socially and spiritually. In the period of the Enlightenment, the more intelligent group was mainly equated with white Europeans, leading on to concepts of master races, be they Jewish, Egyptian, German or British. The alternative view of the 'Polygenesists' was that the variability could only be explained in terms of multiple creations, a view put forward by the French anthropologist Lamarck. This implied that racial superiority was something which was inbuilt, and that Europeans represented the final and most perfect creation.

John Cowles Prichard (1781–1848)

Prichard (**19**) has been claimed as the founder of modern physical anthropology, and his theories form a useful starting point for a discussion of nineteenth-century developments in the study of racial origins. A doctor by training, he had an established practice in Bristol. Leaving aside his contributions to medicine, he had a

19 *John Cowles Prichard.* Copyright
The Bodleian Library, Oxford

wide range of interests, including linguistics and archaeology. He had extensive
international contacts; as previously mentioned, his book on the Celtic languages
was dedicated to Jakob Grimm, and the French historian Amédée Thierry
mentions his correspondence with Prichard in the introduction to the third
edition of his *Histoire des Gaulois.* His books, *Researches into the Physical History of
Mankind* (1813) and *The Natural History of Man* (1843/1973), discussed the
problems of human variability, and brought together a wide range of different
physical types from all over the world. As a confirmed 'Monogenesist' his primary
problem was to explain how this variability could have developed in such a short
period of time (less than 6,000 years since the Creation, and 4,000 years since the
Flood) and the dispersal of humans across the world. His explanation was environmental, that human groups adapted very rapidly to their environment: black
skins in hot countries, white skins in cold countries; in many ways this was a
precursor of Darwin's theory of evolution and the survival of the fittest. But
Prichard was not able to formulate any mechanism whereby the changes might
take place, especially within the short timescale within which he was working. He
at first suggested very rapid mutation, with new populations adapting within a few
generations; consequently, white men would within a century or two produce
black offspring if they moved to a hot climate.

This produced two further questions. Firstly, if one cannot use physical appearance to trace origins, how can this be achieved? His answer was through language,
and this explains his excursus into Celtic linguistics published in 1831. He argued
that the Welsh, Irish and Scots, though all Celtic speakers, had slightly different

physical characteristics, which he saw as a confirmation of his theory. His second problem was chronology, and, as Mike Morse (1999a; 1999b) has recently pointed out, it was physical anthropologists rather than antiquarians who were most interested in developing a chronological framework at this period. Thus Prichard was the first to publish Thomsen's 'Three Age System' in English. Towards the end of his life, he began to realise that the biblical chronology was unworkable; his solution was that the chronology may well be wrong, and that many generations had not been recorded in the biblical genealogies.

Craniology

The linguist Rasmus Rask (1787–1832), at the beginning of the nineteenth century, had already suggested that Indo-European languages may have been late arrivals in western Europe, and so there could have been pre-Indo-European populations which had spoken another, non-Indo-European language; he suggested Finnish, but others were later to suggest Basque. As we have seen, language and race tended to be equated; so, it was argued, speakers of non-Indo-European languages should be distinguishable from the Indo-Europeans in terms of their physical characteristics, the reverse of what Prichard was arguing. Proponents of this approach considered the skull to be the most distinctive part of the body.

The major developments of the theories of craniology occurred in Scandinavia; Daniel Eschricht (1798–1863), Sven Nilsen (1787–1883) and Anders Retzius (1796–1860) showed that there were physical differences between the Neolithic and Bronze Age populations of Scandinavia (they were early converts to the 'Three Age System'). The approach was quickly adopted in Ireland by William Wilde, father of Oscar (1815–76), who, in his book *The Beauties of the Boyne and its Tributary the Blackwater* (1849), claimed to be able to distinguish the two main groups mentioned in the *Book of Invasions*, firstly the pre-Celtic 'Fir-Bolg' (descendants of Magog) and then the Celtic 'Tuatha Dé Dannan' (descendants of Gomer) who he claimed arrived in the Bronze Age. In Britain excavators such as Thomas Bateman started assiduously to collect skulls from their barrow excavations. In Britain the major proponents of the method, John Thurnam and Joseph Barnard Davis, began to publish detailed drawings and measurements of skulls in their *Crania Britannica*, and detected a difference between 'dolichocephalic' (keel-shaped) skulls in the Neolithic population, and a 'brachycephalic' (broad-headed) population in the Bronze Age: long heads in long barrows, round heads in round barrows! This was interpreted as a change in population in the Bronze Age, and for many archaeologists in the late nineteenth century, this change signified the arrival of Celts, a view very clearly expressed by Broca:

But thanks to the remarkable and rapid strides modern archaeology has made, we are on the most perfect scientific ground when we state that the monuments alleged to be Celtic twenty years ago are of two different periods; the stone age on one hand, and the bronze age on the other. Yet others, even more recent, contain some iron objects. Comparative studies . . . have shown that the primary inhabitants of Europe belonged to the stone age, while the use of bronze was introduced by more civilized man, probably of Asiatic origin . . . The Celtic period begins with the bronze age; the stone age period is pre-Celtic . . . In summary: the Celts of History are a confederation of peoples in Central Gaul. The Celts of Linguistics are the people who have spoken and are still speaking the so-called Celtic languages. The Celts of Archaeology are the people who inaugurated the bronze age in Europe. The Celts of Craniology finally, are the people who brought dolichocephaly to the native brachycephalic European population, according to Retzius; whereas according to Thurnman they are, on the contrary, the people who brought brachycephaly to the native dolichocephalic British population.

Broca 1864, in Schiller 1979, 145–6;
information from Margarita Díaz-Andreu.

The chronological chains snap

Since Bishop Ussher propounded his biblical chronology of the world, the dates had appeared alongside the text in most bibles, and had formed a constraint within which all scholars had been forced to work. We have already noted how for physical anthropologists such as Prichard this was becoming an increasing problem, but for geologists trying to deal with long sequences of strata and the recognition of fossils of extinct plants and animals in them, eventually the chronology proved impossible, leading initially to theories of many creations wiped out by many floods. In 1835 Charles Lyell, in his book *The Principles of Geology*, propounded the theory of 'uniformitarianism', whereby he suggested that rocks in the past had been laid down by the same processes observable in the modern world; igneous rocks by volcanoes; gravels by rivers; sand by sea and wind. Some of these were slow processes, and a very long chronology was inescapable.

Though observations had been made on a number of occasions of flint tools and even human remains, such as the 'red lady of Paviland', in geological strata and associated with extinct animals, it was not until 1859 that Robert Prestwich and Sir John Evans assembled the evidence from France and Britain to demonstrate, at least to the satisfaction of the scientific community, that mankind was considerably more ancient than the biblical accounts allowed. Their exposition coincided with the publication of Charles Darwin's *On the Origin of Species*, and though Darwin himself only briefly mentioned at the end of his book the possible implications for human origins, others such as Thomas Huxley quickly followed it up. The impact on science in general was huge, and the principles adopted not only for the living world, but also, as we have seen, by linguists to explain the changes and relationships between languages; by anthropologists looking at the development of society; and by archaeologists looking at the classification and evolution of artefacts (typology). For all these groups, by breaking the chronological constraints, it also gave enormous freedom to explain long-term change.

Source and text criticism

Before exploring how these ideas were to impact on Celtic studies, and especially the rise of archaeology, a few words need to be said on the process of editing the ancient texts and the critical analyses of them. This work had already started in the sixteenth century with scholars such as Joseph Scaliger, and by the nineteenth century a whole series of editions started to appear in which not only were the variations within the various manuscript versions compared and juxtaposed, but attempts were made to clean up texts which had become manifestly corrupt. These texts became the standard fare for all education systems in central and western Europe, at least for the middle and upper classes, a tradition which only died in the middle of the twentieth century. Thus all educated people were expected to know some Latin, if not Greek as well, providing a large market of people to whom the ancient peoples such as the Celts and Germans became familiar through the works of Caesar and Tacitus. The dissemination of the ideals of Greek philosophy and art, or Roman government and justice, were used in the justification of the empire builders of the nineteenth century, but so were classical attitudes towards native populations, the creation of 'the other', with stereotyping of native peoples as backward, bizarre, uncivilised, unchanging unless change was forced upon them by the superior civilisations of Europe. All these were attitudes which were reflected in archaeological theory and explanation.

Earlier historians such as Buchanan had largely accepted the truth of what the classical authors had written, but it was clearly recognised by the nineteenth century that there could be major discrepancies, and the critical approaches of historians had to be applied to the ancient texts as well. One which will concern us directly are the various versions of the invasions of northern Italy by the Gauls. There are two main narratives, that written by Polybius at the end of the second century BC, and that by Livy written in the late first century BC, nearly 300 years after the sacking of Rome in 290/287 BC. Livy dates the invasion to around 600 BC, placing it in the reign of Tarquinius Priscus, and also linking it with the foundation of *Massalia* by the Phocaeans. As Niebuhr pointed out in 1835 there is a major discrepancy between his dates and those of Polybius who implies it took place two centuries later, a major difference when we come to look at the archaeological evidence.

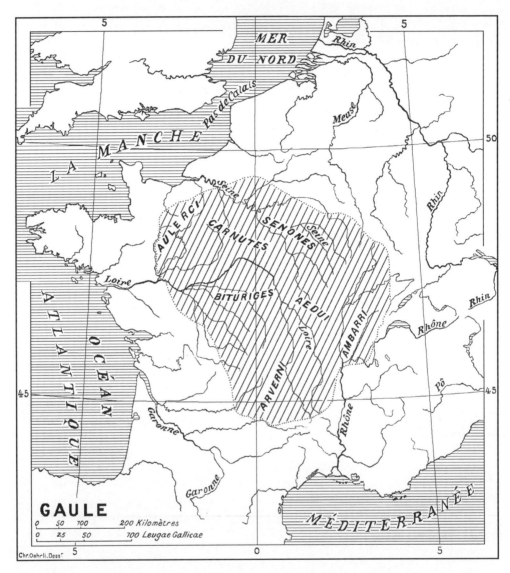

20 *Thierry's concept of the origin of the Celtic peoples invading Italy.* Bertrand 1876

Amédée Thierry

The impact of linguistic, racial and chronological theories on interpretations of the Celts can best be studied by discussing the three main French authors of the nineteenth century to deal with the subject. The Celts, or Gauls, formed a major element in the mythology of the French state, as will be discussed in chapter 9, so Celtic studies attracted a considerable amount of attention as *nos ancêtres les Gaulois*. The major historical work was the *Histoire des Gaulois* of Amédée Thierry, first published in 1827, and subsequently to go through four editions. Though Thierry was aware of the concept of Indo-European languages, and as previously mentioned was in contact with Prichard amongst others (1857, xx), he makes little use of linguistic evidence, and his views of the origins of the Celts are simply to see them as indigenous from somewhere in the early second millennium BC, using the short biblical chronology. He makes no use of archaeological evidence, other than to note in the 1857 edition that the early Gauls used stone axes and flint-tipped arrowheads.

His main sources are Caesar and Strabo for the location of the Gallic tribes, and he envisages that many of these were to be found in the same location at the time of the invasion of Italy (which, following Livy, he dates to around 600 BC) as they were at the time of Caesar in the first century BC (**20**). He makes no conjecture about the date of the arrival of the Gauls, considering them as the original inhabitants who arrived from the east, along with the Iberians (represented by the Ligurians and the Aquitani). However, he implies an early date for this colonisation (around 2000–1800 BC) as he argues that the Celts had invaded Spain by the seventeenth/sixteenth century BC, and that the first Gallic invasion of Italy took place around 1400 BC, represented by the Umbrians, who, on the basis of a statement by Antonius Gnipho he assumed were also Celtic rather than Italic (1857, 26). The first settlement of the British Isles he accepted was by the Gaelic speakers of Ireland and Scotland.

Similarly, on the basis of Caesar's statement about the origin of the Belgae, and Strabo's categorisation of the Armoricans as Belgae, he envisaged a later wave of Gallic settlement emanating from the Cimmerians/Cimbri (who, he argued, spoke a Gallic language and were Gauls) which included the Belgae and the Armoricans, as well as two southern Gallic tribes, the Volcae Tectosages and the Volcae Areconici, on the grounds that *Volcae* and *Belgae* are synonymous terms (1857, 26–7).

Henri d'Arbois de Jubainville (1827–1910)

D'Arbois de Jubainville is one of the key influences on the modern interpretations of the Celts, since it is on his views that archaeological interpretations depend, for instance the association of the spread of La Tène art and culture with the migrations of the Celts. His views represent a major contrast with those of Thierry, as he envisages the Celts as late arrivals in the west, and he lays much heavier emphasis on Herodotus and Polybius rather than on Livy and Caesar.

An historian by training, much of his early writing was on the medieval period in his capacity as the departmental archivist for the Yonne. However, he had already betrayed his interests in the classics in his book *Premiers Habitants de l'Europe d'après les Auteurs d'Antiquités et les Recherches les plus récentes de la Linguistique* published in 1877. Like Thierry his main source of information was derived from the classical sources, but he was more inclined to accept mytholog-ical statements than was Thierry, and especially he made extensive use of linguistic evidence. Archaeology he only refers to in passing as not his domain, stating that archaeologists had demonstrated that early man, like the Cyclops, lived in caves! He used a long, non-biblical, chronology, but probably more because he used classical sources rather than because of any advances in geology and archaeology. Upon his retirement, he took up the post of the first professor of Celtic Studies at the Sorbonne, and most of his later writings are based on the lectures that he gave in Paris, for instance a major compendium of the classical sources which refer to the Celts.

In his 1863 book he suggests four phases of colonisation, usually referring to these as 'Empires'. Quite what he means by this is not entirely clear, but he certainly often envisages a level of social and political organisation by hunter-pastoralists that could never have been supported by such a level of economy. His four phases are:

1. Undated. Cave dwellers living on hunting and pastoralism, epitomised by Polyphemus the Cyclops encountered by Odysseus in the *Odyssey*.

2. 6000 BC. An Iberian empire, with hunters/pastoralists speaking a non-Indo-European language. He conjectures that the Iberians may have been the original inhabitants of Atlantis who were forced to colonise new territory when their land disappeared. He follows Pliny in dating this to 6000 BC.

3. 1500 BC. A Ligurian Empire. He suggests the Ligurians were the first Indo-European speakers to arrive from the East, introducing agriculture, and largely displacing the Iberians.

4. 500 BC. A Celtic Empire. The Celts represent the second wave of Indo-European speakers arriving from the east.

D'Arbois de Jubainville's earlier 'empires' can be dismissed as fanciful conjecture, other than noting that, unlike Thierry, he accepts the presence of pre-Indo-European and pre-Celtic speakers, evidenced in river names such as the *Sequana* (Seine). It is the reasons for his belief that the Celts were late arrivals on

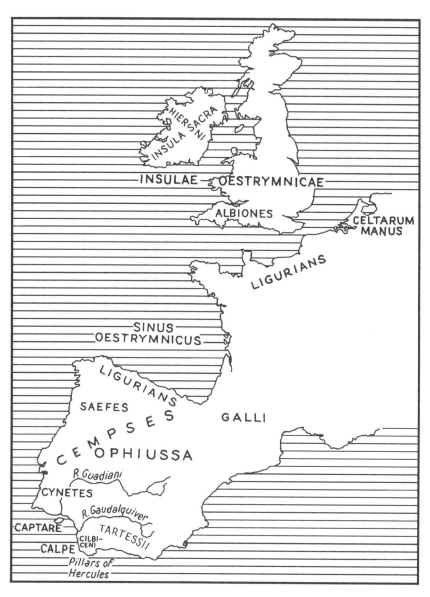

HIERSACRA

INSULA

CELTARUM
MANUS

INSULAE — OESTRYMNICAE

ALBIONES

LIGURIANS

SINUS
OESTRYMNICUS

LIGURIANS

SAEFES

GALLI

C E M P S E S
OPHIUSSA

R. Guadiani

CYNETES

R. Gaudalquiver

CAPTARE

TARTESSII

CILBI-
CENI

CALPE

Pillars of
Hercules

21 *Geographical reconstruction of the Periplus of Himilco. After Dinan 1911*

the scene which need more careful consideration, matters with which he dealt in greater detail in his 1903 and 1904 papers. Firstly there was the evidence of the introduction of Indo-European languages, the assumption of their easterly origin, and their relatively late appearance in western Europe. Secondly he claims to find evidence for population change in the historical record, for southern France, in western Spain, and more contentiously, on the North Sea.

For the south of France and the Atlantic coast his primary sources for a pre-Celtic phase come from the various *Periplus*, instructions for those sailing along the coast of the Mediterranean and the Atlantic. The *Periplus of Himilco*, dating to about 500 BC, only mentions Celts somewhere on the Atlantic coast, north of Britain, and the peoples named in Spain are not those found there at a later date (**21**). When Herodotus was writing around 440 BC, however, there were already Celts on the Atlantic coast adjacent to the Cynetes, so presumably in Iberia. The Massaliote Periplus ('Scylax' in Avienus) also states that the Rhone formed the boundary between the Iberians and Ligurians (i.e. around the fourth century), but when Hannibal and Hamilcar crossed the Pyrenees in the late third century BC, we only hear of Celtic tribes in the south of France. On these grounds d'Arbois de Jubainville suggested that the south of France was taken over by the Gauls around 300 BC (1863, 241).

Avienus mentions the presence of a 'Ligurian Marsh' in Spain near Tartessos which d'Arbois de Jubainville interpreted as indicating the former presence of Ligurians in the Iberian peninsula, as well as those located by Avienus in northern Spain adjacent to the Saefes and Cempses and, quoting Himilco, he also refers to Ligurians being forced to leave areas in northern Gaul due to floods (which d'Arbois de Jubainville interprets as in the Netherlands (1903, 163)). This was his evidence for a former widespread occupation of western Europe by Ligurians, before being replaced by Celts. For the eastern origin of the Celts, he uses Herodotus' assertion about the Danube rising in the territory of the Celts (e.g. in southern Germany) as well as Polybius' statement that the Celts invaded northern Italy from the other side of the Alps (e.g. from the north). D'Arbois de Jubainville thus envisages the Celts/Gauls coming from east of the Rhine where, unlike France, the river names suggested there was no pre-Celtic language spoken. He envisaged an early occupation of the lower Rhine (on the evidence of Himilco), and also of the British Isles because of the word *kassiteros* in Homer (see below), and an outpost in Spain established around 450 BC (**22**). The colonisation of southern France was not completed until some time in the third century BC with the arrival of the Volcae. He also attacked the idea promoted by Bertrand that a distinction could be made between Gauls and Celts. Though he accepted that the term Galli/Galatai does not appear in the written sources until the third century BC, he showed that most authors tend to use the terms synonymously.

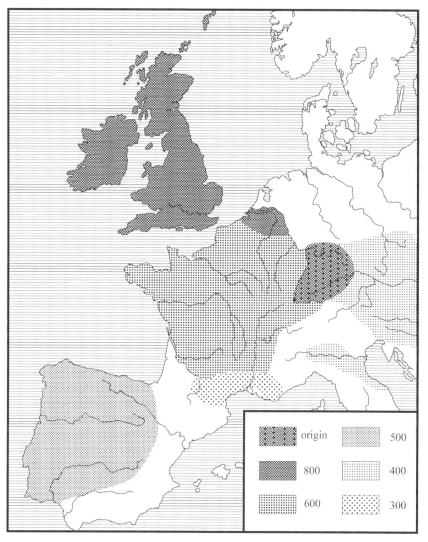

22 *Reconstruction of d'Arbois de Jubainville's theories on the origin and expansion of the Celts.*
Collis 2004

23 *Alexandre Bertrand.* Permission of
Professor Derek Roe

Alexandre Bertrand (1820–1902)

Bertrand (**23**) was director of the Musée des Antiquités Nationales at St Germain-
en-Laye, and was primarily an archaeologist. In two books, one jointly authored
with Salomon Reinach, he made an early attempt to marry the historical evidence
with the archaeological sources, using the newly developed methods of dating
archaeological finds (see the next chapter). He follows d'Arbois de Jubainville in
seeking an origin for the Celts and Gauls east of the Rhine. Ignoring the
Palaeolithic, he envisaged three main phases of occupation in France. The earliest,
given no ethnic name, were the megalithic builders with a Stone Age technology.
Secondly there were the Celts, and following the craniologists, he suggested they
introduced a bronze technology around 2000–1500 BC. Some time during the
Bronze Age, he argued, the Celts arrived in Britain; this he claimed on the
evidence of the use of the word *kassiteros* (tin) in Homer, a Celtic word derived
from the Cassiterides which he assumed to be Britain. In this he was followed by
d'Arbois de Jubainville and Dinan. Finally there were the Gauls who introduced
iron technology, and were characterised by the inhumation cemeteries of the
Champagne area (we have already noted d'Arbois de Jubainville's rejection of this
chronological distinction between Celts and Gauls). In his joint-authored book,
he and Reinach mainly described the Hallstatt-period burials of northern Italy and
southern Germany as the physical evidence for the Celts. Like d'Arbois de
Jubainville he argued for an origin north of the Alps for the Celts who invaded
Italy, and also the later date around 400 BC.

In his earlier book (1876) he noted the patchy distribution of these various archaeological groups. Megalithic tombs were mainly concentrated along the Atlantic coast in western France, whereas the burials with iron weapons were more common in the east and north. This he explained by suggesting that each wave of new invaders did not obliterate the previous inhabitants, and, for instance, the Gauls formed isolated colonies within the Bronze Age Celtic populations. The megalithic builders of western France he suggested survived until the Iron Age, and it is interesting to note that as late as 1923 the excavator of the *allée couverte* at Tressé claimed it was built in the Iron Age, on the basis of Iron Age material found in it (Collum 1935).

Camille Jullian (1859–1933)

The successor to Thierry's *Histoire des Gaulois* was the monumental work of Camille Jullian (**24**), *L'Histoire de la Gaule*, which appeared in a series of eight volumes between 1907 and 1926, a work continued by his pupil Albert Grenier. Though his ideas produced a reaction from d'Arbois de Jubainville, in many ways, in the matters which concern us here, it merely presented the revised interpretations of the Celts developed in the late nineteenth century to a wider public, so that they became the official view in France for much of the twentieth century. Only now are they undergoing major revision, mainly under the impact of archaeological discoveries of the late twentieth century.

24   *Camille Jullian.* Permission of Musée des Antiquités Nationales, St Germain-en-Laye

As we shall see, the interpretations of d'Arbois de Jubainville and of Bertrand were highly influential on Joseph Déchelette when he brought together a wide range of archaeological material for his *Manuel de Archéologie*. However, some of the ideas of these authors still find a resonance in the popular imagination. It is still possible to buy postcards in central France depicting circular drystone huts with corbelled roofs, described as prehistoric Ligurian huts, though most of them in fact are shepherds' and herdsmen's shelters dating to the seventeenth to nineteenth centuries. The distinction between Celts and Gauls also survives among some French archaeologists. My colleague Robert Périchon remarked to me in the 1980s that the absence of La Tène material in the highland areas of the Massif Central was because it was still inhabited by Celts ('les pasteurs des plateaux'), whereas the fertile plains were occupied by the incoming Gauls.

5

ART AND ARCHAEOLOGY

Before considering the major developments in archaeology in the nineteenth century, I should say a few words about the development of ideas on British origins in the eighteenth and nineteenth centuries. The normal term used by authors such as Camden designates the prehistoric inhabitants of Britain as 'The Ancient Britons'. From the early eighteenth century the term 'Celtic' starts to become more common, and by the end of the century it was generally accepted that the early inhabitants of the British Isles had been Celts, and that the Scots, Irish and Welsh are their descendants. Simon James has suggested that this acceptance of the term Celtic was due to an increasing sense of being 'other', especially on the part of the Welsh and Scots, the latter in the wake of the Act of Union in 1707. Though this difference of identity certainly existed, it should not be overplayed; the rebellions of 1715 and 1745 were, after all, not about the independence of Scotland, but about who should sit on the throne of England, and, as previously mentioned, I can detect none of the Welsh nationalism that James sees in Edward Lhuyd's writings. I make no pretence to understanding the complexity of what was going on, and the matter is not helped by the tendency for modern historians to use the term Celtic where their sources may be using terms such as British, Irish or Gaelic. As with the ancient sources, we need to strip off our modern preconceptions, and see what nomenclature these authors were actually using, why, and what it might imply. I see a number of inter-related processes going on.

Firstly there is the impact of John Toland. As a fluent speaker of Irish he had interested both Lhuyd and von Lebnitz in the language and early literature of Ireland. But it was his pamphlet *Christianity not Mysterious*, published in 1696, which introduced the concept of Deism, arguing for the primacy of scientific rationality over belief, and the rejection of myth and fabrication, views which were later to lead on to the radical political beliefs of Thomas Paine and Robert Owen. Though he claimed that by stripping away the irrationalities in Christian belief it would be strengthened, his views produced outrage from the Establishment. To defend himself he turned to 'natural religion', which led him on Pythagoreanism, and then, following the link made by classical authors such as Diodorus Siculus with Druidism, he decided to write a book on Druids. Though it never appeared, his views were widely promulgated through the outlines he prepared in attempts to raise money for the project, recorded in three letters written to Viscount Molesworth in 1719, and finally published in his *History of the Druids* (1746). One opponent to Deism was the antiquarian William Stukeley who had taken holy orders, and in 1730 openly stated that in studying Avebury, 'My main motive in pursing this subject is to combat the deists from an unexpected quarter, and to preserve so noble a monument of our ancestor's piety, I may add, orthodoxy' (Piggott 1985, 104).

Another 'unexpected quarter' in which the concept of Celts was to be developed was in the conflict over the organisation of the Scottish Church, whether it should become Episcopalian with a system of bishoprics as in the Church of England, or whether it should maintain its less hierarchical Presbyterian structure. In part the debate was historical; had Christianity first been introduced into Scotland in the Roman period by the Roman Church with its Episcopalian structure, or was it through the Irish connection with its less hierarchical structure of monks and abbots? This in turn linked in with a debate on the origin of the Scottish state, and the relative importance of the Irish and Pictish components, itself something which pitched Highlander against Lowlander. This took its extreme form in the denial of the existence of a genuine tradition of Irish and Gaelic literature (a position taken up by Samuel Johnson), and opposition to the translation of the bible into Gaelic and Irish on the grounds that such barbaric languages should be suppressed! The Scottish historian John Pinkerton (1758–1826) went as far as to argue that the Gothuni of Buchanan were in fact the historical Goths, and so introduced a Teutonic language into Scotland, the origin of the Lowlanders' dialect, and he poured scorn on the Celtic languages. Inevitably, as one of the main historians who had dealt with the Irish (and Celtic) origin of the Scottish crown, and also as one of the founders of Scottish Presbyterianism, Buchanan was widely read, if not often quoted!

The third intertwining trend was towards romanticism. In the late seventeenth century there was a lively debate over the origin of Stonehenge and Avebury, with it being variously assigned to the Romans, the Danes and the Druids. The main advocate of the latter was John Aubrey in his unpublished *Monumenta Britannica*, a view in which he was followed by William Stukeley. As the Druids were the priestly caste of the Celts, it is not surprising that we begin to find a subtle shift in nomenclature and so Stukeley entitled an unpublished manuscript of 1723 as *The History of the Temples of the Ancient Celts*, the first use of the term in Britain in an archaeological context. Henry Rowlands in his *Mona Antiqua Restaurata*, a history of the Isle of Anglesey published in 1723, likewise uses the term. Smiles has recently discussed the impact of Romanticism on the arts in the eighteenth century, both visual and poetic, such as Thomas Gray's *The Bard* (1757). By the end of the century James MacPherson's fabricated epic poem *Ossian* (1765) had tapped into this romanticism, as did Sir Walter Scott in his Waverley novels (1814) and in *Rob Roy* (1817). The impact of these works was worldwide, and Amédée Thierry was one writer who was influenced by the works of Scott.

Because of the confusion and misuse of the term 'Celt' in modern discussions of the eighteenth century, indeed the failure to recognise that there is a question to be discussed, the uptake and dissemination of the term is not yet well documented. As we have seen, James Parsons in 1767 was familiar with the idea that the British were Celts, even if he rejected the original thesis of Buchanan, but in the Scottish literature in many quarters Buchanan's and Lhuyd's formulation was widely accepted, especially for advocates of the Irish connection, as Lhuyd was suggesting that the Irish and the Scots were the original inhabitants of Britain. James Boswell, in his *A Tour to the Hebrides with Samuel Johnson, LL.D.*, mentions encountering a Scottish priest, the Revd Donald Macqueen of Kilmuir on Skye, who showed him a site he claimed to be the 'temple of Anaistis', a name he had also encountered when reading Pliny and Pausanias writing about Asia Minor (17–18 September 1773). Macqueen goes on to say 'Asia Minor was peopled by Scythians, and, as they were the ancestors of the Celts, the same religion might be in Asia Minor and Skye', implying that the ancient inhabitants were Celts. Though Boswell says that Macqueen on a number of occasions defends James Macpherson's *Ossian*, it is clear that we see here the influence of the Irish texts and of George Buchanan. Boswell mentions him several times, quoting Johnson as saying 'Buchanan had spread the spirit of learning amongst us, but we had lost it during the civil wars' (18 August 1773). They also visited a couple of 'Druid's temples', though Johnson was unimpressed: 'to go and see one is to see that it is nothing, for there is neither art nor power in it, and seeing one is much as one could wish' (30 August 1773).

Thus by the early nineteenth century it was universally accepted that the pre-Roman inhabitants of Britain were Celts, with publications such as Edward Davies (1746–1826) *Celtic Researches on the Origin, Traditions and Language of the Ancient Britons, with introductory sketches on primitive societies* (1804). He and his contemporary Edward Williams (1746–1826) also known as Iolo Morgannwg, can be looked upon as the founders of the modern Welsh Bardic tradition. Nor was this phenomenon confined to Britain; in France La Tour d'Auvergne (1796) promoted the romantic image of the Celts and Druids, which in the early nineteenth century would produce, for instance, Bellini's opera *Norma* (1831). It was against this background that the concept of Celtic art was to be founded.

Chronological precision

One of the major achievements of archaeologists in the nineteenth century was to build up a chronological framework, not only for historically documented periods, but also, to a large extent, for the prehistoric period as well. The first stage in this development was the recognition of increasing technological sophistication in the past, starting with the 'Three Age System' of Christian Thomsen, the Ages of Stone, of Bronze, and of Iron, a theory based on the collections in the Danish

THE CELTS: ORIGINS, MYTHS & INVENTIONS

National Museum in Copenhagen. Though conceived in 1823, it was not published until 1837. As we have seen, it was quickly seized upon by physical anthropologists such as Prichard, and in the 1840s the scheme was widely disseminated by Thomsen's pupil, Johannes Worsaae, who visited both Ireland and Britain. Worsaae himself had divided the Danish Stone Age in two in 1859, contrasting the finds from the megalithic tombs with those from the 'kitchen middens' (what is now labelled as Mesolithic). The system was further developed in 1863 by Sir John Lubbock, who, in his book *Prehistoric Times*, recognised an earlier Stone Age not found in Denmark, but found in the caves and river gravels. This he labelled the *Palaeolithic* in contrast to the more recent period which he called the *Neolithic*.

The second element in the development of a detailed chronology was artefact typology. The classification of the natural world had been pioneered by naturalists such as John Ray and Carl von Linné in the eighteenth century, and the voyages of discovery were usually accompanied by naturalists and artists to describe the local fauna, flora and peoples; Joseph Banks accompanied both Cook and Bligh, and Darwin voyaged to the Galapagos, and these are but the more illustrious examples. Similar traditions existed for art and archaeology, and the illustrations of ancient Egyptian civilisation brought back from Napoleon I's expedition to Egypt in 1798, and a second expedition under Rosellini and Champollion in 1828, had a profound effect on French architecture and design in the early nineteenth century. But no such tradition developed for local artefacts until the early nineteenth century when antiquarians such as Richard Colt Hoare and Thomas Bateman started systematic description, illustration and publication of their finds. The same period saw the establishment of regional and national museums at which large collections of artefacts could be gathered and catalogued (e.g. Sir John Evans' catalogue of Ancient British coins). Comparative studies became an important tool of research, not only through publications, but also through the nineteenth-century tradition of major institutions exchanging artefacts with one another, or the acquisition of major collections of antiquarians and archæologists working in other countries (e.g. the British Museum's acquisition of the Morel collection from Champagne).

The new awareness of the historical significance of archaeology for national and regional prestige and identity meant that public funds were made available not only to purchase items for public collections (as Peter the Great had done in Russia in the early eighteenth century), but also for excavation projects, such as Napoleon III's funding and support for excavations at *Alesia*, *Gergovia*, *Bibracte* and elsewhere in France as part of his researches into Caesar's campaigns in Gaul. For the Iron Age and the study of the Celts, other than Napoleon's work in France, the two major groups of finds were those from Hallstatt in Austria and from La Tène in Switzerland.

Systematic excavations started at Hallstatt in the 1840s under Georg Ramsauer, Bergmeister of the salt mines. His excavations were of a higher standard than the average for the period, and though he did not generally keep the highly fragmented pottery and human bones, the majority of the metal objects can still be assigned to specific graves, largely because of his extensive catalogues supplemented by the illustrations made by a local artist, Isidor Engel, not only of the artefacts themselves, but of the graves in which they were found. Though the majority of the finds were deposited in the National Museum in Vienna, detailed descriptions with hand-produced drawings (*Protokolle*) were produced for interested parties; thus both the museum in Munich and the Society of Antiquaries of London possess their *Protokolle* providing wide access to some of the major finds.

The conditions of the discovery of La Tène were very different. The site, at the northern end of Lac Neuchâtel, emerged during one of the 'corrections' of the lake levels, which involved the lowering of the water level of several of the lakes. It led to the emergence of the famous 'lake dwellings' of Neolithic and Bronze Age date, but Iron Age finds consisted mainly of material which had been deposited, deliberately or accidentally, in the lake and the adjacent rivers. La Tène was discovered in 1857, but was effectively looted by local treasure hunters who literally fished the objects from the lake bottom, and sold them to local antiquarian dealers. The finds were then sold on to museums across central and western Europe, and so it meant that they were very quickly familiar to scholars internationally. Though some of the material was quickly published by Emile Désor and Friedrich Schwab, because the material is so widely dispersed, and not always well documented, even now they have not been published in their entirety. The swords and scabbards, for instance, were only definitively published in 1972 by the British scholar José de Navarro after many years of work collating the finds with the original documentation.

Thus there was an increasing range of artefacts available for study, some of it discovered under controlled circumstances, but many just chance finds from the building of roads and railways, or from the dredging of rivers. It thus became possible to recognise specific 'types' of artefact. It was immediately clear, for instance, that the swords from Hallstatt were different from those from La Tène, as was the style of decoration. Similar sorts of finds could be identified over wide areas of Europe, from Scandinavia to northern Italy, and from Ireland to the Hungarian Plain. In 1874 the Swedish scholar, Hans Hildebrand, suggested these were not differences between regions, but a pan-European phenomenon. Though he is usually credited for making the chronological division between the Hallstatt and La Tène, Gilbert Kaenel has recently pointed out that he only talks about 'styles' and that it was the Swiss prehistorian Désor who first proposed a division of the Iron Age into an earlier 'Hallstatt' period, and a later 'La Tène' period. It is important to note that this was purely a chronological division, and there was no racial or ethnic interpretation of the material.

But artefact typology is capable of greater refinement than merely distinguishing between categories or classes of objects (sword, brooch, axe), or between artefact types (Hallstatt sword, La Tène sword, or Viking sword); it can also pick

25 *The evolution of Iron Age coinage in Britain.* After Evans 1849

out subtle changes within types which can be used chronologically to show its evolution, much like the evolution of living animals and plants, as described by Darwin. In fact artefact evolution had been recognised a decade or more before Darwin published *On the Origin of Species.* In 1849 Sir John Evans published a series of drawings of Ancient British coins showing how they had started as recognisable imitations of the gold staters of Philip of Macedon, and had 'degenerated' into a series of lines and dots found on cast bronze coins from Dorset (**25**); this evolution was supported by the gradual reduction of weight and purity of the coins, from fairly pure gold, through various alloys, to purely bronze. Such 'typological development' is usually functional, like the evolution of the flat bronze axe into the flanged axe (to stop the axe wobbling in the shaft), and finally into the palstave with its stop ridge (to stop the axe splitting the haft when in use). Sometimes, however, it is purely fashion, like the evolution of grandfather clocks in the seventeenth and eighteenth century, or the design of motorcars in the 1950s and 1960s. Sometimes features which were originally functional become purely decorative ('skeuomorphs'), like the cross-hatch decoration on Late La Tène brooches which was where the foot of the brooch was formerly clipped on to the bow (the leading scholar to use typology, Oscar Montelius, showed how the decorative layout of railway carriages in the late nineteenth century in fact reflected their origin in the stage coach). An early example of this methodology, in 1887, was Otto Tischler's division of the La Tène period into 'Early', 'Middle' and 'Late', using different shapes of brooch and scabbard shape (**26**).

This leads on to further principles on which archaeological chronologies are based. Firstly there is the 'type-fossil'; the types of brooch which Tischler identified are the typical 'type-fossils' of their period, so that when they are found, for instance in a grave, they will provide a date for the grave and the other objects found in it. This gives us the second concept, that of the 'association' or 'closed find', making it possible to link together the different stages in one artefact with those of another. In Tischler's case we would therefore expect his Early La Tène scabbards to turn up in association with his Early La Tène brooches. Both of these methods are taken over from geology, but, surprisingly, a third essential method used in geology was hardly used in Iron Age studies until well into the twentieth century, that is 'stratigraphy', the superposition of layers one above another, forming a chronological sequence. This was perhaps because nineteenth-century

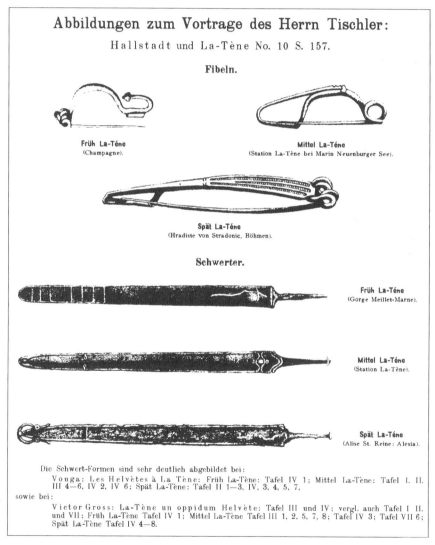

26 *The chronological scheme of Otto Tischler (1885); the Early and Late La Tène swords have accidentally been transposed.* Copyright The Bodleian Library, Oxford

discoveries came mainly from cemeteries where such superposition is unusual, or from river finds or other chance finds, which almost by definition means the objects are out of context. Settlement excavation did not start to become common until the 1920s, and even then, Iron Age habitation sites are often on eroded hilltops where stratified deposits are rare.

Unique to archaeology are the methods used to provide 'absolute' dating, that is providing fixed dates for the sequence established by typology. Three methods were available in the nineteenth century. The first was to excavate historically dated sites, such as the battlefield of *Alesia* where Caesar defeated Vercingetorix in the summer of 52 BC, thus providing a secure date for the coins and weapons found in Caesar's siege works. Secondly there is the occurrence of dated objects, especially coins, in closed contexts such as the Late La Tène burials at Ornavasso and Persona in northern Italy, which in many cases contained Roman Republican coins. The problem is how long those coins may have been in circulation before they were buried.

The third method is 'cross-dating'. This is the association of objects which are imported from sequences elsewhere which can themselves be dated. Ideally one should be looking for a mutual exchange of goods, as happened between Bronze Age Egypt and Crete, so that we can be sure that there has been no time-lag; long survival in the form of heirlooms does occur (a fourth-century BC Italian bronze bucket, for instance, is known from Denmark associated with objects of first-century BC date). Because many goods were being moved around in prehistoric Europe, potentially it is possible to work systematically from one area to another, linking up sequences as far removed from one another as Scandinavia and Egypt, the latter with its historically dated sequences. For nineteenth-century Iron Age archaeologists, the most useful example of this was the occurrence of Attic Red Figure Ware dating to the fifth century BC turning up in graves in northern France and southern Germany, such as Klein Aspergle in Baden-Württemberg, or Somme Bionne in Champagne (**27**). Another example was the brooches and bronze vessels of types found in dated contexts at Ornavasso, which in 1894 Sir Arthur Evans used to date the Late Iron Age burial at Aylesford in Kent (**28**). By 1900 the Swedish archaeologist Oscar Montelius, using these techniques, had built up a chronological framework for Bronze Age and Iron Age Europe which has had to be little modified since.

The definition of the different phases of the continental Iron Age in central and western Europe was the work of the first decade of the twentieth century. In a series of articles the German archaeologist Paul Reinecke divided up the Iron Age, using closed or associated finds from southern Germany. He distinguished six periods, Hallstatt C and D (Hallstatt A and B were used for the preceding Bronze Age, and acknowledged the degree of continuity that could be seen between the two), and La Tène A, B, C, and D. He defined type fossils for each period, and though in some cases these type-fossils have had to be redefined, and though some of his periods have now been subdivided, his nomenclature is that now most

27 (Right) *The Early La Tène burial from Somme-Bionne, which contains imported Greek pottery dating it to the fifth century BC.* Stead 1991

28 (Below) *The burial from Aylesford, Kent, containing bronze vessels and brooches similar to those from Ornavasso in northern Italy, and dating it to the first century BC.* Evans 1890

widely used on the continent, and will be the one used in this book, along with Tischler's more general Early, Middle and Late. At the same time a French archaeologist, Joseph Déchelette, was working on a similar scheme, with Hallstatt I and II, and La Tène I, II and III, his La Tène I corresponding with Reinecke's A and B, or Tischler's Early La Tène.

Celtic art

From the eighteenth century onwards there was an increasing awareness and appreciation of earlier and different styles of art and architecture, rather than simply building, painting and sculpting in the latest style. In the eighteenth century J.J. Winckelmann had started to describe the norms of Classical Greek and Roman art, and architects started consciously to imitate classical and 'Gothic' styles. Napoleon's expedition to Egypt brought the western world's attention to another ancient civilisation with its own distinctive way of depicting the world, and, in France especially, this style became the vogue for architecture and furniture design. At the same time, traders and missionaries were collecting art objects from around the world, not only from the great civilisations of China and India or the Arab world, but also ethnographic material revealing a plethora of styles distinctive of different peoples and cultures, some of which appealed to western taste, and others which offended. Archaeologists too began to recognise different styles from past peoples, and Christian Thomsen was one of the first, in the 1830s, to start distinguishing Bronze Age styles from the later Germanic and Viking styles. It is against this wider development that the art form, now variously labelled 'La Tène' or 'Celtic', was first defined.

The immediate stimulus was the discovery of two outstanding masterpieces. The first was the so-called 'Tara' brooch (in fact from Bettystown in Co. Meath), discovered in 1850 (**29**). It aroused enormous public interest, and Queen Victoria herself had several replicas made to use as personal gifts. The second was the shield from Battersea, discovered in 1857, during the construction of a bridge over the Thames (**30**). It was published by the secretary of the British Association, H.S. Cuming, as pre-Roman and 'Celtic'. He gives no reason for this description other than its association with 'Celtic'-shaped skulls and other objects.

The first definition of the art style was by John Kemble (1807–57). He was a student of Jakob Grimm, and so had a major interest in languages and the peopling of western Europe. His major contribution to archaeology was in the field of post-Roman Germanic (or 'Teutonic') studies. He was the first to link the similarity of cremation urns found in northern Germany and eastern Britain with the historic invasions of the Angles and Saxons, and he was writing a paper on this and the nature of the original (non-Indo-European) language of western Europe, which he argued was probably Finnish. He was also defining 'Celtic art' when he died. However, he had lectured on the subject in Dublin in 1857 (but this was only

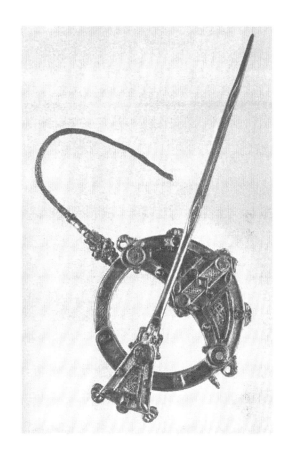

29 (Right) *The 'Tara' brooch, dating to the eighth century AD found at Bettystown, Co. Meath in 1850.* National Museum of Ireland

30 (Below) *The Battersea shield.* As illustrated in Kemble *et al.* 1863

31 *Augustus Franks in 1872; he coined the term 'Late Keltic Art' in 1863.* Permission of Professor Derek Roe

published posthumously in 1863), and we find his ideas first published by Sir William Wilde in the second part of a catalogue of the objects in the Museum of the Royal Irish Academy (1861):

> Shields: bossed plates of bronze decorated with what has been denom-inated the trumpet pattern from its resembling an arrangement of curved horns, and regarded as peculiarly Celtic.
>
> Wilde 1861, 519.

Wilde elsewhere in the catalogue refers to 'Celtic trumpet patterns' (Wilde 1861, 567, 569).

Kemble's work was eventually published by two colleagues R.G. Latham, and Augustus Franks (1836–1897), then a curator at the British Museum (**31**), along with their own papers on these themes. For Kemble, the most distinctive feature of the art form was a triangular shape with curved sides, what is nowadays referred to as a 'trumpet shape' or 'trumpet scroll', which he suggested was entirely distinctive of this art style. He had commissioned a number of plates of objects with which to illustrate the art style, but it fell to Franks to complete this and to add a text. The objects included two shields from Wandsworth and the one from Battersea (**30**), and also that from the River Witham in Lincolnshire, along with other weapons from the Thames and the Witham and various items of enamelled horsegear including some from the so-called 'Polden Hills' hoard (**32**). Franks argued that the style of these objects was neither Roman, Saxon, nor Viking, so the only people to whom they could be assigned were the indigenous 'Celts'. He labelled the finds 'Late Keltic', the 'Late' to distinguish them from the geometrically decorated pottery and metal objects which could be assigned to the Bronze Age (which, as we have seen, was also considered 'Celtic' on the evidence of craniology). As scabbards on which the decoration occurred were of iron, Franks could therefore argue an Iron Age date. He also looked at continental parallels, including the finds from La Tène.

'Celtic' was thus the name given to the art style from the very start, based on the assumption received from linguistics that the early inhabitants of Britain and Ireland were 'Celts'. In 1895 Sir Arthur Evans delivered the Rhind lectures in which he defined the classical origins of the art style. Unfortunately the lectures were never published except as local newspaper reports, and in truncated form in a paper to a local society in Liverpool. The first detailed study of 'Celtic art' was published in 1904 by J. Romilly Allen. He included some of the early Christian finds such as the Tara brooch. He follows normal nineteenth-century interpretation in assigning Bronze Age finds to the Celts, so these are included, as well as later stone crosses with interlace patterns which are better paralleled in Germanic art styles.

This development in Britain was not paralleled on the continent. The one book of the period entitled *Art Celtique* by Charles Roessler and published in 1908 is a hotchpotch of material none of which fits the modern description. In

32 *Late Iron Age harness fitting from various sites in southern Britain.* Kemble *et al.* 1863

33 *The gold bowl from the rich La Tène A tumulus burial at Schwarzenbach, Kr. St. Wendel, discovered by chance in 1849.* Antiken Sammlung, Berlin

the 1860s a rich series of burials were excavated, concentrated in the Hunsrück, south of the Mosel, including the gold torcs from Durkheim and Besseringen. These and many other finds were published by Ludwig Lindenschmidt between 1858 and 1881. In 1874 Hermann Genthe published a work demonstrating Etruscan trade over the Alps as well as Greek trade from Marseilles, and it was in this context that these finds were interpreted. For Lindenschmidt, the Durkheim torc was an Etruscan torc, and when Adolf Furtwängler published the gold bowl from Schwarzenbach (**33**), he assigned it to native workshops in the neighbourhood of Marseilles, an interpretation followed by Reinecke in 1902. Thus, though the ornamented scabbards and some of the bronze enamelled torcs were recognised as indigenous, the great masterpieces were not considered to be of local origin.

Cultures and culture groups

At the same time as these distinctive art styles were being recognised, it was suggested that there were also distinctive types of artefacts which might be diagnostic of specific peoples and perhaps even to document migrations. Kemble's recognition in the 1850s of the similarities of the cremation urns from the Hamburg region of Germany with those found in eastern England, and linking this with the fifth-century AD Anglo-Saxon invasions described by Bede, is possibly the earliest example. By 1869 Rudolf Virchow was identifying the hand-made pottery

34 *Gabriel de Mortillet in 1870.*
Permission of Professor Derek Roe

(*Burgwallkeramik*) found on hillforts in central Europe with Slavic settlement of the fifth to eighth centuries AD.

At the International Congress at Bologna in 1871 Count Gozzadini displayed the finds he had made on his excavations at the Etruscan town of Marzabotto, all of which he considered to be Etruscan. However, both the Swiss archaeologist Emile Désor and the French archaeologist Gabriel de Mortillet (**34**) recognised the finds from some of the burials as being different from the rest, Désor comparing them to the finds from La Tène, and de Mortillet with the finds from burials in northern France. It was left to de Mortillet to publish their ideas in 1871, where he illustrates the finds alongside comparable ones from sites in the Marne (**35**). This he then explicitly links with the statement by Livy that the Senones who inhabited the Marne in the first century BC were among the invaders of northern Italy at a date variously placed at around 600 BC or 400 BC. However, he nowhere makes a more general statement about Gauls and Celts and their material culture.

In the late nineteenth century, anthropologists were defining a concept of 'culture' to signify the differences in the beliefs, ideology and ways of living of different peoples. Culture was something which had both a spatial dimension (the territory occupied by a people) and a time dimension (the transmission of those ideas from one generation to another). Archaeologists felt that this concept could be carried over into the realm of material culture (the ways of decorating pots, the sort of ornaments worn) as well as to burial rites, and house and settlement structures, and so the word 'culture' (in German *Kulturgruppe* and in French *Civilisation*)

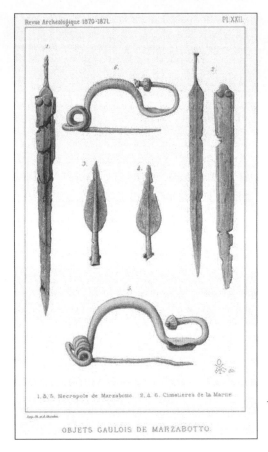

35 *The comparison made between the finds from the Etruscan town of Marzabotto and finds from northern France.* de Mortillet 1870-1. Musée Dechélette, Roanne

was adopted to signify this. In the last decades of the nineteenth century and the first decade of the twentieth the concept had been tacitly accepted – Joseph Déchelette for instance was talking of *les civilisations d'Hallstatt et de La Tène* in 1902. This represents a significant departure from the original formulation by Hildebrand and Désor in the 1870s which was strictly chronological, with no implications of race or peoples.

The first explicit definition of an archaeological culture (*Kulturgruppe*) is universally ascribed to Gustaf Kossinna (1858–1931), and as it directly underlies the modern equation of the Celts with La Tène Art and Culture, it is worth quoting in full:

> Sharply defined archaeological provinces correlate at all times with definite peoples or tribal groups.
>
> Kossinna 1911, translation author.

This was to be more clearly stated by Gordon Childe in the 1920s:

> We find certain types of remains – pits, implements, ornaments, burial rites, house forms – constantly recurring together. Such a complex of regularly associated traits we shall term a 'cultural group' or just a 'culture'. We assume that such a complex is the material expression of what today would be called a people.
>
> Childe 1929, v–vi.

Kossinna's interest lay in the origins and expansion of the German-speaking peoples, and as such he had a specifically nationalistic agenda. His training had been in linguistics, but he turned to archaeology as a means of tracing the origins of language groups in situations where there were no written records. He was impressed with Montelius' demonstration of an apparent continuity of culture in Scandinavia and northern Germany from the Neolithic onwards, and he suggested this represented a continuity of peoples. As the first records showed these peoples spoke Germanic languages, he further suggested that indicated a northern origin for the Germanic languages, if not for the Indo-European language group. He then attempted to demonstrate the spread of the Germans by using distribution maps of specific artefact types. This approach he labelled as *Siedlungsarchäologie*, literally 'settlement archaeology' though the 'archaeology of colonisation' might be a better translation. From the start his views were highly controversial, leading to a major conflict between his own school of archaeology and that of his leading German contemporary, Carl Schuchhardt, a problem which will be pursued in a later chapter.

Joseph Déchelette (1862–1914)

We have been following various threads: the location and origin of the Celts using historical sources; the proliferation of archaeological data; the construction of a chronological framework for archaeology; the concept of culture and its relationship to ancient peoples; and in Britain the definition of 'Celtic art'. All these threads were finally drawn together by Joseph Déchelette in his *Manuel d'Archéologie*, providing us with an overview which has formed the basis on which all more recent syntheses are based.

Déchelette was born in Roanne and entered the family textile firm (**36**). This gave him not only substantial wealth with which to pursue his interests, but also the opportunity to travel; his visits to other countries to sell goods were often supplemented by visits to local museums. He was fluent in several languages, even learning Czech simply so that he could translate into French J.L. Píč's publication of the oppidum of Stradonice whose finds bore a strong resemblance to those of Mont Beuvray. His interest in archaeology was stimulated by his uncle, the wine merchant Gabriel Bulliot who between 1867 and 1895 carried out extensive excavations at Mont Beuvray

36 *Portrait of Joseph Déchelette.* Centre archéologique européen du Mont Beuvray

which he identified as the ancient *Bibracte*, capital of the Aedui; Déchelette took over the excavations between 1897 and 1907. He was also active in the local archaeological societies, publishing finds and preserving sites. His archaeological interests and publications extended from the Palaeolithic to the medieval period.

He developed the grandiose scheme of producing a synthesis of the major archaeological finds of Europe, the *Manuel d'Archéologie Celtique et Gallo-romaine*. In the event, his plans were cut short by the First World War in which he was an early victim (he was shot during an infantry attack in northern France), and the Gallo-Roman section of his work was produced by Albert Grenier in the 1920s. Nonetheless he produced five volumes covering the whole of pre- and proto-history; it is the last three which concern us here, *II–1: Age du Bronze* (1910); *II–2: Premier Age du Fer ou Époque de Hallstatt* (1913); and. *II–3: Second Age du Fer ou Époque de La Tène* (1914).

He nowhere discusses the theoretical basis of his writing, but it is strongly influenced by the concept of culture, and he continuously refers to the *civilisations* of Hallstatt and La Tène, though he is less certain than Kossinna on the racial interpretations of cultures or of material culture. For the identification of the various racial groups his interpretation largely follows that of d'Arbois de Jubainville, seeing a Ligurian population replaced by an incoming Celtic one, disagreeing only over the date when this happened:

> Here we find ourselves in disagreement with d'Arbois de Jubainville who locates the original Celtic territory on the Rhine, the Main and the upper Danube . . . [He believes that the Celts] did not cross the Rhine until around the seventh century. We believe that the

arrival of the Celts cannot yet be fixed exactly, but it was before the Hallstatt period.

Déchelette 1914, 571; translation author.

For the archaeological identification of the various groups mentioned in the ancient sources, he decided that burial rite was the one distinctive feature, and he made the following equations:

Ligurians	=	Crouched inhumation
Celts	=	Extended inhumation
Germans and Belgae	=	Cremation

The Celts he could trace back to the Hallstatt period in western Europe (**37**):

On the evidence of the similarity of the burial rites and the main artefact types, as well as from the anthropological data, in the Hallstatt period people belonging to the same ethnic group seem to have occupied, on the one hand, the southern part of Germany, Bohemia, and perhaps parts of eastern Austria, and on the other hand north-eastern and central Gaul, that is at the minimum Lorraine, Burgundy, the Berry and the Auvergne. In the fifth century the eastern part of

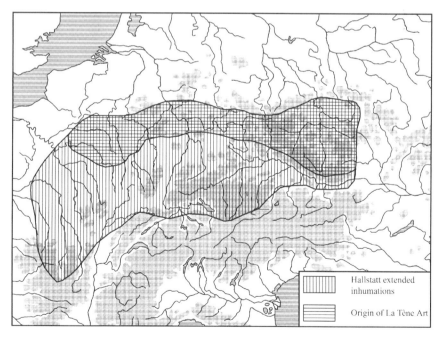

37 *Reconstructed map of Déchelette's theories of Celtic origins and expansion.* Author

this area was, according to the historical sources, occupied by the Celts; the same must be true of the western part. There is no sign of any upheaval in this area up to the end of La Tène II, the time of the Belgic invasion.

Déchelette 1914, 571; translation author.

He also took over the British concept of Celtic art, using both Franks and Romilly Allen as sources, and he assumed an indigenous origin of many of the rich objects from northern France and western Germany. Using the chronology that he had established (Hallstatt I, II, La Tène I, II, III) he was able to assign the earliest of the objects decorated in 'Celtic' style to his La Tène I (**38**, **39**), with a distribution concentrated in an east-west zone incorporating southern Bohemia, Bavaria, Baden-Württemberg, and north-eastern France, largely corresponding to the area which he had assigned to the Celts (**37**). The link between insular 'Celtic' art and the origin of the art style in the continental territory of the Celts was thus made, and though some have preferred to refer to the art style as 'La Tène Art' the term Celtic art has proved the more popular.

The rest of the material culture presented problems. Hallstatt metalwork, for instance swords, has a very extensive distribution which it is impossible to interpret in racial terms; even though the distributions of Hallstatt burial rites, painted pottery, brooch types, etc. are tighter, they still extend across areas which might be occupied by Celts, Illyrians or other groups. For Late La Tène the distinctive swords turn up in contexts which can be labelled both Celtic or Germanic:

> While the Hallstatt culture was shared in common by several peoples and had numerous and fundamental variants, the La Tène culture seems to us to be essentially Celtic, although it did extend beyond the limits of the Celts at the period of their maximum extension, especially on the German side.

Déchelette 1910, 5; translation author.

He finally decided to divide his La Tène into three provinces: Celtic, Germanic and Insular (i.e. Britain and Ireland). For Spain, while he recognised the late date of the Celtiberian cremation cemeteries, he, like most contemporary scholars, labelled them as 'Hallstatt' on the grounds that the principle weapon was the short dagger (as in Hallstatt D in central Europe), and female bracelets were similar to those in Hallstatt contexts in central Europe (Déchelette 1913, 682–92). On the other hand La Tène swords, brooches and art were absent in this area, and for many years afterwards, despite the renown of Celtiberian weapons in the Roman world, and their influence on the arming of the Roman soldier, archaeologists tended to look on these areas as somehow retarded. The only La Tène objects he recorded in Spain were from Catalonia dating to his La Tène II (Déchelette 1914, 1100–02), though he assigns these to the Celtiberians rather than to the Iberians.

This interpretation, of an origin of the Celts on the upper Danube, middle Rhine and northern France, thus becomes linked with the early distribution of La Tène culture and Celtic art, and this forms the basis of subsequent interpretations of the expansion of the Celts: the Iron Age invasions into Britain from the Marne; an eastward expansion into central Europe, bringing with it a La Tène culture and

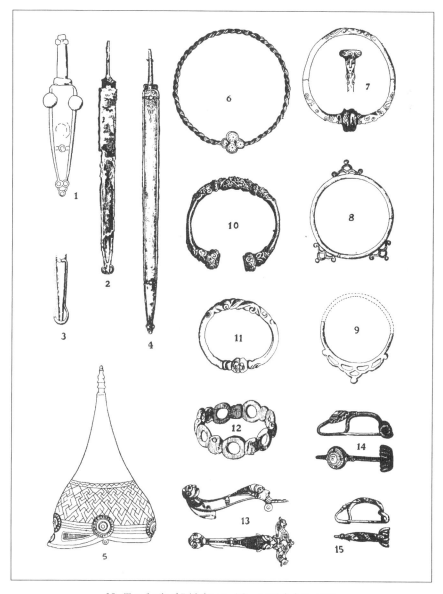

38 *Type fossils of Déchelette La Tène I.* Déchelette 1914

an extended inhumation burial rite; a gradual 'laténisation' or 'celtisation' of western and southern France; and an invasion of Italy around 400 BC from north of the Alps. The validity of these propositions will be explored in later chapters.

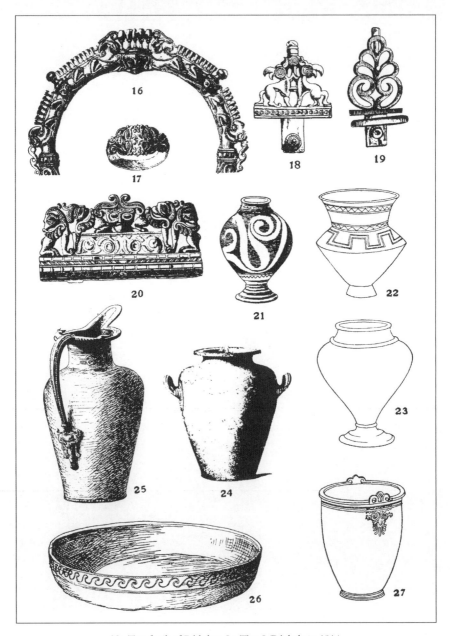

39 *Type fossils of Déchelette La Tène I.* Déchelette 1914

6

LOCATING THE CELTS

Figures **40** to **46** are a sequence of maps with various versions of the origin and expansion of the Celts, and I have deliberately included the original captions. For me they epitomise the problems we have in the development of the twentieth-century concept of the Celts. The first (**40**) comes from Terence Powell's *The Celts* originally published in 1958, but subsequently reissued on a number of occasions; clearly in part it derives from Déchelette. The second (**41**), was published by an ancient historian, André Aymard, in 1954, and reproduced in modified form in Jacques Moreau's *Die Welt der Kelten* (1958). On this map we can immediately detect Déchelette's interpretation of the Hallstatt distribution of the Celts, and southern and western France and central Europe are seen as areas of relatively late colonisation; however, in contrast to d'Arbois de Jubainville, Britain and Ireland have become areas of later colonisation. Arrows signify the areas of expansion or of attack. Those on Delphi and Asia Minor are historically dated and documented, while that on Italy is based on Livy, but with the revision of the date from 600 to 400 BC as originally suggested by Niebuhr in the 1830s. The other arrows to the west are essentially those of Buchanan, but with a nineteenth- or twentieth-century gloss (e.g. the Celts in Ireland come from Gaul, not Iberia).

Aymard's map clearly influenced later maps such as that produced by Paul-Marie Duval in 1977 in *Les Celtes* (**42**), e.g. the area occupied by the Celtiberians in Spain reflects the distribution of place names, not the ancient distribution of the Celtiberians. In his chart (1977, 290–1) he is more explicit about the dates he envisages for colonisation by the Celts; Britain he suggests was not occupied until around 300 BC, an interpretation derived from the ideas developed by Christopher Hawkes from the 1930s (he and Hawkes were close collaborators in the 1960s and later). For Spain he suggests a date around 500 BC. For the exhibition in the Keltenmuseum at Hallein in Austria Ludwig Pauli produced a variation (**43**) which reflected the new finds which were coming out of Austria, which he termed an 'area of fifth-century influence', though his treatment of Britain and Ireland is somewhat bizarre (Pauli 1980, 31). The best-known map is that which appeared in Vincent and Ruth Megaw's *Celtic Art* (1989) based on Duval's, but with the addition of Powell's area of 'origin of the La Tène Art and Culture' (**44**). It is a commonly repro-duced map; it was used for instance in the exhibitions at Rosenheim in 1993 and at

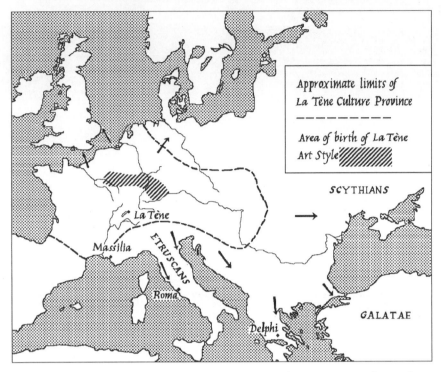

40 *'The expansion of the Celts between the late fifth and the mid-third centuries BC.'* Powell 1958, fig. 15, 'Interpretation 2'

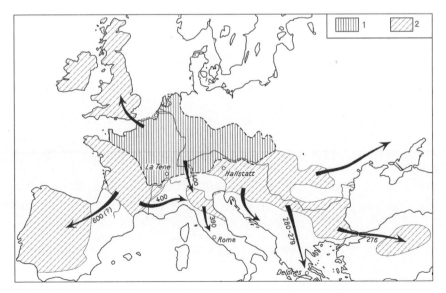

41 *'The Expansion of the Celts. 1: area where the Celts flourished; 2: lands where the Celts settled'.* From A. Aymard and J. Auboyer (eds) Histoire Générale des Civilisations, Vol. II, Rome et son Empire, 1954: 58. *'Interpretation 2'*

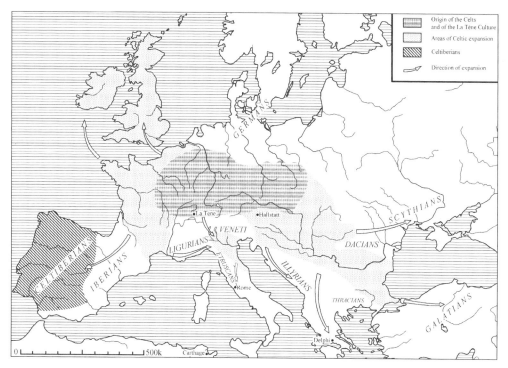

42 *'The Celtic world.'* Duval 1977, fig. 449, 'Interpretation 2'

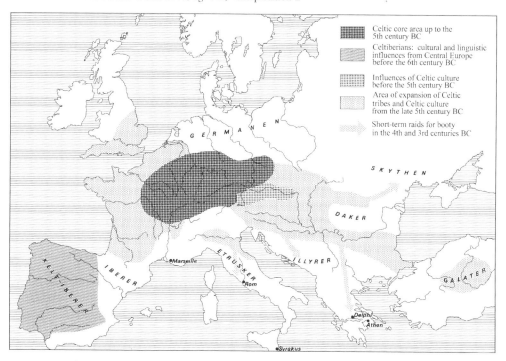

43 Pauli 1980, 31, 'Interpretation 2'

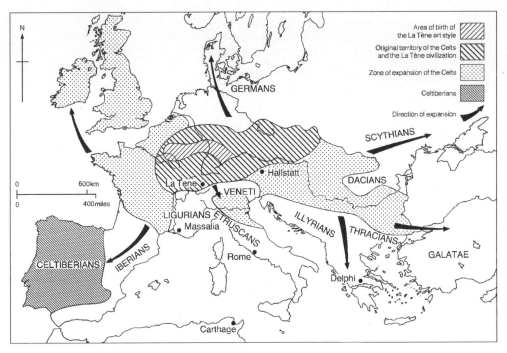

44 *'The territories occupied by the Celts from the fifth century BC until the Roman conquest.'* Megaw and Megaw 1989, fig. 2, 'Interpretation 2'

Troyes (for the conference of the Association française pour l'Etude de l'Âge du Fer in 1995) and by Miranda Green in *The Celtic World* (1995), and in revised form by Barry Raftery in his book on *Pagan Celtic Ireland* (1994). This map thus represents the standard view of the origin and expansion of the Celts as seen in Britain, Ireland, France and Germany. Though the maps distinguish between the territories of the Celts as defined in historical sources, and the origin of La Tène art, the captions and keys make it clear that the two are considered by the authors to be synonymous. This is what I shall call 'interpretation 2'.

The next map (**45**) is that produced by Barry Cunliffe in his 1997 book *The Ancient Celts*; a similar version appears in Simon James' book *The World of the Celts* (1993), and this represents 'interpretation 3'. Here the invasions are coming directly from the north and north-east as well as the north-west (note, however, that the only historical evidence we have of the Boii crossing the eastern Alps is not from south to north in the fifth/fourth century BC, but from south to north following their defeat at the battle of *Mutina* in 193 BC). The invading peoples are shown as coming from the centres of rich burials in Champagne and the Hunsrück-Eifel, and, in the case of Cunliffe, Bohemia as well. In these maps it is the archaeology which has taken over from the historical accounts, that is, the

Celts are being equated with a supposed La Tène Culture which is allowed to over-ride the historical evidence; Livy, the Bituriges and Bourges have been ignored! In fact, in his book Cunliffe almost entirely ignores central France (the 'Celtic' area *par excellence* if we follow Caesar), and it only figures in his maps of the areas where Celtic languages were spoken (figs 206 and 208), not as an area where Celts were settled. In the latest version of this map, produced by Haywood (2001), the archaeological groups are assigned tribal names, Boii, Treveri and Parisii, taking us full circle back to the classical sources, but unfortunately not to the same point from which we started, as neither the Parisii or the Treveri are among the peoples listed by Livy, indeed the Parisii have been misplaced!

The final map is that published by Christopher Pare in 1991, and only deals with the Gallic invasion of Italy (**46**). He tacitly accepts Niebuhr's re-dating to 400 BC, but essentially follows Thierry's interpretation based on Livy in accepting that the Gallic peoples recorded in detail by Caesar and Strabo in the first century BC were already settled in these locations in the fifth century BC (interpretation 1). Thus the invaders of Italy are mainly seen as coming from central France rather than from northern France, and certainly not from Germany or the Czech Republic, though he shows them coming over the passes of Mont Cenis and Great St Bernard rather than Montgenèvre and Great St Bernard. If we follow this interpretation, the supposed direct link between the Celts and the 'origin' of the 'La Tène culture' and 'La Tène art' is broken (there is only a partial overlap), and the

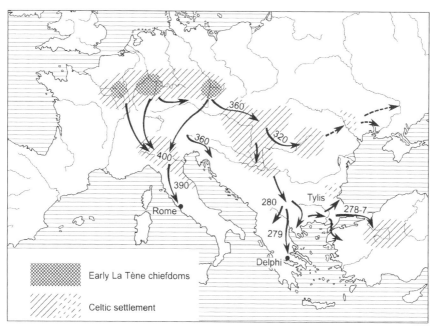

45 *'The principal movements of the Celts, 400–270 BC.'* Cunliffe 1997, fig. 55, 'Interpretation 3'

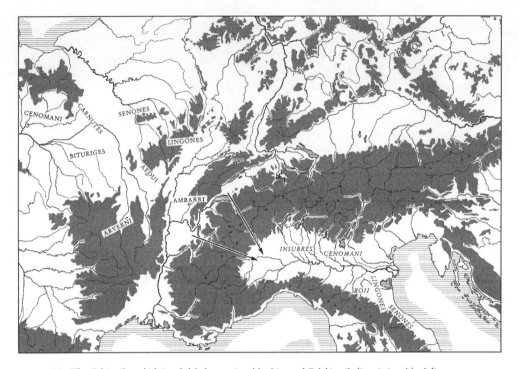

46 *'The Celtic tribes which invaded Italy, mentioned by Livy and Polybius (Italic script) and by Julius Caesar (normal script). The arrows show the routes taken by the Celts over the Great St Bernard and Mont Cenis passes.'* Pare 1991, fig. 10, 'Interpretation 1'

dominant interpretation of the twentieth century needs to be abandoned. When I approached Christopher Pare about this reinterpretation, he was at first somewhat bemused by my statement that it represented a radical departure from traditional interpretations, and said that all he had done was to read the historical sources, and put this on to a map! As we shall see, it is not so simple, so in this chapter I wish to explore which of the three interpretations is more likely. Though, given the nature of our sources, a definitive statement is not possible, I shall, on the basis of both the archaeological and the historical sources, suggest that the Thierry/Pare version is the more likely.

Defining the Celts

The ancient sources use six names to define the peoples about whom we are talking, three in Greek (*Keltoi, Keltai, Galatai*), and three in Latin (*Celti, Celtae, Galli*). The distinction between the male and female endings of the name we can ignore, as only one author, Strabo, makes a distinction between the two. He suggests that the name of the people (*Keltoi*) may have derived from a people or group of peoples called *Keltai* in southern France, and that the Greeks then transferred it as a collective name for the neighbouring peoples:

> This then is what I have to say about the province of Narbonitis whom the men of old called 'Keltai', and it was from them that the Galatai in general were called Keltoi on account of the fame of the Keltai, or the Massaliotes contributed to this due to their proximity.
>
> Strabo, *Geography* 4.1.14.

I shall also, in the first part of the analysis, assume that *Galatai* is equivalent to the Latin term *Galli*, that Latin *Celtae* is the same as Greek *Keltoi*, and that no author will use the term from the other language. This is generally true but there are one or two exceptions. For the Greeks the area roughly equating to modern France was called *Keltike* (though for some such as Dionysius of Halicarnassus it extended east of the Rhine), so if they use a term for the inhabitants of *Keltike*, they would call them *Keltoi*. The Romans, in contrast, called it *Gallia*, and its inhabitants *Galli*. For both the Greeks and the Romans *Galatia* was generally the territory occupied by the *Galatai* (the Galatians) in Asia Minor. We should also note that terms like *Aquitania*, *Keltike* and *Galatia* after the Roman conquest could be used to define administrative areas rather than ethnic areas (e.g. the Roman province of Aquitania extended into central France to include such obviously Celtic peoples as the Arverni).

As already noted in the dispute between d'Arbois de Jubainville and Bertrand, the term *Galatai* appears relatively late, not until the beginning of the third century BC, at the time of the attack on Delphi (279 BC) and the invasion of Asia Minor (278–277 BC); the early texts are mainly derived from Pausanias. The earliest mention is perhaps a quote from Hieronymos Cardanos *c.*370–266 BC who talks about the invaders as:

> These Galatai live at the ends of Europe, near a vast sea the limits of which no ship can reach.
>
> Quoted in Pausanias I.3.6.

The second describes a shield dedicated at Delphi commemorating Cydias, the hero of the second Battle of Thermopylae, who fell fighting against the Galatians (d'Arbois de Jubainville 1902, 8):

> How much this shield regrets the flourishing youth of Cydias, which, after belonging to a mortal, is dedicated to Zeus. Beneath this shield Cydias extended his left arm for the first time when the impetuous god of war killed him in combat with the Galatian.
>
> Pausanias X.1.12.

Finally there is an epitaph of three girls from Miletus who killed themselves rather than fall in the hands of the Galatai or Keltoi (the terms are used synonymously):

> Oh Miletos, dear homeland, we have departed for ever. Thus we have escaped the immoral passions of those Galatai who respect no law. We were three, maidens and citizens, to whom the violent god of war, whom the Celts love, decreed this fate. We have suffered neither dishonourable embrace nor marriage. For fiancé we have found the god of death.
>
> Quoted by d'Arbois de Jubainville 1902, 84.

Logically, as the Venn diagrams on **47** show, there are five possible relationships between the usages of the words *Gaul* and *Celt*:

1. Some Gauls are Celts and all Celts are Gauls. This is the usage which we find in Caesar's *De bello gallico* where there are various groups who live in Gaul and so are called *Galli* (*Aquitani*, *Belgae*, *Germani*), and this includes a group who are called *Celtae*. The most famous quote is that with which Caesar starts his book, but the concept is also to be found in Apollodoros of Athens around 144 BC (quoted by Stephanus of Byzantium):

> The Aidousioi [Aedui], the allies of the Romans in Celtic Galatia.
>
> Müller 1885, 437, Fr. 60.

> The Arverni, the most bellicose people of the Galatai in Keltike.
>
> Müller 1885, 437, Fr. 62.

2. All Gauls are Celts and all Celts are Gauls, that is the two words can be used synonymously and interchangeably. This is quite common in the ancient literature (e.g. the quote above about the girls from Miletos). Hieronymos of Cardia (*c.*360–270), quoted by Pausanias, uses the terms Celt and Galatian interchangeably (Keltoi 11 times, Galatai 21).

3. No Gauls are Celts and no Celts are Gauls. This is what we find in the Greek terminology of Diodorus Siculus quoting Poseidonius:

> It will now be useful to make a distinction which is unknown to most people. Those who live in the interior above Marseille, and those along the Alps, and those on this side of the Pyrenees are called Keltai, whereas those who are settled above Celtica in the area stretching towards the north both in the region of the Ocean and in that of the Hercynian

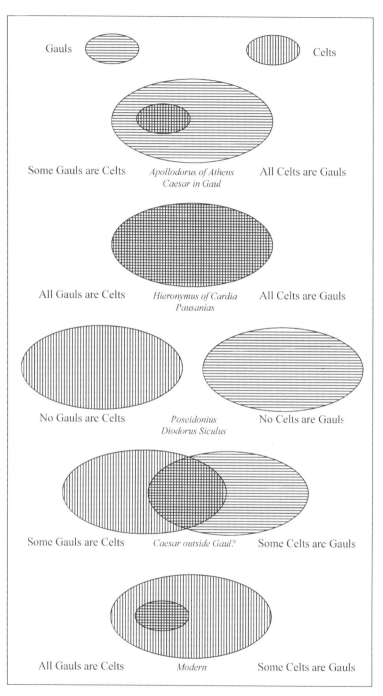

Gauls

Celts

Some Gauls are Celts

Apollodorus of Athens
Caesar in Gaul

All Celts are Gauls

All Gauls are Celts

Hieronymus of Cardia
Pausanias

All Celts are Gauls

No Gauls are Celts

Poseidonius
Diodorus Siculus

No Celts are Gauls

Some Gauls are Celts

Caesar outside Gaul?

Some Celts are Gauls

All Gauls are Celts

Modern

Some Celts are Gauls

47 *Venn diagrams showing the relationship between the terms Keltoi/Celtae and Galatai/Galli.*
Author

> Mountains, and all the people beyond them as far as Scythia are called
> Galatai; the Romans, however, include all these peoples together under
> one name and call them all Galli.
>
> Diodorus Siculus V.32.

4. Some Gauls are Celts and some Celts are Gauls, but not all Gauls are Celts, and
not all Celts are Gauls. This is less easy to document in the Ancient World. It
might have been Caesar's attitude had he discussed the Celts who lived in Spain,
and who were not Gauls because they did not live in Gaul.

5. All Gauls are Celts and some Celts are Gauls. This is an entirely modern usage,
where the Galli, along with the Britanni and the Belgae form part of a larger
group called the 'Celts' (because they speak a 'Celtic' language). It is unknown in
the ancient literature.

From this study two important points emerge: firstly that the ancient usage is not
consistent, and we have to look at each author, if not at each specific context, to
see how the terms are being used; and secondly that we cannot impose the
modern definition on the ancient world.

It has been suggested by Malcolm Chapman (1992), that the ancient Celts may
not have existed as an ancient ethnic group, and that the term 'Celt' is something
which was imposed on them from outside by the Greeks and Romans; indeed
Chapman goes on to suggest this for the modern populations as well, and that it was
only taken on by the people themselves at a later date (c.f. Australian Aborigines
who have adopted the European term as they possessed no collective expression for
themselves). As I have already shown for the modern Celts, the terms were
developed initially by a Scotsman (Buchanan), a Breton (Pezron) and a Welshman
(Lhuyd). In the ancient world there also some evidence that the terms *Galli* and
Celtae were used by the peoples themselves. Firstly we have the statement by Caesar:

> All Gaul is divided into three parts, of which one is occupied by the
> Belgae, another by the Aquitani, and the third by the people called
> 'Celtae' in their own language, but 'Galli' in ours.
>
> *De bello gallico* 1.1.

Secondly we have at least three or four authors whose 'Celtic' or 'Gallic' origin is
assured, and who happily use these terms either to describe themselves, or their
compatriots. Firstly there is Trogus Pompeius who was a member of the Gallic
Vocontii in southern Gaul; his grandfather had served with Pompey in Spain in
the war against Sertorius (76–71 BC) and received Roman citizenship from him;
and his father Gnaeus Pompeius was a senior member of Caesar's staff during the
conquest of Gaul, acting as an interpreter in the negotiations with Ambiorix (*De
bello gallico* 5.36) – though he nowhere specifically describes himself as a Celt or

Gaul, he is happy to use this term for his near neighbours. In contrast the poet Martial in the later first century AD on several occasions described himself as 'half Celtic and half Iberian'. Thirdly there is Sidonius Apollinaris (in the late fifth century AD) who apologises to his brother-in-law Ecdicius, son of the emperor Avitus, for the Celtic accent (or language) of himself and his fellow Arvernian aristocrats. Finally the fourth-century poet Ausonius from *Burdigala* (Bordeaux) describes some of his colleagues as descended from Druids, with an implication of a Celtic background, but not explicitly stated. Other Latin authors also came from areas which we know were occupied by Celts, but who nowhere make any comments on their ethnic origins.

I suggest that the terms Celt and Galatian are used at four different levels of precision:

1. As a specific tribal entity (something only suggested by Strabo *Geography* 4.1.14 quoted above).

2. As a specific group of peoples or states who were called, or called themselves, Celts (e.g. Caesar in Gaul).

3. As a more general group of related peoples, one group of whom were Celts, and a term which was then was extended to the others who may not specifically have been Celts (e.g. Polybius, Livy, etc.).

4. As a very general term to refer to a grouping of people who had different ethnicities, languages, etc., but who were lumped together by outsiders, much as we refer to the aboriginal inhabitants of the Americas as 'Indians', or the inhabitants of Australia as 'Aborigines' (e.g. Ephorus, who in his generalisation would certainly have included the ancestors of the Basques).

Time and precision

We should expect to see a general trend of greater detail and greater precision through time as Greek and Latin authors had greater familiarity with the peoples west and north of the Mediterranean, as they become more acquainted with the geography (**48**). Thus, in Hesiod we merely meet the Hyperboreans, the 'people beyond the north wind'. Aeschylus, in *Prometheus Unbound*, says that the Danube rises in the lands of the Hyperboreans, and even at as late a date as the fourth or third century Heraclides of Pontus uses this term to describe the Gauls who attacked Rome. By the fifth century peoples were being named in general terms (Celts and Iberians), and by the second century distinctions were made between Celts, Galatians and Scythians. With Caesar and Strabo we obtain yet greater precision, with distinctions in Gaul between *Aquitani*, *Celtae*, *Belgae* and *Germani*,

700 - 350 BC				
Hesiod		HYBERBOREOI		
Aeschylus				
Heraclides of Pontus				
500 - 100 BC				
Herodotus		KELTOI		SKYTHAI
Eratosthenses				
Ephorus				
100 - 50 BC				
Poseidonius		KELTOI	GALATAI	SKYTHAI
50 BC - AD 100				
Caesar		BRITANNI		
Strabo	AQUITANI	CELTAE	BELGAE	GERMANI
Tacitus				

48 *From Hyperboreans to peoples; the increasing detail of geography and nomenclature from the seventh to the first century BC.* Author

with fixed boundaries between them, mainly rivers, though whether these were genuine boundaries or a Roman perception or imposition is unclear.

This raises the problems of the Germani as an ethnic group, with many of the same questions we have for the Celts, e.g. how were they defined? For Caesar they were the people on the east bank of the Rhine, except for those on the west! Tacitus mentions Germani who we know spoke Celtic languages (e.g. the Treveri), or where he himself states that they spoke *Britannice*. The earliest mention of the Germani is only just before the Gallic Wars, in the context of the revolt of Spartacus in 67 BC. Sallust writes:

> Crixus and his fellow Gauls and the Germans wished to advance and offer battle, in opposition to Spartacus.

Sallust *Historiae*, quoted in d'Arbois de Jubainville 1902, 213.

Was the lack of previous mention because their territories were so far to the north that Rome had no contact with them until a late date? Or had they been gradually expanding southwards, as Caesar states, taking over territory from peoples such as the Helvetii in the first half of the first century? Or were they simply the *Galatai* of Poseidonius? Where did Crixus' *Germani* come from? Had they been traded from Germanic territories as part of the slave trade, in which case, given the numbers involved in the revolt, there must have been a massive trade, of which archaeology tells us little? These are questions which cannot be resolved from the historical sources.

States and people

With Caesar and Strabo we start to obtain details of the names and locations of specific 'tribes'. 'Tribes' in English is an unfortunate term, as it implies a primitive level of political organisation which is belied by both the classical and archaeological sources. I have tended to use the term 'peoples', though 'state' is a more strict translation of *civitas*, the usual term used by Caesar and other sources, and it is certainly justified for the sophisticated polities of central Gaul such as that of the Aedui, with their state funds, their elected chief magistrates, the *vergobret*, and their *senatus*. It is from these states that individuals took their identity; so Trogus Pompeius introduces himself as a member of the state of the Vocontii, not as a Gaul, though the Vocontii were a bit special, as the one Gallic people which maintained its constitution after the Roman conquest rather than having a Roman model imposed on it. This attitude is confirmed many times over in the Roman period, on dedicatory descriptions and tombstones; the term Celt never appears in this context, and Gaul very rarely (Goudineau 1998, 328).

In Gaul the location of these states is fairly well documented, not only from Caesar and Strabo, but because many of them later became Roman administrative units, and so are recorded by geographers such as Ptolemy. In northern and western France especially it is the tribal name which became attached to the administrative centre, and which survives to the modern day: Paris (*Parisii*); Arras (*Atrebates*); Trier (*Treveri*); Bourges (*Bituriges Cubi*). Though the precise boundaries may be argued in detail, there is an assumption that the pre-Roman ones (as far as they may have existed) continued into the Roman period as administrative boundaries, and these themselves evolved into the post-Roman and medieval bishoprics. Some of these boundaries are supported by boundary names for Roman and modern towns such as *fines* (e.g. Fain) and *aequeranda* (e.g. Iguerande), and from Roman milestones.

Despite this trend towards greater precision, it is also necessary to look at how individual authors use terms like Gallic and Celtic. At one extreme we have Caesar for whom the *Celtae* are a specific group in Gaul, living in a well-defined territory defined by the sea and by rivers; for Ephorus writing in the third century BC, it is a general term for all the barbarians living in western Europe. For him the world outside the Mediterranean was occupied by four peoples, the Celts to the west, the Scythians to the north, the Indians to the east and the Aethiopians to the south. This is very much the same way in which Europeans considered the whole of America to be inhabited by 'Indians'. In locating the Celts we should ignore such general usages, and Ephorus would have been including everyone: Celts, Basques, Britons, Germans, and perhaps other linguistic groups which no longer exist.

We must also remember that, except for the cases of Trogus Pompeius, Martial and Sidonius Apollinaris, we are dealing with the views of outsiders, though it is worth noting that some of the Latin authors, including Pliny and Tacitus, came from northern Italy or southern Gaul, territories occupied by Gallic groups, and indeed they themselves may have had some Gallic ancestry. Seen from outside, it is quite common for groups to be invented or to be assigned to a grouping which would not be accepted by the peoples themselves. Another common usage is to name a larger group after one of the group, usually the closest; thus the Romans called the Hellenes *Graeci*, the French call the Germans (or self-styled Deutsch) the *Allemands* after the Alamanni who settled in south-western Germany in the third century AD; and continentals still tend to refer to the all inhabitants of the British Isles as 'English' (**49**). As we noted, Strabo suggested that this was how the *Keltoi*

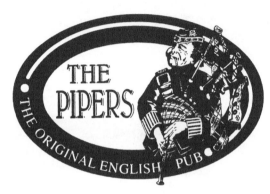

49 (Right) *A beer mat picked up in Alicante (Spain) in 1999. It demonstrates how perceptions from 'outside' (the Spanish) contrast with those seen from 'inside' (the Scots)*

50 (Below) *Strabo's concept of Gaul.* After Goudineau 1998

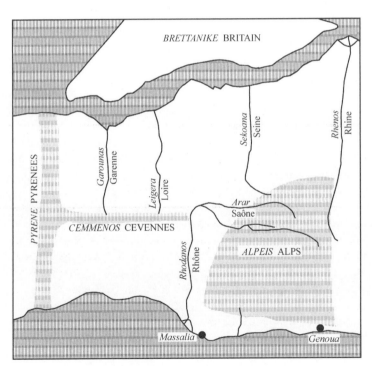

obtained their name, from a Narbonese group called the *Keltai*, though nowhere else do we encounter such a specific tribal usage for the term Celts, except perhaps for the Celtici of western Iberia.

Finally we must remember the geographic preconceptions of our authors, and that their vision of the geography of Europe, even for authors such as Strabo and Ptolemy who were fairly well informed, is not that of the modern world with its atlases. There is a welcome recent trend especially in the German literature to try to present these alternative geographies graphically (**50**).

Migration and colonisation

As the maps previously discussed demonstrate, migration has been a major ingredient of the late first millennium BC, both in explanations in the ancient world and in modern scholarship. In this section I wish to discuss those for which there is good documentation, as well as those where ancient authors have used migration to explain similarities between ancient groups (**51**, **52**). Moving populations was part of Roman frontier policy, and in the period immediately following the conquest of Gaul, two Germanic groups, the Sugambri and the Ubii, were moved from the east to the west bank of the Rhine, partly to give them, as allies, greater protection, and partly to fill some of the settlement voids caused by the decimation of some of the pre-existing population by Caesar, notably the Eburones.

At the time of Caesar's intervention in Gaul, two population movements were underway. The first involved the Helvetii and their allies, the Tulingi, the Latobrigi, the Rauraci and the Boii (who had been displaced from further east by Dacian expansion), totalling some 368,000 people according to Caesar. Their intention was to leave their territory in present-day Switzerland and move to the territory of the Santones in south-west Gaul, which involved traversing the Roman province of Narbonese Gaul. Refused access, and driven off from their attempt to cross the Rhine at Geneva, they moved northwards, only to be defeated by Caesar just south of *Bibracte* (Mont Beuvray). They were forced to return to their homeland, except the Boii who were settled somewhere in the territory of the Aedui. Caesar states that they were under pressure from the north, from German tribes, but he nowhere states that they had lost any territory. However, some German groups had crossed the Rhine in recent years, including the Suebi under Ariovistus, who had come to assist the Sequani in their conflicts with the Aedui, and then, according to Caesar, had attempted to stay as overlords of the Sequani. Caesar says that the Aeduan, Diviciacus, put the numbers of Suebi at 120,000.

Caesar mentions two other movements of population, both concerning the Belgae. He states that the Belgae were immigrant Germans from east of the Rhine who had driven out the native Gauls; he also says that the Belgae had gone to raid Britain and then to settle. For neither does he give a date, though the settlement of Britain is supported by Roman tribal names in central southern England (the

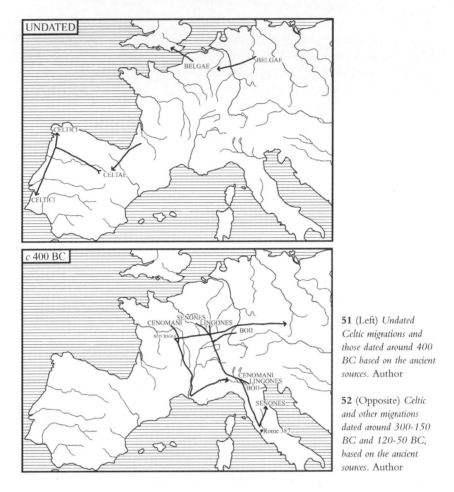

51 (Left) *Undated Celtic migrations and those dated around 400 BC based on the ancient sources.* Author

52 (Opposite) *Celtic and other migrations dated around 300-150 BC and 120-50 BC, based on the ancient sources.* Author

Atrebates, based at *Calleva Atrebatum* (Silchester), and *Venta Belgarum* (Winchester). The other story, however, has more the nature of an origin myth.

Previous to that there had been the movements of the Cimbri and Teutones, of which the later stages are well documented, with the defeat by Marius of the Teutones at *Vercellae* (Vercelli) in 102 BC and the Cimbri at *Aquae Sextiae* (Aix-en-Provence) in 101 BC. The latter were returning from an attack on Spain for which we have no details other than conflict with the Celtiberians, and the Romans had previously been defeated at *Arausio* (Orange) in 105. However, the Cimbri had already been en route for several years, and an earlier Roman defeat is recorded in 114 BC at *Noreia* (probably the site of the Magdalensberg in Austria), and in the same general area they had been repelled by the Boii. They also seem to have attacked northern Gaul, as Caesar records Critognatus reminding the Belgae that they alone had resisted the Cimbri, retreating within their oppida. Caesar adds that the Atuatuci were descendants of a group of Cimbri who had been left behind in northern Gaul to guard the excess booty. Tacitus (*Germania* 37) mentions the massive defended sites along the Rhine as a testimony to their great numbers, though he is probably referring to earlier oppida such as Kirchzarten (near Freiburg in Breisgau). The precise origin of the Teutones and their allies the Ambrones is unclear, but the Cimbri are later recorded in southern Jutland.

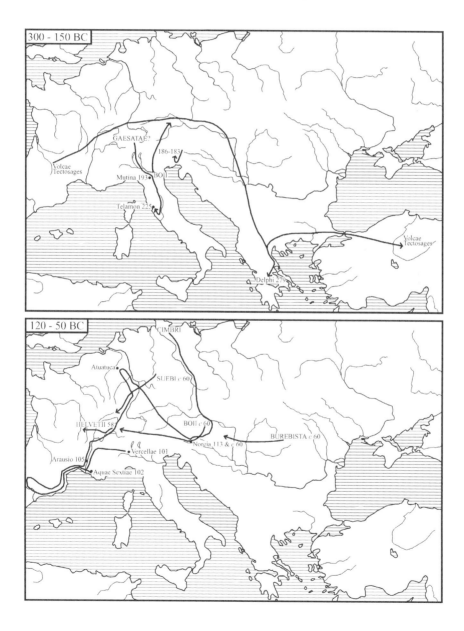

Second- and third-century incursions into Italy are recorded. In 186–183 a group of Celts came over the Carnic Alps, but were defeated and retreated back into central Europe, though not before they had started construction of a new town near Aquileia (Livy 39.22, 39.45). In 193 the Boii were defeated at the battle of *Mutina* (Modena), and retreated over the Alps. The *Gaesati* (a name for a group of special warriors who fought naked in battle rather than a tribal name), came from somewhere in the Alps and played a prominent part in the battle of Telamon in 225 BC.

For the early part of the third century there is the well-documented attack on Delphi by the Galatai in 279 BC. The origin of these groups is unknown, possibly from somewhere around the Hungarian Plain, though most sources say they came from near the Ocean, suggesting the far west. The following year another group of Galatians appeared in Asia Minor, where, after a number of battles, they settled down around *Ancyra* (Ankara) to form a state called *Galatia*. It later became a Roman province, and St Paul wrote a letter to the Galatians. As late as the fifth century St Jerome noted that these people still spoke a language similar to that spoken around Trier. There are also links with southern France, as one of the tribes mentioned is the Volcae Tectosages (who are also recorded in southern Germany), and Trogus Pompeius claims that some of the treasure captured by the Romans at *Tolosa* (Toulouse) in 123 BC originated from Delphi.

The earliest invasion for which we have good documentary evidence is that of northern Italy. However, there are problems about the date. Polybius records of the Keltoi that:

> On their first invasion they not only conquered this country, but reduced to subjection many of the neighbouring peoples, striking terror into them by their audacity. Not long afterwards they defeated the Romans in pitched battle, and pursuing the fugitives, occupied, three days after the battle, the whole of Rome with the exception of the Capitol.
>
> Polybius II.18.

He had earlier dated the attack on Rome as the nineteenth year after the battle of Aegospotami (405 BC), that is in 387–6, and so the invasion of Italy at end of the fifth and the beginning of the fourth century (Polybius I.6).

Livy, in contrast states that:

> It is generally agreed [the Gauls] who besieged Clusium were not the first who had passed the Alps. Indeed it was two hundred years before the attack on Clusium and the capture of Rome that the Gauls first crossed into Italy; neither were the Clusini the first of the Etruscans with whom they fought, but long before that the Gallic armies had often given battle to those who dwelt between the Apennines and the Alps.
>
> Livy V.33.5–9.

Later he says:

> Concerning the migration of the Gauls into Italy we are told as follows: while Tarquinius Priscus [616–579 BC] reigned in Rome the Celts, who make up one of the three divisions of Gaul, were under the domination of the Bituriges, and this people supplied the Celtic nation with a king [Ambigatus].
>
> Livy V.34.1.

He then relates the story of how Ambigatus sent out two groups of Celts to relieve the population pressure in Gaul, under his nephews; Segovesus led one group into the Hercynian Forest (central Europe), and Bellovesus the second group over the Alps to Italy. He then relates how the latter group assisted the Massaliotes to ward off the Salui and to found *Massalia* (around 600 BC).

Of the origin and route he says:

> [Bellovesus] . . . taking out with him the surplus population of his peoples, the Bituriges, Arverni, Senones, Aedui, Ambarri, Carnutes and Aulerci . . .
>
> Livy V.34.5.

> . . . They crossed the Alps through the Taurine Pass and the Pass of Duria [or Julia], routed the Etruscans in battle not far from the river Ticino, and, learning that they were encamped in what was the country of the Insubres, who bore the same name as a canton of the Aedui, they regarded it as a place of good omen, and founded a city there which they called *Mediolanum* [Milan].
>
> Livy V.24.9.

He then relates a series of undated invasions (Livy V.15):

> 2. The Cenomani under Etitovius who took the same route, settling around Brixia and Verona.

> 3. The Libui and the Salluvii who settled around the Ticino.

> 4. The Boii and the Lingones who came over the Poenine Pass (the Great St Bernard), and took over territory occupied by the Etruscans and the Umbrians.

> 5. Finally the Senones who occupied the area between the rivers Utens and Aesis, and these he claims were the ones who attacked Clusium and Rome.

For the migration into central Europe, Livy is very vague, merely naming the Hercynian Forest (the Black Forest) as the intended route.

For Spain the information is even more vague. There are several relevant texts, here in chronological order:

> These two peoples, the Iberians and the Celts, in other times fought one another over the land, but they made peace, and lived together in the same country, and through intermarriage they established a relationship with one another, and for this reason were given the common name.
>
> Diodorus Siculus 5.33.

> The Berones, neighbours of the Conisci, live in the parts to the north of the Celtiberians, and they too took part in the Celtic expedition.
>
> Strabo 3.4.12.

> Marcus Varro records that the Iberians, Persians, Phoenicians, Celts and Carthaginians penetrated the whole of Spain.
>
> Pliny 3.1.8.

> The Celtici who live around the cape [Finisterre] have a common origin with those who live on the river Anas [Guadiana], for, it is said, these people and the Turdali made an expedition there, and had a quarrel after they crossed the river Limaeus [Lima]; and in addition to the quarrel they lost their leader, so they scattered and settled down there.
>
> Strabo 3.5.5.

> Besides Roman soldiers they had active Asturians, and nimble Vettones, and Celts, fugitives from the ancient people, the Gauls, who have mixed their name with the Iberians.
>
> Lucan *Pharsalia* 4.1.9–10.

> It is evident that the Celtici came from Lusitania, from the Celtiberians, as is clear from the religion, their language and the names of their oppida, which in Baetica are distinguished by their surnames.
>
> Pliny 3.1.13.

> However, I think that once upon a time the Celts, passing over the Pyrenees, settled with the natives, and that they acquired the name of Celtiberians in that way.
>
> Appian *Hispania* 2.

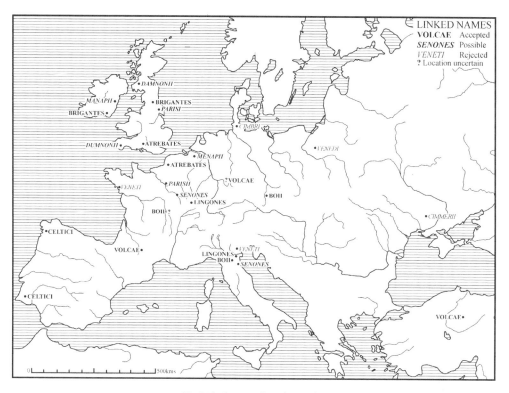

53 *Linked names of peoples.* Author

> The Celtiberians come from the Celtic Gauls, from which the region
> is called Celtiberia. For the Celtiberians are named by mixing the two
> names, from the river in Spain where they settled and from the Gauls
> who are called Celtic.
>
> Isidore of Seville Etymologiae IX.2.113–14.

Thus all the ancient sources explain the origin of the Celtiberians as due to invasions of Celts from Gaul, and Pliny adds to this the suggestion that the Celtici in the south-east of the country came from Celtiberia, and presumably those in the north-west as well who Strabo says split from them after a quarrel. No timescale is suggested, except that, by placing the Celts alongside the Phoenicians and the Carthaginians, Varro implies that this happened some time in the first millennium BC. All the sources, including Martial, suggest that the name was derived from a mixing of the Celts and the Iberians, with the exception of Isidore of Seville who suggests that it came from the name of the river Ebro rather than from the Iberians.

In addition to these specific examples of population movements, classical authors did also conjecture on common origins based on the similarity of tribal names. We have already encountered Pliny's suggestion that the Cimbri were the descendants of the Cimmeri. He also suggests a link between the Veneti of northern Italy with those encountered by Caesar in Armorica, but this is one we would reject on the grounds that one was Italic speaking and the other Celtic speaking. Tacitus in fact records a third group with the same name, though these were likely to have spoken a Germanic or Baltic language given their location in the south-eastern corner of the Baltic. Other such links are more likely to be due to part of a people moving, such as the occurrence of the Atrebates on both sides of the English Channel, further linked with the name Commius, possibly the same person in Caesar and on British coins (though there are chronological problems with the coins being some 30 years later than the events in Caesar). We have already mentioned the Volcae Tectosages in both Asia Minor and southern France, and Caesar also mentions them east of the Rhine. In other cases similar names are less certainly the same, such as the Senones of northern Gaul (short o, short e) and the Semnones or Senones of northern Italy (long o, long e), though d'Arbois de Jubainville suggested that they were named after the river Sena in Italy, not the northern Gallic people. Are the Parisii of northern Gaul to be linked with the Parisi of Yorkshire, and are terms like the Brigantes just general names, or are their specific links? On figure **53** I note such similar names; with some we have historical events to link them, in others we can only conjecture.

Peoples and states

There is a major time-lag between the date when events are supposed to have happened, and when they were recorded, often of several centuries. Thus, Livy gives us the earliest date for many of the Gallic peoples, but he is not writing until the first century BC, and so is not as reliable as Caesar writing about contemporary events. The majority of the names of peoples is, not surprisingly, to be found in Caesar's *De bello gallico*; between him and Strabo (writing in the late first century BC), and Ptolemy (second century AD) we can see some changes in Gaul, notably the disappearance of the Eburones, wiped out by Caesar, but also the appearance of new groups such as the Ubii (who migrated under Roman supervision in the late first century BC), and the Catalauni (what may have only been a *pagus* at the time of Caesar, but with full *civitas* status in the early Roman period). What is more important for us is the earliest contemporary mention of the tribal names. The earliest contemporary mention of a Gallic people is, in fact, a recent archaeological discovery of the name of the Helvetii inscribed on a potsherd from Mantua in northern Italy, dated to *c*.300 BC. The earliest literary source is Apollodoros of Athens around 144 BC who mentions the Roman treaty with the *Aidousioi* (Aedui), and the Arverni, 'the most warlike of the Galatai in Keltike' (see above), followed by Polybius (205–123 BC) writing in the late second century, who not only mentions the peoples of northern Italy and of central Spain, but also one people in Gaul, the Ardyes, presumably the Aedui, living on the Rhone

(3.47); he also names the Allobroges in the context of Hannibal crossing the Alps in 218 (3.49), but no other peoples are mentioned by name. The Arverni appear in the events around the Roman invasion of Provence in 125–123 BC, but Poseidonius' stories of Luernios takes them back to the mid-second century. A later source, the poet Silius Italicus (AD 25–101), mentions that Hannibal encountered the Volcae, Tricastini and Vocontii.

We thus cannot take the tribal names back with any certainty before the second, or at the earliest the third century BC. So, how far can we trust Livy's list made in the first century which gives the names of Gallic peoples for the fifth century if not earlier? Both he and Polybius give us the names of peoples living in northern Italy in the third century, and as several of these names occur in Gaul as well, we must assume that the peoples brought them with them. The list given by Livy includes names poorly recorded or unknown elsewhere, such as the Libui and the Salluvii, suggesting this is not a list taken from a first-century source such as Caesar. The same is true of the importance he assigns to the Bituriges, which does not fit with any later sources, despite the importance of the siege of *Avaricum* (Bourges) by Caesar; as we shall see, there is some strong archaeological evidence to support the pre-eminence of Bourges in the fifth century.

If all these tribal entities did exist in the fifth century BC, it is difficult to imagine some context in which they all moved from some putative homeland in northern Gaul or southern Germany in the fifth century or later, especially if Livy is right about the routes taken. Thus, a central Gaulish (rather than northern) origin would be more logical for the peoples mentioned in the first two waves, which is what we find, whereas the more northerly groups such as the Lingones would logically take a more northerly pass. The one problem would be the Boii who, if they were of central European origin, would have had to move to the west before moving south over the Great St Bernard Pass. There is, however, a problem with Livy's text first noted by Beatus Rheanus (1485–1547), as he talks of the first wave helping the Massaliotes at the time of the founding of the colony, and then crossing via the Taurine and *Juliae* (i.e. Birnbaumer) passes. This latter would be taking them over the Alps via Austria, which would make little geographical sense, and though all the extant manuscripts have this reading, since the eighteenth century the text has been amended to read *Duriae* which would bring them over the western Alps (d'Arbois de Jubainville 1902, 240–7).

However, we know from cases such as the Helvetii and the Volcae Tectosages that major changes could occur, and that names could be imposed by incoming groups who had established a hegemony over an indigenous group. The most elaborate documented tribal group is that of the Boii (**54**). Livy lists them as one of the northerly group who took the Great St Bernard Pass, but we do not know their actual origin. In Italy various sources place them around *Bononia* (Bologna) which takes its name from them. They were involved with various wars with the Romans, but were finally defeated in the battle of *Mutina* in 193 BC, and, according to Strabo, they retreated over the Alps:

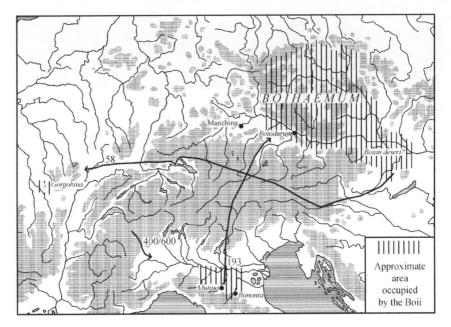

54 *Location of the Boii.* Author

The Boii were merely driven out of the regions they occupied; and after migrating to the regions around the Danube, lived with the Taurisci, and carried on war with the Dacians until they perished, people and all; and thus they left their country, which was part of Illyria, to their neighbours as a pasture for sheep.

Strabo V.1.5, 216.

Strabo also states that in central Europe they had withstood the attack of the Cimbri, and at that time were resident in the Hercynian Forest. The Boian desert, the result of their defeat by the Dacians (in the Augustan period), is mentioned by both Strabo (VII.1.5; VII.5.2) and Tacitus:

Therefore the Helvetii, the furthest of the peoples of Gaul, but formerly the Boii, occupy the territory between the Hercynian Forest, and the rivers Rhine and Main. The name *Boihaemum* still survives and indicates the old memory of the place though the occupants have changed.

Tacitus, *Germania* 28.

This suggests that the territory they occupied extended down to the Danube, and this is confirmed by the name *Boiodurum* recorded by Ptolemy and other sources, the modern Innstadt bei Passau. However, the modern Bohemia, also named after them, also seems to have been part of their territory, as both Strabo (7.1.3) and Velleius Paterculus (II.109) say that Maroboduus and the Marcomanni (who can be located in modern-day Bohemia) took over their territory around 8 BC. There is also a potsherd from Manching in Bavaria with the name BOIOS scratched on it (Rieckhoff and Biel 2001, 220). We have no evidence of them in Gaul until the time of Caesar, when they took part in the migration of the Helvetii (having first attacked *Noreia* the capital of Noricum (Magdalensberg?)), and were settled by Caesar in the territory of the Aedui, based on the unidentified oppidum of *Gorgobina*.

Though we thus have no evidence of the Boii in central Europe until the second century BC, we equally have no evidence of them in Gaul until a much later date. The most logical interpretation is that their original location was in central Europe in modern Bohemia, on the border between Bavaria and Austria, and, following Tacitus, as far north as the Main. They then took part in the invasion of Italy in the late fifth century, but retained their links with the north, hence the retreat over the Alps in 193 BC. Some subsequently, in 58 BC, took part in the attempted migration by the Helvetii before being settled in Gaul, but their main base in central Europe was wiped out by the Dacians and the Marcomanni in the late first century BC. The other problem is that the area assigned to them in central Europe is huge in comparison to the better documented peoples, and territorially the term *Boii* is more on a par with terms like *Celtae* and *Belgae* in Gaul. Thus, though they are one of the best documented of the tribal groups, the details are still very ambiguous.

The home of the Celts

We have so far located two areas where there is good historical evidence that the Celts, however defined, arrived relatively late in the first millennium, that is in Po valley and Asia Minor. We have areas where there was never any mention of Celts in the ancient record (except in the most sweeping and general terms by authors such as Ephorus), and this would include Britain and Ireland, much of the Mediterranean littoral, the North German Plain, and Scandinavia. There are also areas such as central Europe where the information is too vague, and we can neither assume nor discount the presence of Celts from an early date (e.g. Iberia, the Hungarian Plain, the Czech Republic, parts of Austria). This leaves us with southern Germany, Switzerland and the southern Alps, and western, central and parts of southern France, and possibly parts of Spain.

We should recall that we have the three conflicting theories on the location of the Celts in the fifth century, what I have labelled (working from west to east) 'interpretation 1' (central and northern France); 'interpretation 2' (northern Gaul and southern Germany) which has been adopted by the majority of modern authors; and 'interpretation 3' (northern France, southern Germany and

Bohemia). Which one of these we accept has major implications when we come to investigate whether the archaeological 'La Tène culture' and 'La Tène art' is 'Celtic' or not. Usually, in locating the Celts, modern authors tend to start with the earliest sources, but these are the authors who are the most vague because of their restricted knowledge. It would be more logical to start with more recent authors where we are on more certain ground, and work backwards.

Logically, when looking to locate the Celts, we should start with the views of the Celts themselves, but for this we only have two relatively late sources, who may themselves have been influenced by the previous literature. The earlier dates from the first century AD, the poet Martial, from the city of *Bilbilis*, near the modern town of Calatayud in central Spain, who, as a Celtiberian, considered himself half Celt and half Iberian. The other is Sidonius Apollinaris writing in the mid-fifth century AD, and this places us in the territory of the Arverni in central Gaul. This latter fits well with the only other source which purports to give the views of the Celts themselves, that of Caesar who states that this was the name used by the inhabitants of central Gaul for themselves. He defines the area occupied (**55**):

> All Gaul is divided into three parts, of which one is occupied by the Belgae, the second by the Aquitani, and the third by people called in their own tongue the Celtae, but in ours the Galli. These all differ from one another in their languages, their institutions and their laws. . . . The Galli are separated from the Aquitani by the River *Garumna* [Garonne] and from the Belgae by the *Matrona* [Marne] and the *Sequana* [Seine] . . . . One part of the country which is said to be occupied by the Galli has its origin at the river *Rhodanus* [Rhone], and is circumscribed by the River *Garumna* [Garonne] and the [Atlantic] Ocean and the territories of the Belgae. On the side of the Sequani and Helvetii it even reaches the River *Rhenum* [Rhine]; it tends to extend in a northerly direction. The Belgae sit on the furthest limit of the territory of the Galli; they extend to the lower part of the river Rhine; their orientation is towards the north and east. Aquitania extends from the Garonne to the Pyrenean mountains, and the part of the Atlantic ocean which lies near Spain; it faces to the south and the north.
>
> Caesar *De bello gallico* 1.1.

This is the classic definition of *Gallia Comata*; indeed, as Christian Goudineau has recently pointed out, one can actually claim that in this paragraph Caesar invented it. The standard term for this part of Europe from the Roman perspective was *Gallia Transalpina*, Gaul beyond the Alps, but it had never been precisely defined in this way. It is clear that Caesar is approximating the actual territories by using the rivers as the boundaries. However, the two terms are not coterminous, as *Gallia Narbonensis* does not form part of Caesar's definition, and he gives no

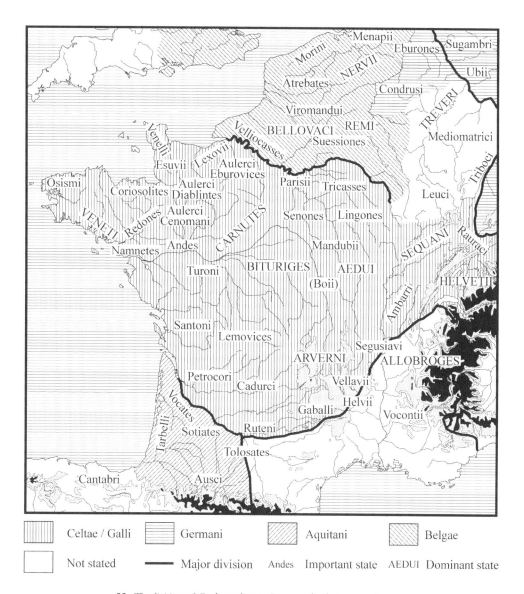

Celtae / Galli	Germani	Aquitani	Belgae

Not stated — Major division Andes Important state AEDUI Dominant state

55 *The divisions of Gaul according to Caesar, with ethnic groups.* Author

southern boundary of Celtic territory, assuming it lies on the boundaries of the Roman province. There are some ambiguities about the boundaries to the north-west between the Marne and the Rhine; exactly where do the Treveri belong? Also, is Armorica really part of Celtic Gaul, or is it an entity in its own right? However, the Germani lie beyond the river Rhine (though we later encounter Germani to the west of the Rhine), and the Britanni are to be found on the other side of the channel, though some of them are Belgae. Strabo is of little help, partly as he follows Caesar quite closely, but also he imposes the Roman administrative boundaries laid down in the reforms under Augustus; thus the Arverni, from being at the heart of Celtica, become part of Aquitania. As Goudineau (1998) has shown, these administrative divisions are based more on preconceptions of the geography of Gaul held in the ancient world (four rivers flowing to the north into the 'Ocean', that is the Garenne, the Loire, the Seine and the Rhine), and a desire to balance up the size of the new provinces (Aquitania was seen as too small) (**50**).

The literary sources of the third and second centuries BC are mainly concerned with the activities of the Galatai in Greece and Asia Minor, in one or two areas around the Black Sea, e.g. the short-lived kingdom of Tylis, and attacks on the Chersonese and Olbia, and especially the attack on Delphi in 279 BC. The kingdom of Galatia was established first in the following year in 278 BC, and was to continue in existence until the Byzantine period. The main sources for the events are Polybius and Pausanias, and there are also poems and inscriptions, both extant and recorded in Pausanias, which are contemporary with the events. From all these sources it is clear that the Galatians were foreign to the region, and originated either from central Europe or from western Europe; contemporary sources talk about the Galatians coming from the far west where they lived next to the Ocean (e.g. Callimachus, *Hymn to Delos*; Hieronymus of Cardia, quoted in Pausanias I.3.6).

Central Europe presents many difficulties as the historical sources are very patchy, and it is likely that the ethnic mix then was as complex as it is today. Herodotus mentions the horse-rearing Sigynne who would seem to be located in eastern Hungary, and to be related to the Scythians on the Black Sea. Other groups in the general area are the Thracians and the Illyrians. It is not until the late second century that we have the first mention of any peoples of Celtic origin, the Scordisci, Taurisci and the Boii, who, according to Poseidonius, warded off an attack by the Cimbri in 113. All were later labelled as Celtic by Strabo (VII.3.2). The Scordisci were located around Belgrade (*Singidunum*), but are also mentioned by Poseidonius as being involved with the kingdom of Tylis, which would push them back to the third century BC (Athenaeus 233d–234c). The Boii have already been discussed, and can be located roughly in modern Bohemia and adjacent parts of Bavaria, and whose presence may also be pushed back earlier by the statement that the remnants of the Boii retreated across the Alps in 192 BC after their defeat at *Mutina* in 193 BC. The Taurisci, we are told by Pliny (III, 133) are the same as the Norici, the kingdom in southern Austria. However, we can dismiss the identification of *Nyrax*, the Celtic town mentioned by Hecataeus, with *Noreia* as a wild guess, as the assumed site, the Magdalensberg, does not start until the late second century BC (it is sometimes claimed that the ancient name was *Virunum*, but this is the name of its Roman successor at Zollfeld, and other than *Narbo*, I know of no other town which took its name when it was relocated). It is usually assumed that these groups arrived in the fourth/third century as part of the expansion of the Celts along the Hercynian Forest as related by Livy, and, in the case of the Scordisci, as part of the invasions of Greece in 279. However, no dates are given by the ancient sources, and there is no reason that the Boii and Taurisci at least should not go back further.

Southern Germany also presents many problems, as by the time we get precise information from Strabo and Ptolemy from the late first century BC onwards, it is occupied by what are probably German tribes such as the Vindelici. Caesar tells us that part of the Hercynian Forest was occupied by the Volcae Tectosages who had sent colonies east of the Rhine (VII.24), but he gives no precise details, and he also mentions the Boii, who had attacked Noricum (I.5), and subsequently joined the Helvetii in their abortive migration to western Gaul. Tacitus mentions the Helvetii as occupying the area between the Rhine and the Main, where they had replaced the Boii (*Germania* 28, see above, p.119), the area later called the *Agri Decumates* (i.e. it was not assigned to a specific tribal group like other adjacent areas), which suggests that something unusual had happened in this area. The size of territories assigned to these peoples, especially the Boii, is much larger than any of the tribal states in Gaul, suggesting we are dealing with fairly vague generalisations. The problem of Herodotus and the source of the Danube I will deal with below.

The picture for northern Italy is, superficially, more simple, as we have good documentary evidence at least of the later phases of Celtic occupation. The standard story is that the Gauls invaded somewhere around 400 BC, captured *Melpum* in 396 (according to Cornelius Nepos on the same day as the Romans took Veii), and renamed it *Mediolanum* (Milan), and then went on to attack Rome (390 according to Roman records, 387 according to Polybius), and then settled a swathe of land in the Po valley from Milan to Ancona on the Adriatic, with, from west to east, Laevi (though Livy considered these Ligurians) and the Lebecii or Libui, then the Insubres, the Cenomani, the Anares, the Boii, the Lingones and the Senones. From the late third century into the early second, in the aftermath of Hannibal's invasion, the Gauls were systematically defeated and driven back by Roman expansion, with some such as the Boii being forced to desert their territory (in fact there is plentiful evidence for a continued Celtic presence, and the Romans called the area Gallia Cisalpina).

However, there is a major problem about the date of the first Gallic presence in Italy. Since the 1830s, the date given by Livy of 600 BC has not been accepted. There are two reasons for this. Firstly, it is tacitly, though not openly, challenged by Polybius' account, and he was writing closer to the events than Livy. He merely says that the capture of Rome was 'not long after' the invasion (III.18). Secondly, Polybius and other sources say that the Po valley was under Etruscan control in the

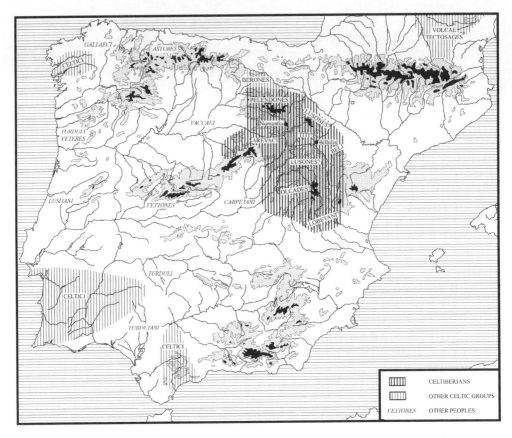

56 *Celtic and related peoples in Iberia according to Strabo.* Author, after Gómez Fraile 1999

fifth century BC (II.17). However, other peoples in northern Italy were often compared with the Gauls. Polybius says the Veneti were similar in their customs and dress, but differed in speech (their languages is now classified as 'Italic'). The Umbrians were referred to as *veteres Galli* (Old Gauls) by M Antonius Gnipho, though again they were Italic speaking. Polybius says that the Etruscans were the neighbours of the Celts (III.17), though he implies that they lived on the northern side of the Alps, though this is due to his belief that the Rhone ran north-east/south-west north of the Alps with its source north of the Adriatic (III.47). The arrival of Celtic languages may also pre-date the arrival of the Celts, and the sixth-century script of the Lepontii, who lived in the Ticino valley, seems to be a Celtic dialect. The name Insubres was already used by one of the peoples near Milan (Ligurian?), which is why the first wave of invaders settled there and called themselves Insubres after one of the sub-peoples of the Aedui.

The situation in Spain is less clear. The major information on the location of peoples comes from the usual sources of Ptolemy, Pliny and Strabo. However, it is not always clear what the ethnic affiliation of the peoples may be. In the east and south there are non-Indo-European speaking Iberians, and in the north the Vascones are probably the ancestors of the modern Basques. Strabo states that the Celtiberians are divided into four groups of which he names two: the Arevaci (with the towns of *Numantia*, *Segeda* and *Pallantia*), and the Lusones; he also says that *Segobriga* and *Bilbilis* are Celtiberian towns (Strabo 3.4.12–13). He talks about the origin of the Celtiberians lying in a migration in which the Berones who lived just to their north also took part, presumably from Gaul (3.4.12), and he says that they were once all called Keltoi and had controlled Spain before the Carthaginians (3.4.5). However, he adds that the rivers *Anas* (Guadiana) and *Tagos* (Tagus) flow through Celtiberia and that the *Dourios* (Duero) and the *Baetis* (Guadalquivir) have their origin in it, and this gives us a rather wider geographical definition of Celtiberia which would include much of central Spain (**56**). The only other group mentioned by Strabo for whom a Celtic origin can be assumed are the Celtici, more a generic name than a tribal name. The main group lived in the south-east between the Guadiana and the Tagus (3.1.6) including the towns of *Conistorgis* (3.2.3) and *Pax Augusta* (3.2.15), but a second smaller group lived in the north-west around the promontory of *Nerion* [Finisterre] (3.3.5); Strabo notes they were closely related and had a common origin.

Ancient Gaul is the best documented of the Celtic areas of Europe, with detailed information from the first century BC to the second century AD, through Caesar, Strabo and Ptolemy, but with additional information from place names and medieval diocesan boundaries from which it is possible to reconstruct the pre-Roman political boundaries with a fair degree of certainty, especially of the tribal *civitates* of central and northern France (**55**). It is also possible to monitor some of the changes brought about by the Roman conquest. The most extensive of these was the drawing of the provincial boundaries under the reforms of Augustus, to reflect administrative needs rather than the ethnic groupings sketched by Caesar. Thus *Aquitania* was greatly expanded at the expense of Celtica (*Gallia Lugdunensis*), as was *Gallia Belgica*, which acquired the Helvetii, the Sequani, Lingones and Leuci, and later the two Germanies were created to encompass the military zone along the Rhine frontier. Some *civitates* disappeared, notably that of the Eburones who had been decimated by Caesar. New ones were created, either with the division of large *civitates* (those of the Bituriges Vivisci, the Tricasses and the Silvanectes), while the Eburones were replaced by the Sugambri and the Ubii who were resettled from east of the Rhine. In *Gallia Narbonensis* the many, often miniscule, 'city states' were amalgamated into larger entities. It was at this time the 'Iberian' and 'Ligurian' ethnicities, already strongly Hellenised, were transformed into an essentially Latin-speaking Roman culture.

Earlier changes are less easy to detect. On the south coast the earlier sources, most notably the 'Massaliote periplus' dating to perhaps the fourth century BC recorded Ligurians to the east and Iberians to the west, with the Rhône forming the frontier between the two; several sources say that *Massalia* was founded in the territory of the Ligurians. However, by the second if not the third century BC there is a strong Celtic presence in the form of the Volcae Tectosages around Toulouse and the Volcae Arecomicii around Nîmes. Polybius, in the context of the crossing of the Carthaginian armies through southern Gaul under Hannibal and later Hamilcar, makes no mention of Iberians or Ligurians (or indeed Greeks), only Celts. Both Thierry and d'Arbois de Jubainville interpret this as signifying a Gallic invasion some time in the third century, but there is no mention of conflict in southern Gaul excepting the on-going conflict between *Massalia* and its neighbours. Strabo, however, implies that they were long established, and that the Tectosages who invaded Asia Minor came from here, though he did consider that they controlled the areas west of the Rhône down to the coast, not just the foothills of the Cevennes. The archaeological evidence which will be discussed in chapter 8 would suggest a complex ethnic mix, but under the Roman reforms it was the Gallic peoples who gave their names to the *civitates*.

Further north the major question is when the political entities which were to become the *civitates* of Caesar first become recognisable. Contemporary documentary evidence starts in the second century BC, with Apollodorus of Athens who, writing some time before about 138 BC mentions both the Aedui and the Arverni. Only slightly later Polybius mentions the *Ardyes* north of the Alps, presumably the Aedui, and in the context of Hannibal's crossing of the Alps in 217 BC, also the Allobroges. The defeat of the Arvernian army under Bituitos by the Romans in 123 BC shows that they were a well-established power by that time, and the story of his father Louernios' potlatch by which he became king would take us back also to the mid-second century. Before that we only have the potsherd from Mantua from an early third-century context which mentions a Helvetian. So, to what extent can we believe Livy, writing in the late first century BC, when he evokes the names of Gallic peoples in the fifth century BC (or seventh century on his chronology)? The only literary support lies in the tribal names which were transferred to Italy, the Cenomani, the Lingones, the Boii, and perhaps the Senones. This does not, of course, mean that they were located in the area where Caesar encountered them later, though we have no evidence that they came from anywhere else; their names are generally unknown elsewhere in Gaul or east of the Rhone, and the exceptions we have, such as the Tectosages, are more likely to originate in the west. Also the relative importance which Livy accords them does not reflect the situation in the first century BC (e.g. the dominance of the Bituriges), all suggesting that Livy had access to sources which are no longer extant. However, if we accept this, it utterly contradicts the dominant theory of the origins and the spread of the Celts in the La Tène period. As we shall see, the archaeology supports Livy.

The third and fourth centuries BC in Gaul are generally poorly documented, as the few mentions are written by Greek authors with little knowledge of the west. The best informed was Pytheas of *Massalia* (*fl.* 310–306 BC) who sailed around Britain, the *Pretannikai nesoi*, the Pretannic islands, but of the Celts he merely says that Britain lies to the north of *Keltike*. Timaeus (352–256 BC) says of the location of the Celts that they lived next to the Ocean (in Diodorus Siculus IV, 56, 4), and that the rivers of *Keltike* flowed into it (quoted by Pausanias in *De placitis philosophorum* III, 17, 4). Other Greek authors such as Callimachus (*fl.* 285–247 BC) and Hieronymus of Cardia (*c.*370–270 BC) say the Galatai came from the far west where they lived next to the Ocean. All these sources imply that the Celts were by this stage in the early third century at least along the Atlantic coast and in central Gaul. For the fourth century BC, the major source for the Celts is Aristotle, but he gives no information on their location, indeed his lack of knowledge on western Europe is shown by his statement that the Danube rises in the Pyrenees (*Meteorologica* I.13, 19, 20), an ignorance also shown by his pupil Heraclides of Pontus who mentions Rome as a Greek city by the great sea attacked by the Hyperboreans (d'Arbois de Jubainville 1902, 52).

This takes us back to the very earliest records that we have of the Celts dating to the end of the sixth and the fifth century: Herodotus, Hecataeus and Himilco. Herodotus writing around 440–430 BC tells us two things. Firstly he says that the Celts are neighbours of the Cynesioi (Cynetes) who were the westernmost people in Europe (**57**). As late as the first century BC most geographers thought that

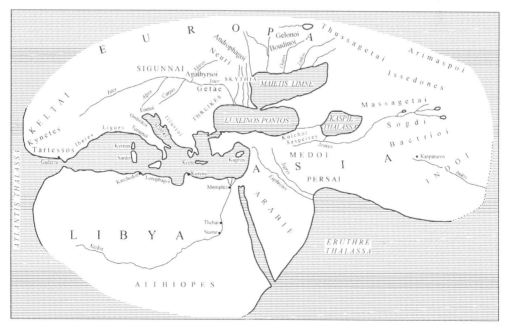

57 *Herodotus' concept of the world c.430 BC*

125

Iberia lay on the same latitude as Gaul, and that the Pyrenees ran north-south (**50**), so this could refer to Celts in either Spain or in Gaul. Secondly he says that if one goes out through the Pillars of Hercules, one encounters Celts on the coast. However, as he makes no mention of the Pyrenees, it is not clear if he is referring to the coast of Iberia or the coast of Gaul. However, most scholars take these two statements to mean that Celts were established in the Iberian Peninsula by the mid-fifth century. The next earliest record that we have of Spain is from Eratosthenes (*c*.275–195 BC), who says that the Celts occupied the coast of Spain as far south as Cadiz (quoted in Strabo II, 4, 4).

Herodotus' third statement, made twice, is that the headwaters of the Danube lie in the territory of the Celts, 'near the town of *Pyrene*'. There are two possible alternative interpretations. The more straightforward is to assume that Herodotus knew that the Danube rose north of the Alps in what is now southern Germany, and *Pyrene* is the name of an important settlement such as the Heuneburg. Proponents of this theory argue that, as there is evidence not only of Greek trade with the Heuneburg and adjacent sites, but also, in the unusual architecture of the site (the use of sun-dried bricks and of bastions, for which the closest parallels lie in the Greek world), that the Greeks were already familiar with these regions if not actually present, and so would not make a mistake (cp. the ignorance of fourth-century writers). The story of the voyage of the Argonauts in which they sail up into central Europe is often quoted in support.

However, Herodotus' conception of the geography of the western world is that Europe and Africa ('Libya') mirror one another, each with a major river flowing from west to east through the middle of them, the Danube in Europe, and the Nile in Africa. Like Aristotle, Herodotus may also have believed that the source of the Danube lay in the Pyrenees as shown by his statement about the town of *Pyrene*. *Pyrene* appears only in one other place, in the *Massaliote Periplus*, where it is described as a market place lying on the coast west of *Massalia*. As there is no mention of the Greek colony of *Emporiae*/Ampurias (literally 'trading place'), two suggestions have been put forward: that the *Periplus* pre-dates the foundation of *Emporiae* (somewhere between 600 and 500 BC); or, alternatively, that *Pyrene* is in fact *Emporiae*, which took its alternative name from the proximity of the Pyrenees. An alternative might be the *Portus Pyrenaei* mentioned by Livy (34.8.5–7), located somewhere north of *Rhode* (Rosas), but otherwise unknown. Thus, surprisingly, the more likely suggestion is that which places the Celts at this time near the Pyrenees in southern France, in the area later known to be occupied by the Volcae Tectosages.

Hecataeus was writing around 500 BC, and is quoted in both Strabo and in Stephanus of Byzantium. Again, there are three pieces of information. Firstly, the town of *Nyrax* is Celtic, but we have no idea where this was (as previously stated, it cannot be *Noreia* as is sometimes suggested). Secondly the Celts live '*kata*' *Massalia*, literally 'above', but usually read as inland, that is to the north. This could be read to fit any of the three interpretations that were introduced at the beginning of this chapter. Finally he says that *Narbo* is 'an emporium and city of *Keltike*'. *Narbo* was a Roman colony founded in 118 BC, but it took its name from an earlier settlement, which on other evidence may go back to the fifth century (there is an Iron Age settlement at Montlaurès at Narbonne), so this need occasion no surprise. However, this is in an area supposedly under Iberian control at this time, but, as Gayraud (1981, 77) has pointed out, Stephanus assigns the expression to Strabo and Marcian, for whom this would have been administratively correct from the first century BC onwards (*Narbo* was the capital of *Gallia Narbonensis*, and so part of *Keltike*), and that this therefore is not statement about the ethnicity of the inhabitants at this time (see chapter 8).

Finally we have the *Periplus* of Himilco. This is only found quoted in later sources, notably in the flowery poem by Avienus written in the fourth century AD, and, as previously illustrated (**21**), it shows a complete contrast with the evidence we have been considering so far, with different tribal names along the Atlantic coast from those which were to follow. The one mention of the Celts is north of the Oestrymnes (variously taken as Brittany or Britain); the Ligurians also appear in the same area as well as in northern Spain. The only linking point is with the Cynetes or Cynesioi of south-east Spain which we also find in Herodotus. It is this document on which d'Arbois de Jubainville's theories of a late arrival of the Celts in western Europe is based, replacing the earlier more widespread Ligurians. Clearly, as a *periplus* it only considers what is happening on the coast rather than inland, and, as we have seen in southern France, there were some changes going on in the ethnicity of some areas. It is impossible to make a decision about how much weight to put on this document, and how to interpret it.

Summing up, we can turn back to our three interpretations presented at the beginning of this chapter, but one can make no final decision (and there is archaeological evidence yet to consider):

Interpretation 1. There is nothing in the earlier sources, even Himilco, to suggest that the Gallic peoples who invaded Italy did not come from central Gaul. There may have been some expansion at the margins, for instance in southern France (though the Celtic tribes are fairly certainly in place by the late third century when Hannibal passes through), and possibly along the Atlantic coast of Iberia (present by the third century if not the fifth), but Herodotus and Hecataeus may even be read as supporting an early Celtic presence in southern France rather than contradicting it. We have vague evidence of Celts along the Atlantic coast in the fourth century, and more certain by the third. It is difficult to see where the peoples of Gaul came from if they came from east of the Rhine as suggested by Interpretation 2. As we shall see, the archaeological record, especially of Bourges, seems to support it.

Interpretation 2. The origin of the Celts is seen as west of the Rhine, and though, other than the ambiguous statements of Herodotus and of Polybius, we have no definite evidence that southern Germany was occupied at an early date by the Celts, let alone who they might have been, or that they were the ones to invade Italy; the later evidence suggests it was occupied by Celts or Galatai up to the first century BC. The evidence for Celts in northern France north of the Seine-Marne is also not clearly stated by trustworthy sources (merely Caesar saying the Belgae came from east of the Rhine and replaced the local Celts). There is no explicit record in the written sources of expansion of the Gauls to western or southern France. This interpretation, while possible from the written sources, needs a fair amount of special pleading.

Interpretation 3. This relies mainly on archaeological evidence, and tribal names such as the Boii and the Senones. It ignores most of the literary evidence that we have, of the routes taken and of the peoples which participated. It is the least likely.

The Celtic languages

Linguistic and place-name evidence is often used in conjunction with the classical sources in documenting the origin and spread of the Celts. Though in some cases the two phenomena are certainly linked, I argue that it is essential for the two types of evidence to be kept clearly apart, as a failure to do this can lead to major misunderstandings. As I have already stated, in the ancient world we have evidence to suggest that language was not a defining factor in assigning ethnicity. The origins of the Celts and of the Celtic languages may be two very different things.

Everyone agrees that the origin of the Indo-European languages lies outside western Europe, coming from somewhere in eastern Europe or Asia Minor; the disagreement lies in when they arrived and in what form. The two extremes are represented by Mallory (1989) who sees the dispersal as happening essentially in the third to second millennium BC on the basis of some shared vocabulary between the main languages, and Renfrew who seeks an earlier dispersal, associated with the adoption of farming in the sixth/fifth millennia. The very short chronologies favoured in the late nineteenth and early twentieth centuries received a shock when it was realised that the language spoken in Greece by the Cretans and Mycenaeans ('Linear B') in the mid-second millennium BC was already recognisable as Greek, and that it had not been introduced by the 'Dorians' in the early first millennium as had been assumed, and that Indo-European languages such as Hittite were already established in Asia Minor by the mid-second millennium BC. This then implies that the adoption and development of other language groups such as Celtic and German were likely to be equally early.

Languages are rarely, if ever, changed without some influx of population, and even Renfrew who, in the 1960s, was one of the major opponents of the migrationist interpretations of the 'Culture-Historical' paradigm in archaeology, himself accepted migration as the main mechanism for the Indo-European language expansion. However, there are no simplistic rules which allow us to assume under what circumstances a new language will or will not be adopted. Thus, in the migration period the Frankish invasions of Gaul had little effect on the local language, with the result that French is Latin based, whereas in England Latin disappeared as a spoken language to be replaced by English in the east, and a revival of the Celtic languages in the west and north. In contrast, the Roman invasion of Gaul produced little change of population, but the adoption of Latin in place of Gallic. In this case we know that the two languages overlapped chronologically, but Gallic had little effect on Latin, as in modern French only some 120 words have been listed in the latest study that owe their origin to Gallic. In contrast, the Norman invasion of England, introducing a French-speaking aristocracy, while it did not produce a language change, nonetheless had a profound impact on the vocabulary. Thus arguments that the lack of Celtic words in English mean that the indigenous population in eastern and southern England were wiped out or destroyed by the invading Anglo-Saxons is not one that can be sustained, at least, on linguistic evidence, and in any case the areas of early Saxon settlement in eastern England were probably Latin- rather than Saxon-speaking.

One major problem with languages is that, as we shall see with material culture, change is not a smooth linear process. Gradual change is happening continuously, but it is punctuated by periods of very rapid change, so chronology cannot simply be established by comparing the closeness or distance of two languages, even if we can find ways of measuring similarity. Generally linguists look for chronology in terms of deviations in a particular language from the norm of its closest relatives. So, certain features are shared in common by all Indo-European languages, and, as a rule these can be seen as the features of the original shared language (be it in terms of vocabulary or of grammatical construction). Thus, it has been claimed that Irish may have been the first of the Celtic languages to break off from the Celtic group because it has more archaic elements in it than, say, Welsh. This does not, however, mean that the language becomes fossilised or a backwater; American English has some archaic features, e.g. the use of past participles such as 'gotten', which have disappeared in UK dialects, but American is still the more influential of the two languages at a worldwide level. It does also not mean that 'archaic' languages stop expanding. At the time when the Celtic languages were finally disappearing in Europe in the post-Roman period, British was in fact expanding into Brittany, and Irish was expanding into south-west Scotland. This in itself warns us that expansion of languages is not a simple linear process, and that the actual process of adoption and contraction can be due to entirely local factors, and that we should be wary of the standard models which link the expansion of Celtic languages with the expansion of the Celts.

The linguistic evidence comes from four sources: the present spoken languages; written and epigraphic sources especially from the first millennia BC and AD;

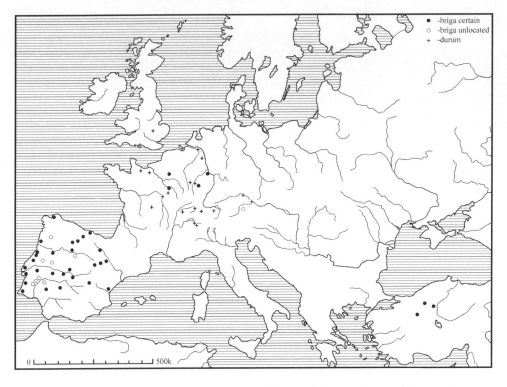

58 *Distribution of place names ending in* -briga *(hill) and* -durum *(fort). It should be noted that most of the names on figures* **58** *and* **59** *are of new foundations after the Roman conquest.* Author

inscriptions on coins (mainly the names of individuals); and from place–name evidence. The modern languages and the post-Roman documents lie outside the purview of this book, other than to note that evidence for earlier Celtic languages must be based on these languages as they are the only ones for which we have an adequate database, and that documents for Britain and Ireland are relatively late, in the second half of the first millennium AD.

The earliest inscriptions we have for Celtic languages come from northern Italy, and start in the sixth century BC, the so-called Lepontic inscriptions from the area around Lake Maggiore, and they continue until the first century BC. None are of great length, mainly inscriptions on pottery or memorials on burial stele. The next earliest date to the third century BC, and come from the area east of the Rhône in the territory inhabited by Ligurian peoples; again they are mainly burial stele. There is also a scatter of inscriptions from Gaul, mainly of early Roman date, curses on lead tablets from Chamalières at Clermont-Ferrand and from Larzac, inscriptions on plates from the samian producing centres of La Graufesenque and Lezoux, and, most famously, the calendar from Coligny near

Lyon. There are no Gallic inscriptions from Aquitania or from the Iberian area around Narbonne. Coinage is found in the same areas of southern, central and northern Gaul, but also includes south-eastern Britain; the distribution of place names extends the areas of Celtic languages much further, throughout Britain and Ireland, northern Gaul, southern Germany and much of central Europe (**58, 59**).

From the territory of the Celtiberians there is a series of short inscriptions on pottery and stone dating back to the third century BC, and, dating to the second/first century BC are two bronze legal documents which are the longest inscriptions in a Celtic language from the classical world. However, Spain is more complex than other areas as inscriptions in three other languages are found in the peninsula. Most common are those of the Iberians found down the Mediterranean coast from the Hérault to the upper Guadilquivir. They cannot be read, but it is certainly a non-Indo-European language. From the south-west there are inscriptions in a language simply known as 'south-western'; it too cannot be translated, but also seems to be non-Indo-European. Finally there are four inscriptions which are referred to as 'Lusitanian', which are probably Indo-European, but not Celtic. In addition we must assume that in the north the

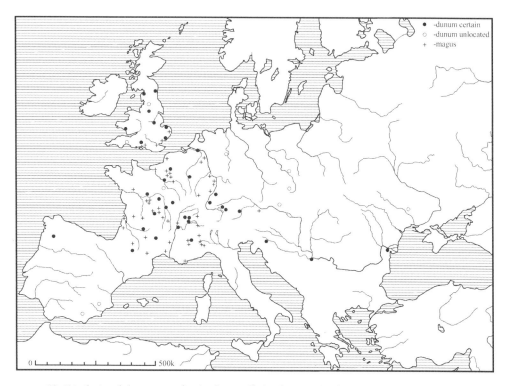

59 *Distribution of place names ending in* -dunum *(fort) and* -magus *(market).* Author

language ancestral to Basque was being spoken; there is no evidence that it was related to Iberian. The place-name evidence in Spain, however, suggests that the Celtic languages were more widely spoken than Celtiberia, and encompassed much of the centre and west of the peninsula, including the areas in which the Lusitanian and south-western inscriptions are found, suggesting that some of the populations may well have been bilingual.

7

THE NATURE OF THE
ARCHAEOLOGICAL SOURCES

Since the end of the nineteenth century archaeology has increasingly been used to define the origins and spread of the Celts, but as already indicated in chapter 5, much of the methodology used is of doubtful value, and often we encounter simple misuse and misunderstanding of the archaeological evidence. In this chapter I wish to explore the archaeological data in more detail, what they can, and cannot, tell us.

Deposition

One of the fundamental problems with archaeological data (as with the written sources) is how well they survive. Though there are natural processes of erosion and decay, for instance the rotting of organic materials, for the Iron Age the major factor is the cultural activities of the Iron Age people themselves. Some of this is obvious. Did they bury their dead in a way which archaeologists can detect, in graves (e.g. in holes in the ground), or did they expose the dead, or cremate them and scatter the ashes? Did they dig pits in which to store their grain or to quarry materials for building or agricultural activities, or did they enclose their settlements with ditches, holes in the ground which can act as traps for rubbish, or be picked up in aerial photographs? Often distributions maps do not show the area where a certain type of pottery or metal object was in use, but of burials or ritual sites where they are likely to have been deposited. They are thus still maps of material culture, but at one stage removed, reflecting as much beliefs and ideology.

Burial rites
There is a large zone in western Europe in which burials are rare or unknown in the Late Bronze Age and the Iron Age, or, if burials do appear, the tradition is relatively short-lived. This zone encompasses the whole of Britain and Ireland, western and central France, western Spain and Portugal. Even in areas where there

BURIAL TRENDS IN THE NEUWIED BASIN			CREMATION GRAVE GOODS				INHUMATION GRAVE GOODS			
			TOTAL GRAVES	POTTERY ONLY	POTTERY + METAL	METAL ONLY	TOTAL GRAVES	POTTERY ONLY	POTTERY + METAL	METAL ONLY
HA C	LAUFELD		262	243	17	0	14	2	8	1
HA D	HUNSRÜCK - EIFEL	I	19	11	7	1	218	38	60	120
LT A		IIA	29	16	9	4	161	47	78	24
LT B-C		IIB	11	10	1	0	23	3	9	11
LT C-D	NORTH GALLIC	I	33	9	24	0	1	0	1	0

60 *Numbers of burials in the Hunsrück-Eifel in Hallstatt C to La Tène D. Collis 1977*

is plentiful evidence, there are periods when burials are relatively rare. Figure **60** gives the figures for one part of the Hunsrück-Eifel, showing a major fall-off of numbers of burials in La Tène B and C, but with all other periods fairly well represented. This is the pattern not only for the central Rhine-Mosel area, but also for Champagne, areas which in the past have been considered important for the ethnogenesis of the Celts; figure **61** shows Déchelette's map of Early La Tène burials in France showing a marked concentration in the north, and the situation since has not changed radically. These areas, with some of the Celtiberian areas of central Spain, are the only ones where we have a fairly continuous burial record throughout the first millennium, though even so with some fluctuations.

In the areas which concern us there are many very localised burial rites that appear and disappear, or where there are only one or two burials known, but there are also long-lived or widely spread traditions which can be identified.

1. In Celtiberia and other parts of central Spain cremation is dominant throughout the first millennium, increasing in numbers towards the end of the period. Burials may be marked by stele or small cairns. The later ones may be in large cemeteries associated with urbanised oppida, as at Numantia (near Soria), or Las Cogotas and the cemetery of La Osera at Charmartín (near Ávila). According to Silius Italicus (3.340–3) describing the Celtiberians, and Claudius Aelianus (X.22) in the case of the Vettones, warriors who died in battle were left to the vultures, a rite which is also depicted on the local painted pottery (**62**).

2. Over much of central Europe (Austria, Bohemia, Bavaria, Baden-Württemberg, northern Switzerland, eastern France), there is a long parallel development (though with local variations) starting at the beginning of the first millennium with simple urnfield burials in cemeteries, with pottery, but few metal

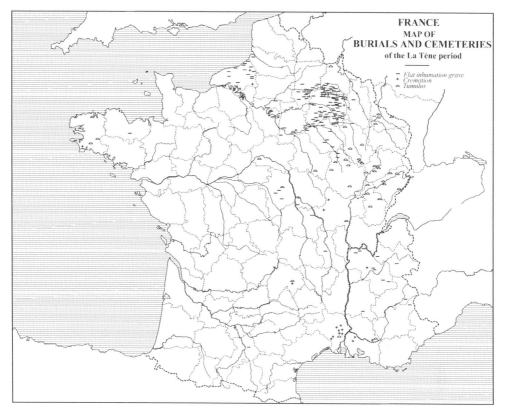

61 *Map of the distribution of Early La Tène burials in France.* Déchelette 1914

goods or other signs of individual wealth. During Hallstatt C in the late eighth and seventh centuries BC differentiation starts to appear with burials in wooden chambers, accompanied by four-wheeled vehicles, swords, rich pottery, and personal ornaments, mainly in bronze. The richest burials tend to be inhumations, a trend which is also documented in central Italy (Etruria and Latium). By the sixth century inhumation is almost universal (some poor burials and those of children continue the cremation rite). The female graves tend to have a rich array of bronze ornaments (anklets, bracelets, brooches), especially young females who may also have 'amulets' (bronze pendants, stone axes or flint arrowheads which were ancient when they were buried); the men often have a weapon: a dagger, a spear or, in some areas, an axe (**63**). With the burials of Hochdorf and the Hohmichele in south-western Germany and Vix in eastern France, this burial rite reaches an extreme, with imported Mediterranean imports, local ceramics and ornaments, gold objects, but rarely weapons.

62 (Left) *Dead Celtiberian warrior being consumed by vultures.* Jimeno Martínez 2002

63 (Below) *Examples of Hallstatt D burials from the Magdalenenberg, southern Germany. Burial 86: 1., 2. bronze armlets; 3., 4. bronze bracelets; 5. bronze belthook; 6. bronze torc; 7. pottery vessel. Burial 90: 8. belthook; 9. pottery vessel; 10. iron arrowheads; 11. bronze fitting from quiver; 12. iron dagger in a bronze sheath.* Spindler 1976

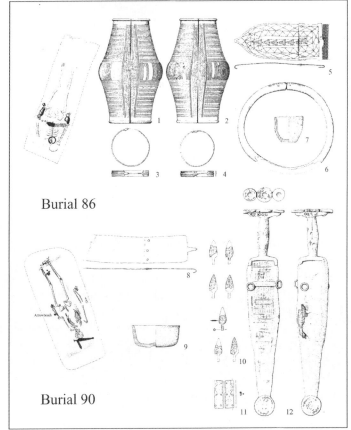

Burial 86

Burial 90

3. In central and southern France in Hallstatt C and D extended inhumation usually under a tumulus is common in the highland areas of the central Massif and the Garrigues. Swords are well represented in male graves, sometimes with imported bronze vessels in Hallstatt C, but wagon and harness burials are unknown; however many male burials are unaccompanied. The male rite disappears during Hallstatt D, but female inhumations with personal ornaments, also under tumuli, appear (**64**).

4. In central Germany, southern Poland and Moravia the tradition of cremation cemeteries continues into Hallstatt D (Lausitz Culture), but the number of pottery vessels increases hugely. Metalwork is rare, but does occur occasionally (e.g. the bronze Gündlingen sword from Platénice in Bohemia).

5. In Hallstatt D and La Tène A the late Hallstatt tradition of extended inhumation becomes dominant in eastern and northern France ('Marnian Culture') and on the central Rhine-Mosel (Hunsrück-Eifel Culture), as well as the Ardennes, northern Bavaria and southern Bohemia. Many men are buried with weapons and women with ornaments, now commonly including a torc. In the southern part of the area (Switzerland, Baden-Württemberg, Burgundy) the tumulus burial rite continues, but in Champagne flat inhumations cemeteries are the norm. The richer burials contain two-wheeled vehicles, rich goldwork and imported bronze vessels from northern Italy and Etruria.

64 *Hallstatt D burial from Pâtural, Clermont-Ferrand, France.* Association pour la Recherche sur l'Âge du Fer en Auvergne

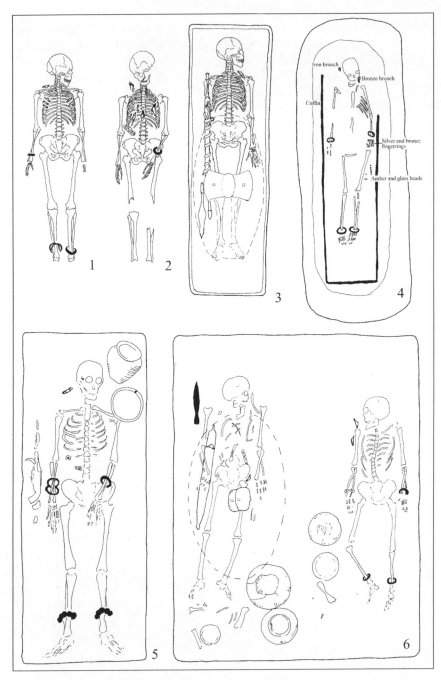

65 *Early and Middle La Tène male and female flat inhumation burials. 1., 2. Andelfingen, Switzerland, graves 6, 9; Vevey, Switzerland, grave 26; Libenice, Bohemia; 5. Vel'ká Maňa, Slovakia, grave 28; 6. Bucovice, Moravia, grave 14. 1., 2., 3. Wyss 1974; 4. Rybová and Soudský 1962; 5., 6., 7. Filip 1956*

6. A similar burial rite, but generally lacking the rich burials, is found throughout much of central Europe (**65**): the Swiss Plateau, southern Bavaria, northern Bohemia, southern Moravia, Slovakia, southern Poland, eastern Romania, the Hungarian Plain, lower Austria, and Slovenia. These 'flat inhumation cemeteries' start locally in Switzerland and Austria in La Tène A (e.g. Münsingen), but are more typical of La Tène B (the 'Dux horizon', see below, p.148). The rite dies out during La Tène C.

7. In La Tène B and C in northern France the focus of visible burials shifts away from Champagne to the Aisne Valley and the Paris Basin, as well as East Yorkshire (the Arras Group with crouched inhumation under a tumulus). In all these areas there are some richer graves with two-wheeled vehicles, and, especially in northern France, weapon burials.

8. In later La Tène C and especially D cremation becomes dominant in a zone which encompasses western Germany (Hesse, Hunsrück-Eifel) northern France (Champagne, but with outliers in Lorraine and Burgundy, such as Mont Beuvray), and in south-eastern England (Aylesford-Swarling Culture). Pottery vessels are the most common grave goods, but on the continent weapon graves also occur. Other than brooches, ornaments are rare, but toilet instruments (razors, chatelaines), are relatively common. The richest burials include imported Italian bronze vessels and wine amphorae.

These are naturally simplifications. Different communities have their own interpretations of the norms, and these can also shift, almost imperceptibly, over time. There are few firm boundaries either geographically or chronologically, and one tradition outlined above can evolve into one of the others. Even in areas where a rite may be dominant, it may not be universal. Rich burials usually indicate rich areas, but the lack of rich burials or of burials at all, may not indicate poverty; according to Poseidonius the Arvernian Luernios was the richest man in all Gaul, but we have no rich burials from the Auvergne dating to the second century BC. Also, even in areas such as the Champagne not everyone was buried in the cemeteries; children and babies are under-represented or absent, and some adults were buried on the settlements.

Burials also need to be studied in their local context. In Bohemia the appearance of the flat inhumation cemeteries was interpreted as representing the arrival of the Celts; however, with the complete excavation of settlements sites such as Radovesice, a hamlet occupied from Hallstatt D until the end of La Tène D, the cemetery was only used for a brief period of time (La Tène B–C1), but without any break in the settlement. The case of Owslebury (Hants) is similar, a settlement which starts in the fourth century BC continuing until the fourth century AD, and with a 'Belgic cemetery' in use between 50 BC and AD 120. The wealth of cemeteries must likewise be interpreted in context. At Münsingen burials become poorer and poorer, with weapons disappearing during La Tène B, at the moment when weapons started to be deposited in large numbers on the nearby cult site of La Tène.

Hoards and watery places

In Atlantic Europe (western Iberia, western France, Britain and Ireland) and also in Scandinavia (Denmark, Sweden, northern Germany), there are numerous hoards of bronze and gold objects dating to the late Bronze Age. These traditions disappear in the eighth century; in Britain, for instance, there are some late hoards such as Llyn Fawr which contains an iron sword and bronze horsegear. For most areas the deposition of hoards does not reappear until the second/first century BC; hoards of iron ingots (currency bars) are the one exception, concentrated in southern Germany and in southern Britain. It is only with the advent of coinage in the third and especially the second century BC that hoards start becoming common again, mainly gold coins, but often accompanied by gold torcs. There are also local traditions such as the hoards of bronze harness found in southern England, of helmets in Austria, or iron agricultural tools such as scythes in central Europe. Such activity makes little sense in the traditional invocation of 'periods of unrest' and a ritual context seems more appropriate for most of these finds.

Deposition in bogs had a very long tradition in Denmark, starting in the Neolithic if not the Mesolithic, though the nature of deposition changed radically over time. By the Iron Age the most common offerings were human bodies, but there is also the boat at Hjortspring with its La Tène weapons, the cauldrons from Gundestrup, Rynkeby and Brå, and the vehicles from Dejbjerg (the last three all in La Tène art style), and the imported Italian bronze jug from Kærumsgaard. But hoards of personal ornaments, so common in the Late Bronze Age, had largely fallen out of fashion. Finds in bogs occasionally occur elsewhere, especially in Ireland and Britain (Lindow Man, Llyn Cerrig Bach or Deskford), and more rarely in Germany (Kappel, Kr. Biberach in Baden-Württemberg).

In western Europe, generally deposition in rivers was more common. Though sometimes these finds were concentrated at a specific spot, as at La Tène in Switzerland, more normally finds are spread out along the length of the rivers. The most important of such rivers are the Thames and the Witham in England, the Rhine and the Saône, but there are many single or small groups of finds from other rivers, especially in Switzerland. The Seine has produced one of the outstanding examples of La Tène art, the gilded iron helmet from Amfreville (and in this context, we should remember the helmet from a pit in the cave at Agris in the Charente, also likely to be some sort of ritual offering).

The best documented of all the rivers is the Thames where deposition of metal finds started with bronze 'rapiers' in the Middle Bronze Age and reached its zenith in the Late Bronze Age, especially with bronze swords. Though in the Iron Age the quantities declined, it continues through Hallstatt D and La Tène A with various daggers, and probably throughout the period, with the Battersea shield, the helmet from Waterloo Bridge, or the shields from Wandsworth. The density of finds is clearly in part due to activities such as dredging and the quarrying of sand and gravel, and so is biased towards the major rivers, but no one has yet looked in detail at the negative evidence to see where such activities have still failed to produce finds, for instance on the lower Rhône or the Trent.

Ritual sites

Ritual and ceremonial sites are common throughout much of Europe in the Neolithic and Early Bronze Age, but after that they virtually disappear from western Europe until around the third century, with rare exceptions such as the sixth-century site of Závist near Prague or the cult enclosure at Vix in Burgundy. From then onwards, they become more and more common, many continuing into the Roman period. In central Europe there are the *Viereckschanzen*, square enclosures with shafts and cult buildings, though most are now being interpreted as partly or wholly domestic. In northern France cult sites such as Gournay-sur-Aronde and Ribemont-sur-Ancre have produced huge quantities of finds. These vary from site to site, some mainly producing weapons (in some cases miniaturised), human and animal remains, coins, personal ornaments, etc. By the Late Iron Age the tradition had spread to southern England, for instance Hayling Island, and also occasionally in central Europe, the temple site on the Frauenberg bei Leibnitz near Graz in Austria.

Defended sites

Settlements with earthen or stone ramparts, be they for defence, for display, or both, are the most visible aspect of the European Iron Age, though their size and function is extremely variable, from farms to towns, temporary refuges, storage centres, centres of production or cult. Despite this visibility, there are no overall syntheses for many areas (e.g. parts of Spain), let alone the whole of the area which concerns us. In southern France and eastern Spain defended sites started appearing in the Late Bronze Age and remained in use up to and beyond the Roman conquest, many taking on urban characteristics, comparable to the city states of Greece and Italy. In contrast, in northern Germany and Scandinavia defended sites are virtually unknown in the first millennium BC. The exception is eastern Germany and Poland where defended sites occur in Late Urnfield and the Hallstatt periods (especially Hallstatt C and D), of which the lake fort of Biskupin is the most famous, but in the La Tène period this areas joins the rest of the North European Plan in the absence of defended sites.

In the broad swathe from Slovakia across to Britain and Ireland there is a thin scatter of Late Bronze Age defended sites, but most are abandoned around the seventh century (Hallstatt C). The sixth century, in contrast (Hallstatt D), sees the hillfort at its most extensive, both chronologically and in geographical extension, encompassing the Alps, the Czech Republic, southern and central Germany, eastern France and Belgium. They are also found in widespread areas of Britain, northern, western and central Iberia, and in many of these areas they remain in continual use up to, and beyond, the Roman conquest. In central Spain many of the larger ones such as Numantia take on urban characteristics. In central Europe most are abandoned by the fifth century; the Hunsrück, northern Bavaria, and Bohemia are the exceptions, and by the fourth/third century they are distinctly rare, the completely excavated site of Bundenbach in the Hunsrück being a notable exception. However, certain areas are noted for a general absence of hillforts, for example central and south-western France. In the second century defended sites reappear, the oppida, noted for their large size, and in some cases, urban characteristics, though again there are areas where they are surprisingly absent, such as south-western France.

Enclosed and open settlements

The vast majority of the population of Europe in the first millennium lived in small villages and farms, and concentration in defended sites only occurred in specific periods and specific places. The identification of non-defended sites by archaeologists depends on five main factors:

1. *Stone-built structures.* These survive especially in highland areas where stone was used for domestic buildings, but they are also areas where defended sites are most common: western Britain, Brittany, central, western and northern Iberia. Only locally do non-defended sites exist, e.g. in Cornwall.

2. *Enclosure.* The enclosing of sites with non-defensive earthworks or palisades is relatively unusual, but if it occurs it makes sites very visible from aerial photographs even when the banks have been ploughed out. Ditched enclosures are especially common on the chalklands and gravels of northern France and southern England, but ditched fields and settlements are now beginning to appear in central France as well, for instance in the fertile Grande Limagne in the Auvergne, while in southern Germany the late Iron Age *Viereckschanzen* are still a prominent feature in the landscape.

3. *Pits and quarries.* The most common type of pit, especially in Catalonia, southern and northern France and south-eastern England are pits for storing grain. Both these and quarries for building materials and liming the fields can be visible from the air. Wells are a feature of sites in the Grande Limagne, but are generally rare.

4. *Distinctive wooden buildings.* On the loess soils of the Czech Republic small sunken houses (*Grubenhäuser*) are a regular feature of certain phases of the La Tène period, while in central France there are rectangular pits interpreted as cellars. In parts of Britain round houses may be provided with a drainage gully. Otherwise we depend on substantial postholes to recognise rectangular buildings such as the

long houses of the Netherlands, northern Germany and Denmark. However, many types of construction are difficult for archaeologists to recognise, such as the use of turf and cob, log cabins, houses built on sill beams, or the wattle and daub 'stake' houses of southern England in the Middle Iron Age.

5. *Ceramic scatters*. The survival of material culture relies substantially on the digging of holes in the ground which can act as traps in which material will collect and survive. But systematic survey can reveal sites which are only visible from surface scatters, with few, if any, subterranean features. However, systematic field walking has only been undertaken in a few parts of Europe; Poland is the only country where substantial parts have been walked as a concerted national research project over the last 30 years. However, in some areas ceramics are not highly fired, and will not survive weathering, and we also have areas, notably northern and western Britain and Ireland, where ceramics were rare or not used at all. Barry Raftery has claimed that there is not a single Iron Age potsherd from Ireland. Other such blank areas are known in Europe, such as parts of the Massif Central in France in the La Tène period; were they really not occupied, or simply not using much pottery?

In the early stages of the development of archaeology the study of settlement sites did not excite the same interest as hillforts and burials, and though there have been honourable exceptions (e.g. Bersu's excavation of Little Woodbury in the 1930s), it was not until the arrival of the 'New Archaeology' of the 1960s when there was a new impetus to study animal bones and seeds, or to place hillforts in their wider context with approaches such as 'Central Place Theory' or 'Site Catchment Analysis', that settlement archaeology came into its own. Large-scale systematic survey became increasingly important to understand 'Regional Systems' of settlement and production, and the arrival of the mechanical excavator has allowed large-scale stripping of settlements to obtain plans and sequences. From the 1980s there has been an increasing interest in the processes of deposition, with the recognition that the material culture found on these sites is not necessarily simply discarded 'rubbish', but includes deliberate selection and 'placed' material, from feasting and ritualised activities, including the deposition of partial and complete human bodies.

Even so, our knowledge of the smaller settlements is still very patchy. In part this is due to differences in the theoretical orientation of archaeologists; those brought up with a traditional approach in culture history or art history still tend to excavate burials at the expense of settlements, and also it depends on the impact of individuals working in their own research areas. Even so, this only accounts in part for the absences in the archaeological record. My own experience in the Auvergne underlines this problem. The earliest systematic field walking produced plentiful evidence for the Late Bronze Age and the Roman period, but little in between. Part of the answer seems to be that settlement in certain periods appears to cluster in specific areas of the landscape. So, more recent field walking has started to produce early Iron Age sites in areas not previously walked, while recent excavations have produced dense occupation of the third and second centuries BC under the airport and suburbs of Clermont-Ferrand which were inaccessible to field walking. The ditches and pits of these periods produce huge quantities of finds, but Late Hallstatt and Early La Tène finds are still rare, and also the first century BC is almost unrepresented outside the defended oppida. Though large-scale excavations are redressing the balance, certain periods will still be under-represented when settlements only consist of small pits and postholes, without ditches and large pits in which material can be deposited.

Other evidence

Only rarely do such things as field systems and territorial boundaries survive; this is especially a feature of British archaeology, due mainly to the unusual history of land use in the post-medieval period. Field systems, such as the so-called 'Celtic fields' of the English downlands, have occasionally been recognised on the continent, in Denmark and Holland, but elsewhere most traces of early field systems have been destroyed in the land hunger of the eighteenth and nineteenth centuries.

Stone sculptures are also a feature of certain areas, most notably the verracos of central Spain, standing figures of boars and bulls, up to 3m high, the most famous being the Toros de Guisando. They seem to act as territorial markers, on boundaries, routes or around the best pasture. Over 400 are known, though few in their original setting, with a marked concentration in the tribal territory of the Vettones around Ávila. More enigmatic are the stele of Brittany and Ireland; some mark burials, but most have some other function, and occasionally they are highly decorated with La Tène ornament like the Turoe stone. Human sculptures are also known, but are difficult to date unless there is a specific context or something distinctive about the stylisation (e.g. the head from Mšecké Žehrovice). Standing figures and stele were used to mark tumuli, a characteristic of the Hallstatt and Early La Tène periods in western Germany (e.g. Hirschlanden and the Glauberg).

Otherwise there is a large category of 'chance finds' whose context is simply unknown. Many come from the activities of metal detectorists, and, for instance, coin finds show distribution in areas for which we have little other archaeological evidence (e.g. south-western France). Many certainly derive from settlements, but many are likely to be deliberate depositions well away from areas of settlement. We may not be able to categorise them but we should not ignore them.

The Natural Sciences may also supply supplementary information, indeed sometimes it is the only evidence. This is especially true of pollen evidence which, in many upland areas, demonstrates continued forest clearance and agriculture in regions where there is minimal or no other archaeological evidence.

Synthesis

The maps reproduced in chapter 6 showing the 'origin and spread' of the Celts use the archaeological data described in this section. However, much of it is taken out of context, or simply takes the data at face value. Thus, the appearance of flat inhumation cemeteries in central Europe has been interpreted as representing the arrival of the Celts from western Europe, but the settlement evidence tells a very different story. The wealth of burial evidence from the Champagne and central Rhine area has turned it into the perceived epicentre of Celtic expansion, and the reduction of finds in La Tène B as due to the migration of the population to the east and south.

Yet the classic textbook on prehistory which all German students were expected to read, Hans-Jürgen Eggers' *Einführung in der Vorgeschichte* (1959), dealt with precisely this problem of the interpretation of distribution maps, and how they were affected by cultural activities in the past as well as processes of discovery. He was mainly attacking the preconceptions of the *Siedlungsarchäologie* of Gustaf Kossinna, which dealt with the supposed expansion of the Germanic peoples from Scandinavia. Kossinna's approach was to map what he considered diagnostic

	HALLSTATT D					LA TÈNE A					LA TÈNE B				
	Hillforts	Settlements	Burials	River finds	Hoards	Hillforts	Settlements	Burials	River finds	Hoards	Hillforts	Settlements	Burials	River finds	Hoards
SW France	•	•				•	•	•				•			•
Berry		•	●				●	●				●	●		
Auvergne		•	●				•					●			
NW France		•	•				•	•				•	●	•	
Wessex	●	•				●	•	•			•	●			
Thames valley	•	●		•		•	●		•		•	●			
Champagne		•	●			•	•	●				•	●		
Hunsrück-Eifel	•		•			•	•	●			•		•		
Baden-Württemberg	●	•	●				•	•					•		
Swiss plateau	•		●			•		•					●	●	
N Bavaria			●			•		●							
S Bavaria	●	•	●					•				•	●		
N Bohemia	•	•				•	●	•		•		•	●		•
S Bohemia	●		●			•		●					•		

66 *The nature of the archaeological record in selected key areas of central and western Europe.* Author

Germanic characteristics (burial rites, specific sword or vessel types), irrespective of the context in which they had been deposited. In the post-war years scholars were keen to counteract the excesses of the 1930s, and especially the theories concerning the Germans, but the Celts were put under no such scrutiny, even though precisely the same methodological criticism can be applied.

On figure **66** I have tried to demonstrate the nature of the archaeological evidence of some of the key regions, and these are described in greater detail in chapter 8. This should make it obvious that, like the historical written sources which have, sometimes by pure chance, only survived in a small part to the present day, there are also great gaps in the archaeological record which we will never be able to fill. Evidence can switch on and off like traffic lights; we can get different combinations of evidence surviving, but never do we get the full range of data in any area from burials, settlements and the various kinds of deliberate deposition (e.g. hoards). The more evidence we have, the more we can say, but, as I have written on a number of occasions, it is especially the silences which we need to try to understand.

Chronology

One of the tasks of archaeologists is to place this mass of data, from chance discoveries to controlled excavations, into some sort of meaningful pattern from which a history, in the broadest sense of the word, can be written. As we have seen, one of the first concerns of archaeologists faced with an object is 'how old is it?'. Until the latter part of the twentieth century the only way of doing this in the Iron Age was to find objects on sites which could be dated (e.g. the battle-field of *Alesia*), and then extend these dates to similar objects elsewhere. As the best historical records lay in the Near East and the East Mediterranean, archaeologists working in central and western Europe were dependent on finds of Classical Greek goods, notably Black and Red Figure Ware imported from Athens in the sixth and fifth centuries, and found in graves in south-western Germany and Champagne. For most periods of the Iron Age scientific methods of dating have not had a huge impact on absolute dating of the Iron Age. The last half of the first millennium corresponds with a period when the correlation curve between C14 content and calendar years is very flat, so that carbon from dates 200–300 years apart can have statistically similar C14 contents, giving less accurate dates than more traditional forms of dating. Its main impact has been in areas such as northern and western Britain where there is little material culture, demonstrating, for instance, that the beginning of hillfort construction was much earlier than had been assumed.

Likewise with dendrochronology. It is capable of very precise dating if the outer tree rings survive. However, survival of wood in useful contexts is relatively rare, and again, for the periods which concern us most, the sixth and fifth centuries, there has been no great change. The one exception is the dating of the final gateway of the Heuneburg to the late sixth century which has resolved a long-standing debate about the date of its abandonment (see below). The date of the beginning of the Hallstatt Iron Age has also been pushed back by about a half century and refined, but otherwise the main impact has been on the date of La Tène D, placed at 50–40 BC in the 1960s, 90–80 BC in the 1980s, and now 130–120 BC, if not earlier.

Another presumption of earlier scholars was 'time-lag', that is that new ideas and innovations, and especially 'culture groups', have a specific origin from which they 'diffuse'. These 'origins' are based on traditional preconceptions that innovations spread from areas of higher civilisation, e.g. the Near East, Greece or Italy, or are associated with the spread of 'peoples': the Thraco-Cimmerians from the steppes; Hallstatt warrior aristocracy from central Europe; Celts from southern Germany and northern France, etc. Thus Pittioni assumed that La Tène A material from Austria had to be dated to post-400 BC when the Celts 'arrived', and Hawkes assumed considerable time delays for the arrival in Britain of 'Hallstatt elements' (c.550 BC) and 'Marnians' (300 BC); comparable dates based on contemporary chronologies would be 750–700 BC, and 475–450 BC. We now assume (and can demonstrate) that ideas spread very quickly, and it is better that like objects in different places be given like dates until it can be demonstrated otherwise. Nor should we assume where specific ideas may have had their origin; this too needs to be demonstrated (see the case of Braubach pottery below).

These dated objects then have to be applied to a wider range of material. This is done in two ways. The first is 'association', that is objects found together in a grave or a pit which can be assumed, as a working hypothesis, to be contemporary. Exceptions will be encountered: the bronze flagon from Waldalgesheim which was an 'heirloom'; the flint arrowhead and stone axe in the burial of Reinheim which seem to be 'amulets'; or earlier rubbish which finds its way into later pits. Such associations ('closed finds') can then be placed into a local sequence using such techniques as typology (see next section), and these sequences linked with one another to produce the more general chronologies used in this book.

However, there are different ways of constructing these chronologies and these different ways of conceiving chronology have a profound impact in the interpretation of the archaeological record. I envisage three different concepts:

1. *Type fossils.* The earliest attempts at refined chronologies in the nineteenth century followed techniques pioneered by geologists who dated deposits from 'typical' and 'distinctive' animal and plant fossils. Like the geologists, early archaeologists had to deal with major gaps both geographically and chronologically, so distinctive sword or brooch types with wide distributions but narrow chronological ranges were most useful. Associations of type fossils together would thus allow a number of objects to typify a period, that is a series of boxes built up to provide a chronological succession, the German *Stufen*. The first division of the

Iron Age into Hallstatt and La Tène by Désor was of this kind, as was the first subdivision of the La Tène period by Tischler, using brooch and scabbard types to distinguish between Early, Middle and Late (see chapter 5). This was refined by Déchelette, and especially by Reinecke who provides the basic nomenclature used today, though his phases have been redefined and subdivided. An important paper was by Giessler and Kraft in 1942 where they correlated the sequence on the Swiss plateau (e.g. Münsingen) typified by the Marzabotto brooch, and that of the central Rhine and Bavaria with zoomorphic brooches in La Tène A.

2. *The horizon*. The second major way of simplifying chronology is to take a clear indicator (an artefact or an historical change) and treat it as a synchronous marker over a considerable area. The best-known Iron Age examples are Filip's 'Dux' and 'twisted belt' horizons which he used to distinguish between the earlier and later phases of the 'Celtic flat inhumations' of central Europe. The Dux brooch is a distinctive Early La Tène brooch, a type fossil of La Tène B, named after an unusual hoard find at Duchcov in northern Bohemia (**67**), which for Filip was an introduction from western Europe, and which represented the arrival of the Celts in central Europe. It is widely distributed across Europe from central France to Romania. The 'twisted belt' is found in male burials dating to the Middle La Tène, part of the fittings for the sword scabbard. The approach is still widely used in central Europe (e.g. Waldhauser's ceramic horizons in northern Bohemia based on the finds from Radovesice).

Though he did not use the term 'horizon', the concept forms the basis for Hawkes' chronology for the British Iron Age. A set of ideas is introduced from the continent by an immigrant group, and these cultural innovations gradually spread outwards from the initial areas of colonisation. Iron Age A saw the introduction of Hallstatt swords and razors, new ceramic types and hillforts. Iron Age B was the 'Marnian' invasion, with Early La Tène brooches and metalwork, fine angular and black-burnished pottery, and, in Yorkshire, inhumations with chariots. Iron Age C saw the arrival of the Belgae with cremation burials, coinage and wheel-turned pottery.

3. *Seriation*. The reality is much more complex. Different types of artefact, or burial rite, etc. have different life spans; they do not appear and disappear at the same time (as implied by the type fossil), nor are they suddenly introduced over wide areas as implied by the horizon. Most artefact types initially appear rarely as an innovation; they can then become the mode; finally they become old-fashioned and disappear, which is symbolised by 'birth', 'maturity' and 'death'. The most elegant demonstration of the method has been in the styles of tombstones in colonial New England, in this case conveniently dated by the year of death of the deceased. Plotted over time, the number of occurrences shows a 'battleship' curve, the 'prow' by the first appearance of a new fashion, and the stern its disappearance as new fashions replace it.

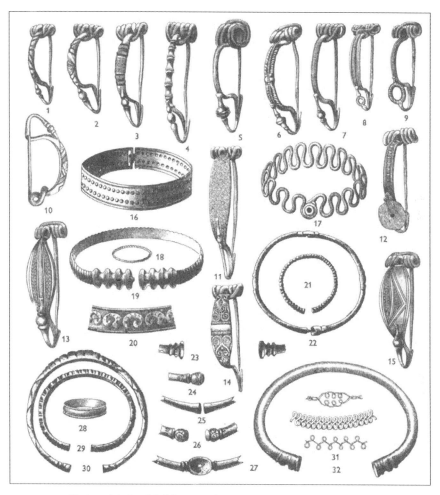

67 *Part of the hoard find from Dux (Duchcov), northern Bohemia.* Filip 1956

The method requires a good data set, with a number of rich associations of groups of finds extending over a considerable period of time, conditions that are rarely met in the Iron Age of central and western Europe. The best example is Hodson's study of the cemetery at Münsingen on the Swiss plateau, which provides the basis of the chronology from La Tène A to C2 for much of Europe. Hodson used sophisticated statistical methods to define the artefacts, and also to sort the graves out in their most likely chronological order based on associations of different artefact types in the graves, which could then be checked against the 'horizontal stratigraphy' of the layout of the cemetery.

The type fossil approach, and especially the horizon, impose breaks in the archaeological sequence and are especially associated, as we have seen, with theories of migration. Seriation emphasises continuity. Though seriation represents a greater reality, only rarely is it possible to invoke it, especially if there is little material to classify, or if there are gaps, e.g. in the burial sequence. Also, to provide a nomenclature for the chronology, it is still necessary to divide a continuity into phases by imposing artificial breaks. Thus Hodson defined phases of development at Münsingen by letters of the alphabet (A, B, etc.), and these were then correlated with Reinecke's nomenclature.

The culture group

The original division between a Hallstatt and a La Tène Iron Age had been purely chronological, but, as we have seen, already from the mid-nineteenth century others such as Kemble, Franks, Virchow and de Mortillet had begun to assign ethnic meanings to some of the characteristic features such as the art style or the weapons and ornaments. At the same time anthropologists were describing different sorts of societies, mainly in terms of languages, customs and kinship, and, especially in North America, in terms of material culture. To explain the mechanism whereby specific, sometimes unique, characteristics were passed from individual to individual, from community to community, and from generation to generation, the abstract concept of 'culture' was conceived, and eventually this term was extended to the societies themselves in the form of 'other cultures'.

The way in which the term was gradually applied to archaeology is documented in part by Margarita Díaz-Andreu (1996) and, as we have noted, in his writings in the early twentieth century Joseph Déchelette was already using the idea, though not the nomenclature, when he talked of '*les civilisations de Hallstatt de La Tène*'. However, as with most of his contemporaries (e.g. Romilly Allen), the term 'Celtic' could be applied to Bronze Age metalwork and ceramics, to Hallstatt material culture as well as La Tène. The *civilisation de Hallstatt* could encompass Celts and Illyrians, and that of *La Tène* Celts and Germans, and though he used other ethnic indicators (e.g. 'Ligurian' Bronze Age hoards, typified by large quantities of sickles), the burial rite was the main diagnostic feature. The same gradual shift can also be seen in the use of the type fossil. In 1875 de Mortillet drew up a chart of French prehistory in which he characterised and named each chronological period by the use of a type site, following the practice of geologists. For the Palaeolithic, terms like the Acheulean, Gravettian and Solutrean have stayed in the common vocabulary, but those for later phases (e.g. the Beuvraysian for the Late La Tène) never took off. But as there was an increasing need to make geographical as well as chronological distinctions, with the recognition that the archaeological record did not just consist of a series of stages of social and technological development, so the periods in their local facies slowly became 'cultures' and individual type fossils became cultural indicators as well.

In the history of archaeology, the shift from chronological phases to culture groups is generally taken to be marked by the publication by Gustaf Kossinna of his paper *Zur Herkunft der Germanen* in 1911. In it he makes his famous statement that behind all culture groups there lies a racially distinct group, an interpretation which infamously became the basis for his theories of Germanic expansion, and laid the foundations for the nationalistic and racial interpretations of German prehistory in the 1930s. However, the methodology need not necessarily be nationalistic, and in the English-speaking world it was Gordon Childe, avowedly Marxist, who took up Kossinna's methodology and promulgated it. It is worth stating yet again his famous and often quoted definition of a culture taken from *The Danube in Prehistory*:

> We find certain types of remains (pots, implements, ornaments, burial rites, house forms) constantly recurring together. Such a complex of regularly associated traits we shall term a 'cultural group' or just a 'culture'. We assume that such a complex is the material expression of what today would be called a people.
>
> Childe 1929, v–vi.

Throughout the 1930s, and culminating in his great overview of earlier European prehistory *The Dawn of European Civilisation*, Childe systematically applied the culture concept to the whole of the Neolithic and Bronze Age. Childe in part followed the usage of type-sites to identify cultures (Vinča, Sesklo, Chassey, Aunjetitz/Únětice, Mycenae), but increasingly some distinctive feature of the material culture, especially, though not exclusively, ceramics (Bell Beaker, Corded Ware, Battle Axe), or occasionally regions or river basins (Danubian, Wessex). Smaller sub-culture groupings might be termed a 'group' (German *Gruppe*), while larger entities might just use the plural (Beaker Cultures, Megalithic Cultures) or a more general term (Western Neolithic, Nordic Bronze Age), though German nomenclature often refers to a *Kreis* ('circle'): the *nordische Kreis* for the Scandinavian and north German Bronze Age; or the *Blechkreis*, referring to Early Bronze Age groups using a simple technology of making copper objects by hammering. The origins and developments of these cultures were explained in terms of migration and diffusion of ideas ('influences'), and most archaeological papers were devoted to studying these phenomena.

In contrast to this systematisation of nomenclature and methodology for the earlier phases of prehistory, Iron Age studies were more heterogeneous (Childe never focused his attention on the European Iron Age). Part of the ambiguity lay in the historical evidence and its racial implications. Iron Age studies in the 1930s were dominated by the German school, and within that the theories and methodologies of Kossinna predominated, indeed were politically obligatory. In a famous paper published in 1941, Ernst Wahle suggested that, in the then prevailing state of knowledge, it was impossible to distinguish between the material culture of Caesar's Celts west of the Rhine and that of his Germans east of the Rhine. It was an overt attack on the Kossinna methodology and so of the National Socialist Party's interpretation of prehistory. But for the intervention of some of his pupils in positions of influence in the Party, Wahle would have suffered dismissal from his professorial post, if not worse.

The other problem was how to deal with Hallstatt and La Tène. Were these cultures in their own right, with specific origins followed by diffusion, or were they overarching terms like the 'western Neolithic' in which separate cultures could be identified? In general the former seems to have been accepted, and though the specific origins of the 'Hallstatt Culture' could not be easily defined except, as Reinecke's terminology implied, as a general evolution from 'Urnfield cultures' of central Europe, particularly southern Germany and Austria, the origins of the 'La Tène Culture' were sought within western Germany, and the Hunsrück-Eifel in particular. Nonetheless local groups and cultures were defined on the basis of burial rites and ceramics for the Hallstatt period: Horakov in Moravia, Platěnice in northern Bohemia, Kalenderberg in Austria, and the *Westhallstattkreis* to encompass the rich burials and *Fürstensitze* of southern Germany and eastern France. For the La Tène period with its more 'Celtic' implications, such divisions were of less interest, except in the definition of origins. Thus, only two groups are usually referred to for the Early La Tène: the Hunsrück-Eifel, phase I of which is assigned to Hallstatt D and IIA and IIB which equate with La Tène A and B respectively; and, following de Mortillet's nomenclature, the 'Marnien' dating to Early La Tène. With the publication of the cemetery of Chouilly–Les Jogasses in 1936, the 'Jogassien', dating to Hallstatt D, was defined as the precursor of the 'Marnien'. Elsewhere the term La Tène or simply Celtic was preferred, and its 'diffusion' linked with the Celtic migrations.

This change from a purely chronological to a cultural approach is nowhere better exemplified than in Britain. In 1931 Hawkes abandoned the Hallstatt/La Tène terminology on the grounds that it was impossible to apply them in an insular context; the material, though reflecting continental trends, was too different, especially the ceramic styles. Instead he proposed three major horizons: A (= Late Hallstatt); B (= Marnian); and C (= Belgic). Though this represented a broadly chronological sequence, he was at pains to point out, using his own emphasis, 'A, B and C are a series of *cultural* entities induced simply from the archaeological material' (Hawkes 1960, 3). Thus, on his interpretation, by the first century BC the Belgae of 'C' had colonised the south-east of Britain and were expanding their influence north and west into areas still occupied by people with a Marnian 'B' Culture, while in the highland zones of Wales and northern England residues of the earlier Hallstatt 'A' populations still lingered on. This presents a classic use of the 'horizon' concept, linked with time-lag, discussed previously.

In a series of papers published between 1960 and 1964, Hodson attacked the whole theoretical, methodological and factual basis of the Hawkes system, and he proposed a return to the Childe's classic 'culture group' approach (**68**). In Britain he recognised one possible and two 'foreign' cultures, both defined by their

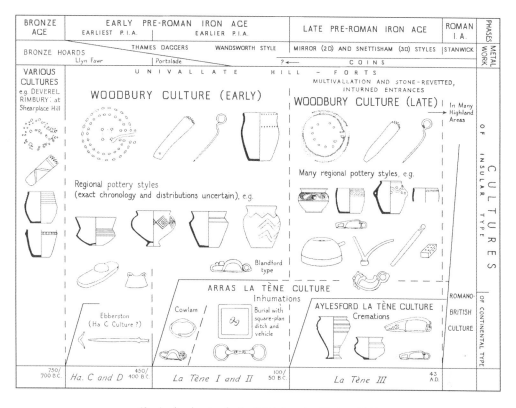

68 *A cultural system for the British Iron Age.* Hodson 1964

distinctive burial rites: a poorly defined period of Hallstatt C influence; the inhumation burials of the Arras group in east Yorkshire; and the 'Belgic' Aylesford-Swarling Culture of south-east Britain with its cremation burials. The rest was a hotchpotch of different ceramic types, house forms and other artefacts, but he recognised three distinctive and widespread common elements: the roundhouse; ring-headed pins; and the bone or antler weaving comb; and he could trace the culture of the roundhouse back at least as far as the Middle Bronze Age. He therefore proposed to call this indigenous culture after a well-known site, the 'Woodbury Culture'. He suggested further refinement might be possible by plotting the distributions of specific artefact types, especially pottery, and so define regional groups. This was done by Cunliffe in the 1960s, generally using the names of type-sites, except for the final period for which he preferred the documented tribal names; he also preferred the term 'style-zone' to 'group'.

The most sophisticated approach to the concept of culture groups is found in the work of David Clarke in the late 1960s. He accepted that the correlation between archaeologically defined culture groups and other types of definition (linguistic, political, social) posed major problems but he considered that grouping by using material culture has as much validity as any other. However, he rejected the traditional 'intuitive' way of defining artefacts or culture groups as 'unscientific', and proposed, firstly, that archaeologists should recognise a nested hierarchy of entities (from 'attribute', to 'artefact', then 'assemblage', to 'culture group' and finally 'techno-complex'). Each level would be made up of different combinations of attributes or artefacts. One assemblage would not contain all the artefacts typical of a culture, but this would vary according to context (e.g. rubbish pit, hoard, burial). Equally, one artefact type might not be unique to one individual culture (as was assumed by earlier scholars such as Kossinna, and implied by terminology which employs a specific artefact type, e.g. Bell Beaker), but could be shared with surrounding cultures. It would be the combination that would be unique. Clarke labelled the Kossinna/Childe approach as 'monothetic', his own as 'polythetic'. The difference would mean that boundaries between cultures and groups would be woolly and indistinct rather than sharp, unless there was some natural barrier preventing contact.

Clarke's ideas have never been directly applied to the Iron Age; indeed, younger people such as myself rejected it as a useful way forward, though I suspect he would have considered Hallstatt and La Tène to be what he called techno-complexes. The main reason was that the period around 1970 marked a change in paradigm, a shift from the 'culture-history' approach with its emphasis upon cultures, migrations and race (or ethnicity as the new terminology demanded), and Clarke was himself one of the prime movers of this change. The New Archaeology was concerned more with economic and social reconstruction, and archaeologists split into two factions, those who espoused the aims of the New Archaeology, and those who followed the traditional methodologies. In the 1970s in Iron Age studies the main battleground was in Britain, and did not really extend to continental Europe until the late 1980s and 1990s.

Typology

Another major contribution of nineteenth-century archaeologists was to develop ways of describing and classifying artefacts. This lay in the studies of the natural world, the detailed drawing of, and comparisons between, plants and animals to be found in the work of eighteenth-century botanists and zoologists which were the basis of the classifications of Ray, Linné and others. Antiquarians were slower in developing similar techniques for artefacts, but after modest beginnings we start encountering detail in, for instance, Sir John Evans' study of 'Ancient British' coinage published in 1864, or in the description of 'Late Keltic Art' by Kemble and Franks. Much classification can be done intuitively (anyone can distinguish a horse from a cow or an axe from a sword), but training and knowledge is needed to distinguish between different types of warbler, or socketed axes.

Typology is classification by description, but the salient points for the description are selected according to the questions being asked. Thus Kemble identified the 'trumpet shape' as something with which to distinguish the art of the indigenous Celts from that of the immigrant Anglo-Saxons, though instinctively he may have also recognised other criteria and the general context; Germanic square-headed brooches have curvilinear zoomorphic art on them, but not the trumpet shape. Tischler, in trying to divide up the La Tène period, would be able to see the logical development in the brooch types (unattached foot, strapped on foot, cast-on foot), and their associations with different shaped chapes and scabbard ends (what Carl-Axel Moberg simplified as O, V and U ends), and this then gave him a basic chronology in which other features could be ignored or tacitly assimilated.

In the 1960s Hodson carried out various experiments in classifying brooches from the Münsingen cemetery. In one he asked various scholars (including non-archaeologists) to place a group of brooches in chronological order. Even among the specialists the results were different, as each person laid different weight on different criteria: decoration on the foot, the height and length of the bow. He advocated a statistical approach recording as many criteria ('attributes') as possible, and then trying various experiments for measuring the similarity between one brooch and another, or one brooch to a previously defined group of brooches. In a subsequent experiment he looked at ways of distinguishing a typical Hallstatt C bronze sword, the Gündlingen type, which is found over much of central and western Europe, from a variant most commonly found in the Thames. In fact only one criterion was needed, the ratio between two measurements on the hilt, and the rest of the information was redundant.

The detailed statistical approaches used by Hodson, Clarke and others in the 1960s have not been extensively used since, despite the greater availability of statistical packages on more powerful computers, partly because the data sets are often not available; the Münsingen cemetery has no equivalent in its size, the date range and the horizontal stratigraphy which can be used to check the chronological schemes devised for it. Also classification tends to be more problem-oriented; indeed part of the reason for non-adoption of some of the methods is that the questions have changed. Thus, for pottery, function will be based on simple dimensions and ratios, or on scientific criteria such as the presence of lipids to show what they contained; production will be studied by the presence of distinctive minerals or the chemical characteristics of the fabric; style will be studied by the nature and location of the decorative elements.

Continuity and change

A fundamental assumption which lies behind archaeological theories on the migrations of the Celts is that we can detect breaks in the archaeological sequence which mark a change in the population, or the arrival of a group sufficiently numerous or powerful to assert their authority, and who introduce new ideas and a new direction for social development. In part these migration theories were based on historical evidence or historical parallels: the Celtic invasions of northern Italy and of Asia Minor; the documented expansion of Germanic-speaking peoples in the post-Roman world, the Vikings, the Magyars, etc. But it is also based on pre-conceptions of the colonial world of the nineteenth century, a belief that 'primitive' peoples had not changed in the past and were incapable of change without external immigration. Left to themselves, natives just degenerate, as the simplification of high foot-pedestals on vases to simple ring-base was suggested to happen in Iron Age Sussex after the Marnian invasion. The following quote from the Danish prehistorian Johannes Worsaae epitomises these attitudes:

> We know that races at the lowest rung of the cultural ladder, e.g. the Eskimos and many savage tribes in the South Sea Islands and in America, remain at the same level for thousands of years; at least they do not develop except through a prolonged and considerable outside influence and perhaps also miscegenation.
>
> Worsaae 1859/2002, 53.

So, in the 1930s, virtually all change and innovation was explained in terms of migration and invasion. By the early 1970s, under the New Archaeology, different mechanisms were being invoked such as trade, social competition, internal economic and social innovations induced by such factors as overpopulation; 'core-periphery' and 'World Systems' which studied the relationship between the resource-hungry states of the Middle East, and, later, the Mediterranean world; or 'peer-polity interaction' which envisaged competition between states or groups of equal size or power. At the extreme, proponents for these new approaches tried to deny migration as a factor for change, or where the historical evidence is over-whelming, play down its significance. As one who promoted the new ideas in Iron Age studies, I never saw them as more than giving different (and often better) alternatives to the traditional explanations for cultural change. However, as we have seen, and as will be described in greater detail in the next chapter, changes can be more apparent than real when the nature of the archaeology changes (appearance and disappearance of burial traditions, hoard deposition, etc.), and we must be careful when arguing from a lack of information. 'Continuity' and 'change' have been invoked in many ways, in terms of settlement patterns, burial rites, the typological development of pottery or metal types, language, or, more recently, genetics). Yet rarely do we see total change; even if an earlier population completely disappeared, there is likely to be continuity in some aspects of the use of the landscape. Thus, at the end of the Roman period in Britain, with major changes in language and material culture, some features are found in both Late Roman and Early Saxon contexts such as chip-carved belt fittings. Saxon burial rites changed under the impact of Christianity, but not the population or the language. In Gaul Iron Age oppida evolved into Roman towns and the language changed from the native Gallic to the local version of Latin that evolved into modern French. Dublin was founded by Germanic speaking Vikings and later inhabited by the native Gaelic speakers (the name itself is Gaelic), but despite continuity of population, it is now largely English speaking. These are cases where we have an historical basis, but for prehistory such contextual evidence is lacking.

Yet it is precisely such evidence, dragged out of context, which is used to define the area of origin of the Celts, and also to signify their arrival (e.g. the flat inhumation cemeteries of Central Europe). The big divide is seen as the division between the 'Hallstatt Culture' (mainly conceived as non-Celtic), and a 'La Tène Culture' which is equated with the Celts. If, it is argued, we wish to find the origin of the Celts, we need to locate areas where the Hallstatt Culture evolves into the La Tène Culture, and where continuity can be demonstrated. The main area which has been claimed has been western Germany. In Baden-Württemberg, even though the major *Fürstensitze* of Hallstatt D seem to collapse (the Heuneburg and Asperg), in the burial rites of the poorer inhumations are found many of the characteristics of the subsequent Early La Tène burials: extended inhumation, men buried with weapons, women with personal ornaments, young women with amulets. The brooch and scabbard types show a continuous evolution between Hallstatt and La Tène, and this also links in with the supposed early mention of Celts on the Danube by Herodotus in the fifth century. As we shall see in the next chapter, there have been alternative views of what happened here in the fifth century.

However, there is one area in which continuity has been universally accepted since the 1930s, the Hunsrück-Eifel, and the nomenclature has also reflected this. The earlier phase, Hunsrück-Eifel-Kultur I, is dated to Hallstatt D, and Hunsrück-Eifel-Kultur IIa to La Tène A. Again continuity is mainly claimed in the burial rites (extended inhumation under barrows, burial of vehicles, etc.). The other area depicted on most maps showing the 'origins' of the Celts is Champagne. For many years French archaeologists assumed a break at the beginning of La Tène, with the arrival of the Celts from the East, but the excavation of the cemetery of Les Jogasses showed many of the characteristics of Early La Tène burials in the preceding Hallstatt period, and also the scabbards and brooches show clear evolutionary continuity, so that, from the 1950s, this area too has been considered one of the points of origin of the Celts or at least as a major centre of diffusion.

It is the Hallstatt–La Tène transition that has been seen as crucial for the arrival of the Celts, but, as we have seen, when Hildebrand and Désor first made the division, it had no such significance. The Celts were thought to be, if not indigenous, at least present from the Bronze Age, and the concept of the archaeological culture was still in its infancy. By the time we reach Déchelette, the cultural gulf had already come into existence, defined largely by the adoption of La Tène art, but also brooch and sword types. But, as many authors have argued, the adoption of this new art style in central and western Europe was part of a process known as orientalising: the adoption of plant motifs such as the palmette and lotus flower, and of mythical animals which have their precedents in the art of the Near East. In most areas such as Greece it is assumed that this betokens no change in the population; Etruria is one exception, but few would now argue for a population change here at the end of seventh century, so why should it imply such a change in central Europe?

In south-western Germany and eastern France, it is clear that the Hallstatt D/Early La Tène transition is associated with profound social and economic changes, and probably a shift of power to areas to the west and north. However, there is little evidence that there was also ethnic and linguistic change. The other major feature of the change is the adoption of La Tène art style. Does this have any significance other than an elite group absorbing the fashions from further south, adopting and adapting them to their own local requirements? In Greece the mythical animals which appear in eighth-/seventh-century orientalising art (sphinxes, winged horses and lions, etc.) also appear in mythological stories explaining the dominance of elite families in their city-states. The Megaws amongst others have argued that La Tène art should be interpreted in religious terms, and Pauli has done the same for the burial rites, and their spread into central Europe.

However, some of the distinctive ornaments of the fifth-century Early Style have distributions which are more indicative of status symbols rather than ethnic or religious significance. The distinctive iron and bronze openwork belt plates decorated with a design derived from the classical palmette show a marked concentration in the Hunsrück-Eifel and Marne, not unexpectedly as they are rarely found outside burial contexts; the distribution map (**69**) is as much one of burial rites as the original distribution of the objects (central and western France, for instance, have few burials of this period). Their distribution extends from southern France to northern Italy and central Europe, and they certainly cross linguistic boundaries. Most come from Celtic-speaking areas, and they have been taken as one of the 'type-fossils' of the 'La Tène culture', but the wearers of these belts also spoke Iberian (e.g. at Ensérune), Venetic in north-eastern Italy, Etruscan in central Italy, Lepontic in the Ticino Valley, while in the central Alps the language was probably Raetic, a non-Indo-European language. In central Europe we do not know the languages (possibly Illyrian, Celtic, or even Germanic). Otto-Hermann Frey (1991) has discussed the problems of their interpretation (for instance, do they represent an earlier Celtic intrusion into northern Italy, or mercenaries at Ensérune?). However, it would be much easier to presume that they were not necessarily indicators of Celtic ethnicity, and that these examples of 'Early Celtic art', were international in their manufacture and usage. It would then leave open the choice of interpretation in each specific case: objects which were traded or formed prestige gifts; or individuals moving around in Europe for whatever reason; or local versions of a widely recognised symbol of status (they are used mainly for belts for La Tène swords); or that they are indeed ethnic indicators (which I doubt). This undermines the automatic assumption that Early La

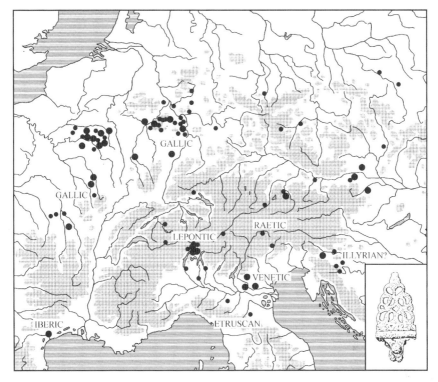

69 *Distribution of belt-hooks decorated with palmette decoration, and dating to La Tène A (fifth century BC), and showing the languages likely to have been spoken by the wearers, if not the craftsmen who made them. Frey 1991*

Tène art is to be ascribed to the Celts (the main concentrations on the Rhine and in Champagne are areas which in later times were ascribed to the Belgae rather than the Celts).

Summary

In this chapter I have reviewed the basic nature of the archaeological record which is used to define the ancient Celts, and the methodologies applied, concepts such as 'culture' and 'culture groups', 'continuity' and 'change'. We have noted that the concept of the archaeological culture is something which 'New Archaeologists' in the 1970s were rejecting as a useful heuristic device, but that this had not generally been taken up by Iron Age specialists on the continent, and by more traditional archaeologists in Britain. It has taken even longer to start to impact on those outside the discipline such as historians and linguists, and this has led to a long survival of flawed methodological approaches in general books on the Celts. In the mid-1980s and 1990s we have seen another paradigm shift to so-called 'Post-Processual' archaeology in which there is greater emphasis on ideological approaches to archaeological data and 'the past as lived'; in fact, in some ways almost a return to the original concept of 'culture' as formulated by anthropologists in the late nineteenth century.

In the next chapter, in a series of case studies, I wish to look at some of these propositions, not only in the supposed core areas, but also in areas supposedly peripheral to the main developments.

8

THE ARCHAEOLOGY
OF THE CELTS

In this chapter we shall look at a sample of the areas supposedly forming the original homeland of the Celts early in the Iron Age, or colonised by them during the course of it. We shall briefly consider the historical evidence for the specific areas and the theories that have been put forward locally, and especially in terms of the maps of Celtic expansion as shown on figures **40–46**. I shall start with the 'core areas' where the Celts are supposed to have originated.

The Hunsrück-Eifel

At the time of Caesar the area either side of the Mosel was occupied by the Treveri. Although powerful, they were not considered by Caesar as one of the most important of the Gallic states. He relates some of the internal politics: there was apparently some sort of oligarchic state, with popular assemblies, but with individuals contending for overall monarchic control. It is unclear whether Caesar considered them to be *Celtae* or *Belgae*, probably the latter, as his boundary between the two ethnic groups is unclear in the area between the Marne and the Rhine. Tacitus even says they considered themselves to have been *Germani* (*Germania* 28). However, they spoke a Celtic language, and St Jerome writing in the fifth century noted the similarity between the native language spoken around Trier (in the Late Roman period the imperial capital of the Western Roman Empire) and that of the Galatians of Asia Minor.

Since the 1930s this has been considered as the core area of the 'La Tène Culture', and so of the Celts. In Hallstatt C the burial rite was cremation (the 'Laufeld Group') continuing Urnfield traditions, but with bronze ornaments becoming more common among the grave goods. In Hallstatt D this shifts to inhumation under a tumulus (Hunsrück-Eifel Culture I), though in the acid soil uncremated bone rarely survives, so we know nothing of the age and sex of the dead other than from the grave goods and by analogy with other areas. Some of these Hallstatt burials contain four-wheeled vehicles (e.g. Bell im Hunsrück) and

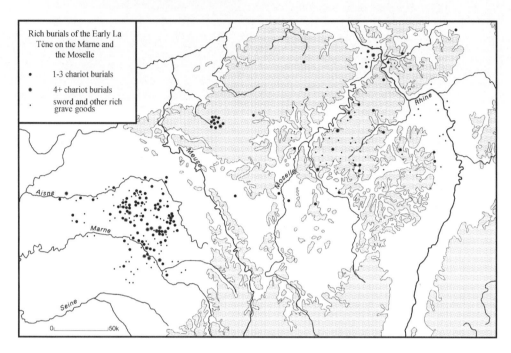

Rich burials of the Early La Tène on the Marne and the Moselle

• 1-3 chariot burials

• 4+ chariot burials

· sword and other rich grave goods

70 *Distribution of chariot and other rich burials in the Marne and in the Hunsrück-Eifel.*
After Diepeveen-Jansen 2001

especially bronze buckets, some of which may be of local manufacture, but others of north Italian origin.

La Tène A represents a continuity of this burial rite (Hunsrück-Eifel Culture IIa), and in some cases of the same cemeteries, though the richest burials tend to be isolated from the rest (**70**). Rich burials are noted not only for the two-wheeled vehicles, but also the relatively common Etruscan bronze vessels (two-handled *stamnoi* and beaked flagons), swords and daggers, and, especially in female graves, rich goldwork. These objects form the major group of 'Early Style' La Tène objects, and also the widest range of decorative motifs (curvilinear, plant, geometric) in fifth-century La Tène art, with masterpieces such as the Schwarzenbach bowl (**33**), the bronze flagon from Reinheim, and the gold torcs and bracelets from Bad Dürkheim, Reinheim and Rodenbach. Styles of pottery are very localised, though one or two potters had started using the potter's wheel. The richest burials are on the upper reaches of the river Nahe, an area agricultur-ally poor, but with mineral resources, especially haematite iron ores. Distributions of imported objects in graves, and also some of the styles of pottery, suggest close links with northern Italy, especially the Ticino valley.

In La Tène B and early La Tène C numbers of burials drop dramatically (**60**) and the richest group of burials disappears, with the notable exception of

Waldalgesheim. Occasionally male burials contain swords. Initially pyre burials, and then cremations in urns, become the dominant burial rite in late La Tène C and La Tène D, when cemeteries again become common, as well as rich burials with Italian bronze vessels, fine pottery, and in some cases wine amphorae. With the wider use of the potter's wheel, ceramics become much more homogenous from La Tène B onwards, with the adoption of the Braubach bowl with its stamped decoration (**79**).

Except for some of the löss areas such as the Neuwied Basin, settlement evidence is rare, but the population seems generally to have lived in small open settlements. A fair number of hillforts can be dated to late Hallstatt/Early La Tène, but their function is very varied, and none produces evidence of intensive occupation. Befort in Luxemburg seems to be a defended elite farm. The most extensively excavated, Bundenbach, starts as a palisaded farmstead, but the later buildings, dated mainly to La Tène B and C, are mainly four- and six-post structures, more likely to be for storage of crops than for habitation. Small hillforts continue into La Tène D, but from the end of the second century BC the settlement hierarchy is dominated by the defended oppida such as the Titelberg in Luxemburg.

The Hunsrück-Eifel is thus an important area in the development of Early Style La Tène art, but this does not mean that we should exclude other areas where the burial evidence is not so rich. It may also be one of the areas where the Waldalgesheim style may have developed, but the idea of a 'Waldalgesheim Master', who was adapting the decoration on the Italian bucket found in the burial, is clearly simplistic. The hand of several different artists can be detected in the objects in the grave, and an equally strong case can be made for the origin of the style in northern Italy. We simply cannot be specific in tying down the origin of art styles to one particular area, let alone to a specific craftsman.

Other aspects of the so-called 'La Tène Culture' are even less clear. The burial of vehicles is found in some groups and not in others into the fifth century and later. Though we may find many similarities in the burial rite in La Tène A in the Hunsrück-Eifel-Kultur with the burials we find later in central Europe, in common with other areas with rich La Tène A burials, the burial rite changes in La Tène B at the time it is being adopted in other areas – indeed, burials simply become less visible. To suggest that the reduction of burial numbers in La Tène B–C is due to emigration to the south and east as part of a Celtic expansion would need confirmatory evidence such as pollen evidence for the wholesale abandonment of settlements (there is no such independent support). The pottery and brooch types (plate brooches and zoomorphic *Tierkopffibeln* brooches) do not form part of the subsequent major trends in brooch typology. The same is true for the pottery. Only in La Tène B, with the adoption of the simpler Dux and Münsingen brooches and of the Braubach bowl does the Hunsrück-Eifel join the main trend of fashions across central and western Europe. Other artefact types such as the swords and the elaborate pierced belt fittings are simply shared in common with adjacent areas, and we can claim no priority for them in the central Rhine–Mosel area.

In conclusion we can suggest that this area had an important, but probably not exclusive, role in the development of the art styles, but it is less important in other aspect of the material culture. Thus it cannot be labelled as the 'area of origin' of the 'La Tène Culture'.

Champagne

The chalklands between the rivers Marne and Seine have the richest sequence of Hallstatt and La Tène burials of anywhere in Europe. Even so, some periods are not well represented. Hallstatt C burials are relatively rare, though one or two tumulus burials with typical bronze swords are known. In Hallstatt D inhumation cemeteries such as Les Jogasses at Chouilly appear, with occasional richer burials with four-wheeled vehicles, daggers, etc., though poor in comparison with Burgundy further south. The similarity of Hallstatt and Early La Tène burials rites has been the basis of claims of continuity, and so of Celtic origins, in this area.

In La Tène A virtually every commune has one or two inhumation cemeteries, and numbers of graves per cemetery can be over 100 (**70**). Men are buried with weapons, especially swords and spears, women with their bronze jewellery. Imported Attic Red Figure Ware and Etruscan bronze vessels are rare, as is gold, in comparison to the Hunsrück-Eifel. However, vehicle burials are much more common (**27**), and have elaborate bronze and iron fittings and harness. Though curvilinear decoration in Early La Tène style is not uncommon, it lacks the range of motifs found in the Hunsrück-Eifel-Kultur, and geometric ornament is more common. Some graves have rectangular enclosures or wooden structures, but tumuli, if they existed, have long disappeared. By La Tène B2 vehicle and sword burials are rarer and generally peripheral to the main distribution in La Tène A. Occasional cremations occur in La Tène A, and by La Tène C and D it has become universal. As in the Hunsrück-Eifel, this includes some richer burials with Italian bronze vessels.

Settlement archaeology has tended to take second place after cemetery excavation until the 1980s. The settlement pattern is dominated by generally unenclosed farms and hamlets, but they are highly eroded, and only storage pits, quarries and large post-holes survive. Only one has been extensively excavated to show the relationship between settlement, cemetery and cult areas, the complex village of Acy-Romance which dates mainly to La Tène C and D. There is as yet no general synthesis of the settlement patterns and changes covering the whole of the Iron Age in the area. Defended sites are rare; the large valley fort of La Cheppe dates to Early La Tène, but its function is unknown, and defended oppida too are rare. The core of Champagne was the territory of the Remi whose chief oppidum was *Durocotorum* (Reims). We have no information about the Remi until the period of the Caesarian conquest of Gaul, at which time he considered them one of the two most powerful states of Belgic Gaul. Caesar stated that the Belgae had come from east of the Rhine and replaced the Gauls, but he places no timescale on these events.

The personal ornaments found in the fifth-century graves tend to be distinctive to the Marne region; the pierced belt fittings discussed on p.159 are an exception, but this is likely to be due to the lack of burials in much of northern France and Britain. The brooches, however, with types such as the Marzabotto, fall into the mainstream of European developments. The swords and daggers have parallels from the Thames. The ceramics of Late Hallstatt and earliest La Tène are of high quality, with angular vases and cups with incised decoration and a few with painted designs, but pottery becomes rarer in graves and less well made in the later phases of Early La Tène. Generally the styles conform to the main general trends in central and northern France and in south-eastern Britain, but with no independent chronological dating (there are almost no dendrochronological dates for this period in France and Britain), we cannot suggest priority for the Marne areas as has often been claimed, nor can it be seen as the origin of the 'La Tène Culture'.

The drop in the number of burials in La Tène B2 has been claimed as evidence for migration from the area in the fourth century, but as we have seen, this is a widespread phenomenon from southern Bavaria to Champagne, and there is no supporting settlement evidence. The appearance of cremation burials is often tied in with Caesar's statement about the Germanic component, which on this evidence is placed in the third century. In fact, cremation already appears in the fifth century, though it is rare, and it is a shift in fashion which equally appears in Caesar's 'Celtic' areas, e.g. at Mont Beuvray and in the Auvergne, and so we can ignore the simplistic interpretations which survive from Déchelette's outdated racial interpretation of burial rites.

Baden-Württemberg

Bounded by the Rhine and Lake Geneva to the south, the Rhine to the west, and the Main to the north, Baden-Württemberg also includes the upper course of the Danube. We have no unambiguous evidence of the presence of the Celts other than Herodotus' problematic statement that the source of the Danube lay in the territory of the Celts near the town of *Pyrene*. Despite claims that perhaps the Heuneburg was *Pyrene*, the greater likelihood is that Herodotus, like Aristotle, was confused about where the Danube rose. The south-eastern part was occupied by the Rauraci, clients of the Helvetii, whose Roman administrative centre was at Augst, but for most of the area we have no names of the tribes who lived there, though there are hints from Poseidonius and from Caesar and Tacitus that the territory of the Helvetii formerly extended north of the Rhine, but was, by Caesar's time, occupied by Germani. Even when the area was incorporated into the Roman Empire, it is known merely as the *Agri Decumani*, the tithe lands. However, place names such as *Tarodunum* (probably Kirchzarten near Freiburg in Breisgau) suggest a Celtic-speaking population in the late Iron Age. The area was certainly German speaking from the late third century AD when it was ceded to the Alamanni.

The area presents much of the classic sequence of the Hallstatt and La Tène periods, though there are local differences, especially in the La Tène period. Urnfield cemeteries were replaced by Hallstatt tumulus burials, including some with wooden chambers with rich pottery finds, and occasionally iron swords, but vehicle burials are not found this far west during Hallstatt C. Right at the beginning of Hallstatt D exceptionally rich burials under huge mounds make their appearance, the Magdalenenberg, Hochdorf and the Hohmichele, the latter certainly, the others probably, associated with a high-status hillfort. The Magdalenenberg was a short-lived centre, but in the mound there was a large number of secondary extended inhumations (**63**), the men with weapons, in one case a dagger, but mainly with spears, and the women with personal ornaments, especially bracelets, anklets and brooches. Already we can see a diminution of the burial of ceramics which had been so important in Urnfield and earlier Hallstatt graves. The *Fürstensitze* of Asperg and the Heuneburg have clusters of rich tumulus burials around them, all, with one exception datable to Hallstatt D, with gold objects, elaborate four-wheeled wagons, and imported goods from Greece and Italy. Wagon and dagger burials occur in other tumulus cemeteries, but lack the gold and foreign goods.

The system collapses at the end of Hallstatt D; the Heuneburg is certainly burnt and abandoned around 500–480 BC, though occupation continues into La Tène A on one of the open settlements just to the south of the fort. For Asperg we have no evidence from the possible site of the hillfort (it is inaccessible under a more recent castle), but we have one rich burial, Klein Aspergle, with imported Attic Red Figure Ware, a *stamnos* and local goods, including two gold drinking horns, decorated in Early La Tène Style. The burial is two generations later than the latest Hallstatt burial, though some features like the drinking horns show continuity in some aspects of the ideology. It can interpreted either as showing the continuity of the Asperg as a *Fürstensitz*, or as an outlier to the Hunsrück-Eifel burials to the north-west. The La Tène A settlement discovered under the Hochdorf Museum has also produced imported Red Figure Ware, and other indications of high status. A number of cemeteries show similar continuity between the Hallstatt and La Tène periods, either with secondary burials (Hirschlanden), or new tumuli (Bargen). However, there is a marked drop in the number of burials in La Tène A, as well as of settlement sites. In La Tène B–C developments are more localised. Some areas (e.g. Breisgau) produce little evidence until the foundation of the oppida in La Tène D (Kirchzarten); in others *Viereckschanzen* appear, dateable to La Tène C–D. Only on the lower Neckar is there plentiful evidence for the standard small flat inhumations cemeteries of La Tène B–C (e.g. Nebringen).

The ceramic traditions of the Hallstatt period are typical for central Europe, with a range of bowls, plates and storage jars richly decorated with incised, stamped and painted motifs (e.g. Alb-Salem ware). The tradition disappears at the end of the Hallstatt period. Wheel-turned wares with cordons and raised pedestal feet, which are probably ancestral to those of La Tène B, already start appearing as early as Hallstatt D at major centres such as the Heuneburg; the sword and brooch types of the Hallstatt period are clearly the antecedents of those of the La Tène period. Thus, though we can point to major changes in the settlement pattern and also perhaps in the social structure at the transition from Hallstatt to La Tène, e.g. the disappearance of the very rich burials, the disappearance of at least one of the major centres (the Heuneburg), in other respects (burial rites, cemeteries, typology of artefacts) one can demonstrate considerable continuity of culture from the sixth to the fifth century. Though the interpretation of the drop in the number of burials as indicating a drop in population requires confirmation from other sources, it is something that might be predicted from a 'systems collapse', the demise of a highly structured and hierarchical society which had previously been able to support and encourage greater specialisation, and so a higher density of population.

However, recent discussion of the chronology of the Late Hallstatt period and Early La Tène produced a fundamentally different story, initially put forward by one of the major excavators of Hallstatt cemeteries in Baden-Württemberg, Hartwig Zürn, and further developed by Ludwig Pauli, and by Egon Gersbach, excavator of the Heuneburg. It started as an attempt to explain the relative lack of La Tène A burials, at least in comparison to those of Hallstatt D. The theoretical and methodological basis for it lay in the Culture-History paradigm, but also in the concept of *Stufen* (type fossils) as the basis for the chronological division. Zürn argued, as did many archaeologists working in the Culture-Historical paradigm, that Hallstatt and La Tène were not so much chronological divisions, but two different 'culture groups', and though locally one may *evolve* into the other (e.g. in the Hunsrück-Eifel), in most areas Hallstatt was *replaced* by La Tène. Though some elements of Hallstatt culture might still be found, these were to be explained as Hallstatt 'influences' or 'survivals'. So, he suggested, the Hallstatt Culture survived longer in Baden-Württemberg than in the Hunsrück-Eifel, and with the two different cultures co-existing, it should be possible to identify La Tène imports from the Mosel turning up in Hallstatt graves further south. He listed a number of graves where he thought this had happened, what he called *Mischgräber* (culturally mixed graves). Finally, after a generation of this co-existence, Baden-Württemberg adopted a full La Tène Culture (**71**).

Zürn envisaged an overlap between the final phase of Hallstatt D (Hallstatt D3) and the earliest La Tène (La Tène A). Pauli went further, suggesting an even greater overlap, with La Tène A in the Hunsrück-Eifel overlapping with Hallstatt D2 in Baden-Württemberg, and D3 with La Tène B. This he argued partly on the evidence of artefacts typical of La Tène B elsewhere turning up in Hallstatt

HUNSRÜCK-EIFEL Reinecke	BADEN-WÜRTTEMBERG		DATE
	Zürn	Pauli	
Hallstatt D1	Hallstatt D1	Hallstatt D1	— 600
Hallstatt D2	Hallstatt D2		— 550
Hallstatt D3		Hallstatt D2	— 500
La Tène A	Hallstatt D3		— 450
		Hallstatt D3	
			— 400
La Tène B	La Tène A	La Tène A	
	La Tène B		— 350

71 *Comparison between the traditional chronology of Reinecke and those of Zürn (1972) and Pauli (1972) for Baden-Württemberg*

contexts in Baden-Württemberg. It was also linked with his theories on the development of certain cemeteries, notably that at Mühlacker where tumuli were found to cover small, possibly family, cemeteries. Pauli proposed that this was a 'matriarchal' society ('matrilineal' would have been a better term), in which the primary burial of each cemetery was an older woman, and around her were clustered her husband and her children. With the death of another 'matriarch', a new cemetery would be established, and the old one covered by a tumulus. Thus, a woman with La Tène ornaments might have a secondary later burial with only Hallstatt artefacts. In fact, there is no stratigraphical relationship other than the assumption that the one at the centre of the enclosure is the earliest.

Working on these assumptions, it would mean that the Heuneburg would have survived to about 400 BC (and so the end of La Tène A in the Hunsrück-Eifel), and thus on the Heuneburg Gersbach referred to the final phases of occupation as 'La Tène' even though there is no Early La Tène material from the defended site. However, it would seem strange that a site where most scholars suggest trade was the basis of its wealth should have the typical Black Figure Ware of the sixth century, but not the Red Figure Ware of the fifth century, especially when nearby sites such as Asperg were acquiring it (one argument was that there was one Black Figure Ware sherd early in the sequence, so the majority which turned up in Hallstatt D3 contexts must be 'heirlooms' or rubbish survival). The nomenclature for the Heuneburg sequence thus confuses and conflates the two different usages of the terms Hallstatt and La Tène: as purely chronological terms; and as different cultural entities.

The matter has now been resolved, as there are dendrochronological dates for the construction of the final gate at the Heuneburg of around 520 BC, and it was burnt down not long afterwards, say around 500–480 BC. The idea of a long local survival of the 'Hallstatt Culture' is thus false, though confusions still appear in the literature, indeed of two recent books on the Iron Age in western Germany, one still talks of a La Tène period on the Heuneburg (Diepeveen-Jansen 2001, 10), and the other in one place talks of destruction of the site at 480 BC, and elsewhere at 400 BC (Rieckhoff and Biel 2001, 88, 375)! These different dates have implications for theories which link the invasions of Italy around 400 BC with the collapse of the 'Hallstatt chiefdoms'; either this simply does not work or the dates of the invasion must be back-dated to around three generations earlier. The problem of 'Hallstatt' objects turning up in La Tène contexts (and vice versa) is resolved in two ways: some of the graves really are *Mischgräber* (they have been badly excavated and the finds mixed!); and some of the objects which are being used as type fossils simply do not fit nicely into their little boxes, and have a life which can span two or three of Reinecke's divisions (i.e. we should look at seriation as a better concept of dating).

The end of the La Tène period in southern Germany is marked by a drastic drop in the number of finds, the disappearance of some of the major settlements such as Manching in Bavaria, and a different material culture, which includes a reversion to mainly hand-made pottery. In this case the marked change in culture is best explained in terms of ethnic change, and Sabine Rieckhoff, in a recent study, has looked for the origins of the new population in central Germany.

The Berry

In Livy's story of the Gallic invasions of northern Italy and the Hercynian Forest (V-xxxiv), the Bituriges Cubi played a key role with their king, Ambigatus, sending out his two nephews, Bellovesus to Italy and Segovesus to central Europe, taking with them the surplus population not only of their own tribe but also of other tribes over whom he had some sort of suzerainty (*in imperio eius Gallia . . .* under his rule Gaul . . .). Livy links this story in with the foundation of *Massalia* and dates it to the reign of Tarquinius Priscus, that is around 600 BC, and thus approximately to the transition from Hallstatt C to Hallstatt D. This has been revised by modern scholars to 400 BC, the end of La Tène A. At the time of Caesar the territory of the Bituriges lay in the modern Berry, with their chief oppidum at *Avaricum* (Bourges). Though the siege and capture of *Avaricum* is one of the major events in the Gallic wars, the Bituriges were not considered by Caesar as in the first rank of the Gallic states, which suggests that Livy's view of their importance at this earlier date must come from some independent source. However, he gives us no indication of where they lived at this period.

Hallstatt C is poorly represented in the Berry, but by Hallstatt D a major centre had come into existence at Bourges, and it continues to provide evidence of considerable wealth until the end of La Tène A. No defended site has yet been identified as a *Fürstensitz*, but there are areas of occupation under the modern town which have produced signs of dense occupation including a building with painted wall plaster dated to Hallstatt D, something unparalleled at this time in non-Mediterranean Gaul and central Europe generally. In the vicinity of the modern town there are also other areas with important remains of settlement, including workshops engaged in the manufacture of bronze objects. This includes Hallstatt brooches of minute dimensions which could only have functioned with extremely fine cloth, as well as pins, more common here than on other Hallstatt D sites, decorated with imported amber or coral. These sites have produced the widest range of imported pottery such as Black and Red Figure Wares, Massaliote amphorae, of any of the *Fürstensitze*. It was also manufacturing the wheel-turned pottery and the painted wares associated with high-status sites elsewhere. However, in the area there are no rich burials comparable with those of southern Germany or eastern France, or of the Hunsrück-Eifel. There are graves with imported Italian bronzes, and a recently excavated robbed tomb has produced a gold pin in Early Style, but there are few La Tène A decorated objects.

The site loses its pre-eminence in La Tène B, though there was still a concentration of activity around the site, including areas with large storage pits, burials, etc. The Berry was an early importer of Greco-Italic amphorae, probably from the end of the third century, and shows signs of early urbanisation at sites such as Levroux and Chateaumeillant. Unlike their Arvernian and Aeduan neighbours, the settlement pattern of the Bituriges was relatively dispersed with a number of small oppida rather than one major centre. The oppidum of *Avaricum* at Bourges, however, has proved elusive.

In conclusion, the story of Livy does fit with the archaeology, but there are major problems with his chronology. However, if we re-date the events to the fifth century, then it fits better, though there is no evidence of the over-population mentioned by Livy as the cause of the migrations.

The Auvergne

The Arverni are mentioned by Livy as one of the tribes which took part in the invasion of Italy. By the second century BC they were, according to Poseidonius, the most powerful tribe in Gaul, controlling an area from the Atlantic to the Rhine, and southwards into Provence. By about 150 BC they had entered into a formal treaty with Rome. Their king, Luernios, was the 'richest man in all Gaul', and he became king through prodigious public largesse, scattering gold and silver coins from his chariot, and setting up enclosures with food and drink for everyone to participate. After the defeat of Luernios' son Bituitos by the Romans on the River Isère in 123 BC where he had been opposing the invasion of Provence, the Arverni seem to have lost their leading role, as Caesar says that by his time the control of central Gaul was being contested by the Aedui and the Sequani. They played no part in the Gallic wars until 53 BC when the Arvernian noble, Vercingetorix, took over the anti-Roman revolt, defeating Caesar at the Arvernian oppidum of *Gergovia*. As late as the fifth century AD, according to Sidonius Apollinaris who was bishop at Clermont-Ferrand, the Arverni considered themselves Celts, though he also claims a Trojan origin for them.

The archaeological evidence from the Auvergne comes from two main ecological areas, the uplands of the Massif Central, mainly volcanic, and nowadays mainly supporting a pastoral economy, and the fertile plain of the Allier valley, notably the Grande Limagne to the east of Clermont-Ferrand. In common with much of the Massif Central, the highland areas are largely devoid of archaeological evidence, except in Hallstatt C and D when there are numerous extended inhumation burials in tumuli. Hallstatt C is dominated by male burials, including several with typical iron Mindelheim swords (**72**); in contrast early Hallstatt D is characterised by female burials with bracelets, anklets and torcs. Elsewhere in the Massif Central such burials may contain imported bronze vessels and occasional small gold objects, and local painted pottery, but these are rare or unknown in the Auvergne.

Otherwise the Iron Age archaeology is mainly concentrated in the Grande Limagne; field walking and chance finds have produced little in the other basins. The Hallstatt and Early La Tène periods are poorly represented even on the Grande Limagne. The one small Hallstatt D inhumation cemetery at Le Pâtural was rich in female ornaments (anklets, bracelets, see figure **64**), but the male burials were generally unaccompanied. Settlements were not enclosed, and generally consist only of small pits and post-holes, and so are difficult to locate. The fine pottery of Hallstatt C includes the painted, stamped and incised wares found elsewhere to the east (e.g. in southern Germany), but by La Tène A the area belonged to the more western tradition epitomised by the Marne (e.g. fine angular vessels, painted decoration, etc.). However, a precise chronology is difficult as associated metalwork is rare, especially Hallstatt D and La Tène A brooches. Imports are rare, though one site on the northern fringe of the later territory of the Arverni, Bègue near Gannat, has produced a couple of sherds of Red Figure Ware.

In the later part of La Tène B a major complex of sites starts to develop around Aulnat just east of Clermont-Ferrand, including ceremonial and cult sites on which large quantities of Italian amphorae are found and a rich array of other imports especially ceramics, and La Tène metalwork (brooches, sword fragments and occasional objects decorated in Waldalgesheim Style). From this time onwards the presence of pits, wells and boundary ditches facilitates the location of sites, and they produce large quantities of finds. Pottery styles

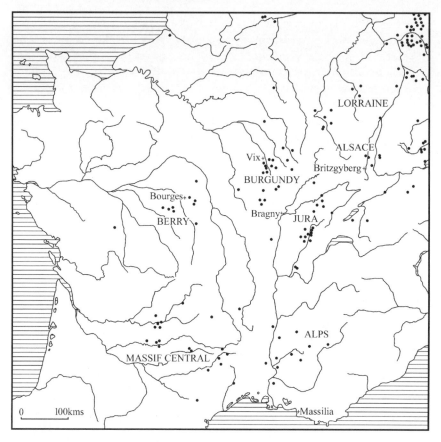

72 *Distribution of burials with iron Mindelheim swords in Hallstatt C and of major centres of Hallstatt D in Gaul.* Gerdsen 1986 and author

change radically during La Tène B with the disappearance of the fine Marnian-style vessels, but by the third century new styles of wheel-turned pottery, including painted wares, appear which later spread across much of western and central Europe during La Tène D. In the Auvergne the best painted wares have La Tène motifs (e.g. Waldalgesheim derived scrolls) and highly stylised animals in addition to the more normal geometric patterns (**73**). In late La Tène D1, around 120–100 BC most of these sites in the Grande Limagne were abandoned, and three successive oppida were established (Corent, Gondole and Gergovie), but all are small by European standards. All have associated cult activity or evidence of feasting (large quantities of smashed amphorae, human and animal bones, some probably sacrificial). Burials are rare until La Tène D, and are usually found singly or in small groups on the settlement sites. Extended inhumation is the norm, but there are occasional cremations. Grave goods are limited, mainly ceramics and small personal ornaments such as glass beads;

swords are rare. Rich burials only appear in the Augustan period, but the pottery (including large number of amphorae) and metal objects are highly burnt, and only survive if they are thrown into a pre-existing ditch.

Déchelette included the Auvergne in the 'Celtic' area on the basis of the Hallstatt extended inhumations, but it was not included in the area of the origin of La Tène Art. Later authors have considered it to have been colonised by Celts probably during La Tène B (e.g. Guichard 1986). However, as we have seen, this interpretation is largely due to the lack of Early La Tène burials, the difficulty of locating early Iron Age settlements, and the lack of metalwork on them. It is thus impossible to argue from negative evidence, and this problem is underlined by the presence of rare Mediterranean imports dated to the fifth century despite the lack of burials. The subsequent wealth of imported finds dating from the second century, and the numerous signs of conspicuous consumption link in well with the documentary evidence, despite the lack of rich burials. This lack of evidence, especially of metalwork, is a major problem across much of central and western France, and it is only unexpected finds such as the Agris helmet that warn us not to take this lack of information at face value.

73 *Painted vase from the second century BC from Aulnat in the Auvergne, typical of the period of Luernios.* Association pour la recherche sur l'âge du Fer en Auvergne

Narbonne and Catalonia

At the beginning of the Iron Age all the written sources such as the Massaliote Periplus assign the coastal area between the Hérault (if not the Rhône) and the Pyrenees to the Iberians, as well as the eastern coast of Spain south of the Pyrenees. By the time of the Roman conquest it was occupied by Celtic tribes, the Volcae Tectosages (around Toulouse) and the Volcae Arecomici (around Nîmes). The coast was colonised by the Massaliotes during the sixth century BC, with settlements at *Agathe*/Agde, *Emporiai*/Ampurias and *Rhode*/Rosas. Supposedly the earliest description of the area is the Massaliote Periplus, re-formed by Avienus in the fourth century AD in his *Ora Maritima*; as previously mentioned, this has been dated to the sixth century or earlier by the absence of any mention of *Emporion*, but instead we have the enigmatic site of *Pyrene*. Various authors have in fact argued that *Pyrene* is an alternative name for *Emporiai*. We also have the supposed statement by Hecataeus that *Narbo* was a Celtic town, but as we have seen above, there is reason the doubt this interpretation of the quotation made by Stephanus of Byzantium. The Roman colony was founded in 118 BC, and the name *Narbo* must have related to an earlier Iberian settlement, and been transferred to the colony.

The archaeology of the region at the beginning of the first millennium in the coastal areas was dominated by the so-called Urnfield Culture. Though there are some similarities in ceramics and the metalwork with areas further north and east, it is the cremation burial rite which has encouraged the parallels with the Urnfields of central Europe, along with poor excavations of heavily ploughed sites. Modern excavations show that in fact most of the burials are under small tumuli. As elsewhere in Europe (Greece, Italy, central Europe), early graves have little more than an urn, but in later graves the number of vessels increases and metalwork becomes more common. In one case, the Cayla de Mailhac, a site controlling the Carcassonne Gap which links Narbonne to Toulouse, a succession of cemeteries surrounds a defended hilltop settlement which later became a small town, in a way comparable with the early Etruscan settlements such as Veii, or Greek towns such as Athens. The seventh-century burials have also encouraged comparisons with central Europe in the presence of horsegear and some 'Hallstatt' artefacts such as razors; the ceramics, however, are local in character, as are the weapons (short iron daggers rather than swords). Similar cremation burials are found south of the Pyrenees in Catalonia.

With the foundation of the Greek colonies from the sixth century onwards, many defended sites with urban characteristics began to appear in their hinterland, such as Ullastret a few kilometres from *Emporiai*, and Ensérune just east of Narbonne. The painted ceramics from these sites resemble those from the Iberian sites of eastern Spain, and graffiti on the pots are written in Iberian (**74**). However, by the fifth century Ensérune was following central European trends in its metalwork, for instance in the use of pierced iron belt fittings in orientalising style.

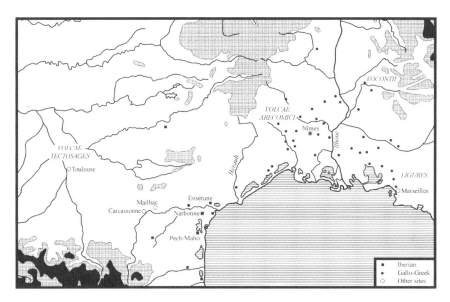

74 *Distribution of Iberian and Gallic graffiti and of major sites mentioned in the text in the south of France.* After Py 1993

Slightly later cremation graves have produced a rich array of Early La Tène swords and other weaponry; such swords are also known from Ullastret south of the Pyrenees. Both areas were using local versions of La Tène brooches.

As in most areas of western France, the early Iron Age archaeology of the upper Garonne is poorly understood, but from the second and first centuries there was considerable consumption of Italian wine amphorae, especially around Toulouse where there are ritual and burial shafts which produce Late La Tène swords and other metalwork, imported Italian table wares and bronze vessels, as well as large numbers of smashed amphorae. It was one of the centres of production of the *monnaies á la croix*, local imitations of the silver coins of Rhode. Toulouse was also the site of a famous treasure deposited on a temple site and captured by the Roman general Caepio in 106 BC. According to Strabo and Trogus Pompeius it included material looted from the Celtic attack on Delphi in 279.

While we can dismiss *Narbo* as a Celtic town in the fifth century BC, it is not so easy to dismiss the presence of Celts, the Volcae Tectosages, in the vicinity of the Pyrenees (or '*Pyrene*') at such an early date. However, Thierry argued for a late arrival of both the Tectosages and the Arecomici (third century or later) as part of the Belgic expansion (he considered *Volcae* and *Belgae* as synonymous). D'Arbois de Jubainville followed him in this, arguing that the Iberians were replaced by the Gauls around the third century. Bosch Gimpera suggested that the appearance of the 'Urnfields' represented the final foreign cultural intrusion into Iberia, and that this must represent the arrival of Celtic languages from central Europe. In this interpretation he has been followed by most Spanish archaeologists up to the modern day. There are several problems with this interpretation, even if we can accept that pots (and burials rites) equal people:

1. Can we accept these burials as the same as the Urnfields in central Europe, or are we simply looking at more general trends which happen over a wide area (not only Catalonia and Languedoc, and central Europe, but also much of Italy and parts of Greece). But as mentioned above, they are not proper Urnfields.

2. If they are all to be linked together, do we need to assume that it represents a single linguistic group? In Italy the cremation burials occur in areas which spoke Italic dialects (Latin, Venetic), Celtic (Lepontic), and non-Indo-European Etruscan.

3. The area where the Urnfields of Catalonia and Languedoc appear was, three or four centuries later, Iberian speaking. In Catalonia, the names claimed by Bosch Gimpera as Celtic are in fact later, e.g. those ending in −ac or −á are late if not post-Roman in Gaul.

The earliest mention of the Volcae in southern Gaul is as late as the early second century BC (Cato, quoted in Pliny III, 130), whereas earlier sources such as the Massaliote Periplus do not mention them. The reason, however, is perhaps that they were not based on the coast; the major centre of the Volcae Tectosages was *Tolosa* (Toulouse), and of the Volcae Arecomici *Nemausus* (Nîmes), both well inland. Perhaps, rather than 'arriving' these Gallic tribes were simply part of the rich ethnic mix in southern France (Greeks, Iberians, Ligurians) and had been present from a relatively early date, but, in the reorganisation of the province in the first century BC, it was their centres which became two of the major administrative centres. Py (1993, 159-60, 166-8) has discussed the evidence for a 'Celtic invasion' in the third century BC. East of the Hérault and in Provence, one can only see expansion of the settlements, in some cases with the development of open settlements or expansion of the defended sites. Inscriptions start appearing at this time, mainly in Gallic. West of the Hérault the story is much the same, though at least one site, Pech Maho, was violently destroyed around 225 BC, but it is an exception. There is no new influx of 'La Tène'-style objects, as in both areas these had already been adopted in the fifth century.

The mixture of 'Iberian' ceramics and 'Celtic' metalwork demonstrates clearly the failings of the Culture-Historical approach. The 'Iberian' culture has been defined by finds from eastern and south-eastern Spain, the 'Celtic' culture from western Germany and northern France, both far from the Mediterranean coast. Both had been defined before the discoveries in southern France, and therefore archaeologists have tended to interpret southern France as a 'mixture' of the two cultures, or of imports from one or the other area (e.g. the La Tène swords as imports from further north, perhaps carried by Celtic mercenaries). The idea that

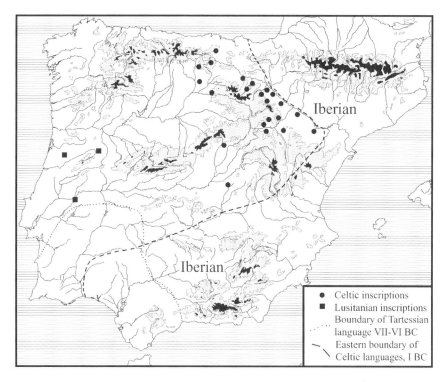

75 *Distribution of language groups in the Iberian peninsula.* Based on publications of J. Untermann

they represented a 'mixture' would perhaps have surprised the people themselves; it is a concept imposed entirely by the modern observer. It also suggests that the manufacture and use of La Tène objects was not the exclusive preserve of speakers of Celtic languages. What we do see, however, is a connection between western Languedoc and areas to the north and west that is long-lived: the similarity of the pottery in the Late Bronze Age, the Hallstatt and La Tène metalwork, and the *monnaies á la croix* (the 'Tectosages cross') variants of which also turn up in southern Germany; the connections of Provence are more with the Swiss plateau.

Celtiberia

The ancient sources claim that the Celts arrived in Spain from Gaul, but no date is given, nor any details of where they might have come from; the story has the air of a foundation myth, as does the suggestion that the people represent a mix of the two dominant ethnic groups in Iberia, the Iberians and the Celts. On most maps of the origin and spread of the Celts, the Celtiberians present a major diffi-culty, as it is assumed that, following Herodotus, they should have arrived on the

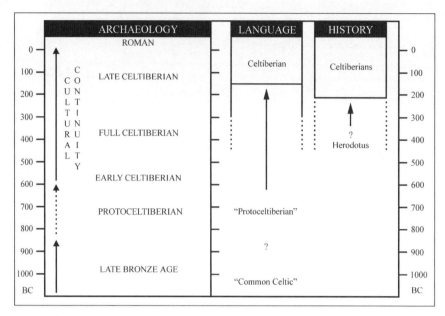

76 *The development of the Celtiberian culture.* Lorrio 1997, 371

Atlantic coast by the fifth century, and they are certainly well attested there by the third century in authors such as Eratosthenes. However, if we accept that in Himilco's time there were no Celts on the coast, as d'Arbois de Jubainville did, they must have arrived in the earlier fifth century, though that does not say when they may have arrived in the centre of Spain where we find the Celtiberians. However, if we follow the standard view of the expansion of the Celts, then southern Gaul was not colonised until much later, so the Celtiberians are very isolated from contemporary fifth-century Celts.

Many attempts have been made using linguistics and archaeology to resolve the problem, from explanations which have envisaged an invasion from central Europe, to suggestions in the 1920s from Bosch Gimpera that the mechanism may have been via the Urnfield Culture of Languedoc and Catalonia, and Urnfield burials are known as far south as the valley of the Ebro. However, as I have already said, the evidence for Celtic place names in Catalonia is not very acceptable, and is very late, and there is no reason to assume that there is an equation between the Urnfields and the Celts (or any other Indo-European group) as in Italy the predecessors of the Etruscans used urnfield burials, and Catalonia and Languedoc are Iberian speaking when we first have evidence. Geographically there is almost no overlap between the Celtiberians and the urnfield cemeteries on the Ebro, and at most one can only suggest that the Celtiberians may have adopted the cremation rite from this quarter. Spanish prehistorians are thus beginning to reject the idea that the Celtic (and Indo-European) languages may have come via this route, and to look more to the west and the Atlantic, especially if one accepts the longer time-scale which Renfrew's theories might suggest. And all this presupposes that we are happy to equate pots and people (or rather, burial rites and languages). We should also distinguish between the Celtiberians (and Celtici) and the distribution of Celtic languages; as I have already argued, these are not necessarily the same thing (**75**), and it would seem from place-name evidence that groups like the Lusitanians and the Vettones who are never called Celts were speaking Celtic languages.

The earliest mention of the Celtiberians is by Polybius in the third century (**76**), but it is likely that some of the 'Celts' who appear as mercenaries in Sicilian and Carthaginian contexts in the early fourth century may have been from Spain, as they regularly turn up in the same context as Iberians. The area which they occupied is not well defined, nor is it possible to place securely the various peoples which are included under the name; only the Pelendones and the Arevaci (and their town of *Numantia*), and perhaps the Belici can be fixed with any certainty. There is also variation from one author to another about who are included as Celtiberians; the Vaccei, Olcades and Carpetani are slightly ambiguous. In cultural terms the origins of the Celtiberian culture are complex. In the Celtiberian area there is something of a blank in the eighth/seventh centuries (as in other areas which were part of, or affected by, the Atlantic Bronze Age), so it is unclear how the society and culture evolved from the so-called 'Las Cogotas I Culture' typified by pottery with excised decoration. As I have suggested for the Hallstatt – La Tène 'transition', changes in ceramics are perhaps more connected with their production, function and social role rather than as an indicator of population change.

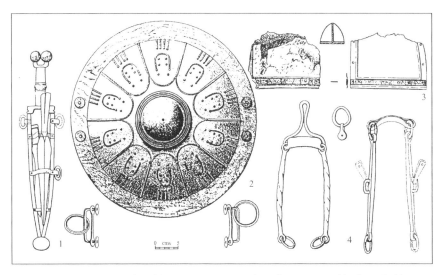

77 *Alpanseque, Soria, Spain, burial 20, street III, grave goods. 1. dagger, spear and knife; 2. shield fittings; 3. fragments of bronze helmet; 4. horse harness.* Lorrio 1997

The cultural sequence in the various parts of what is later Celtiberia is different. Around Soria the early phase from the sixth century is typified by hillforts, but very few burials; the north-western part on the River Ebro is the one area with Urnfields, which continue into the Iron Age. The typical Celtiberian burial rite starts earliest in the highland areas on the headwaters of the rivers Tagus, Duero and Jalón, an area mainly suited to the keeping of livestock. Here the earliest cremation burials contain weapons (spears) but not the daggers and swords found in the later burials; it is also in this phase that iron working is adopted, and the Celtiberian area is rich in iron ores (and salt sources). Some of these cemeteries are laid out within parallel lines of standing stone stele ('streets'). Several of the early cemeteries are in use for a long time, as late as the second century BC, clear indicators of 'continuity'. In the 'Classic' phase of Celtiberian Culture there is increased evidence of social differentiation in the burials though the relative numbers of burials with weapons varies from region to region and cemetery to cemetery. The richer ones have the typical dagger (often in a highly decorated scabbard), spear, shield, knife, and perhaps helmet and horsegear (**77**). In the final phase (Late Celtiberian), dating to the second to first century BC, major urban sites appear, along with fine painted pottery, and the first of the inscriptions in the Celtiberian language.

Thus, there are considerable logistical problems in the traditional view of the origin and expansion of the Celts, to get them from central Europe to Spain sufficiently early for either the historical sources, or the widespread distribution of Celtic languages, or the archaeological evidence from Celtiberia. A relatively early date would suit the arrival of the languages, even if Celtiberian identity evolved somewhat later. However, I find much of the terminology in use in Spain not particularly helpful, terms like 'Proto-Celtic', and 'Proto-Celtiberian', as we do not know when either appeared, nor such concepts as an 'indigenous substratum' as it implies Iron Age immigrants; contacts there were with areas to the north, but no evidence of any major Iron Age incursion. I also reject the idea that the Urnfields were the mechanism for getting Celts and Celtic languages into Spain. The problems are unresolved, but I certainly look at a long time-scale, though not necessarily as long as that as suggested by Renfrew.

Britain

As previously stated, the ancient sources never refer to the inhabitants of Britain as Celts, but from the beginning they are either Pretannoi or Britanni. Caesar writes of Belgae coming to raid and then to settle, and these cross-channel affiliations are confirmed by various later sources: Winchester is *Venta Belgarum* and Silchester *Calleva Atrebatum*, and most links in the archaeological record are with Belgic rather than Celtic Gaul. One exception may be the Parisi of eastern Yorkshire, if they are the same as the Parisii of northern France. Caesar says the people of south-east Britain resemble the Galli most, but Tacitus notes the physical resemblance between the Silures of south Wales and the inhabitants of Iberia.

In the 1920s R.A. Smith suggested three main phases of continental influence, bringing in respectively Hallstatt, Early La Tène and Late La Tène material culture and burial rites. This was subsequently translated into Hawkes' three cultural invasions, designated A (Hallstatt), B (Marnian) and C (Belgic). By 1958 when Hawkes revised his scheme he recognised multiple origins for his Early La Tène invasions. The scheme was attacked by Hodson, but he too accepted three foreign groups, all typified by the introduction of continental burial rites (**67**). The Hallstatt influence was ill-defined, with the supposed burial at Ebberston in North Yorkshire; the Arras Culture on Eastern Yorkshire with its chariot burials was Early La Tène; and the Aylesford-Swarling Culture of eastern England was the Belgae. He underlined the essentially indigenous nature of most of the British Iron Age, the 'Woodbury Culture' though it gradually absorbed Hallstatt and La Tène material culture. However, even the apparently foreign Arras Culture was using much of the same material culture as the rest of Britain, such as roundhouses and the metal fittings of the chariots, and the burial rite has no close parallel on the continent. In a later paper Hawkes talked of 'cumulative Celticity', by which he meant a gradual adoption of continental ideas rather than anything that was specifically Celtic.

The indigenous nature of the British Iron Age is now generally accepted, but with continuous rather than punctuated contacts with the continent followed by periods of complete isolation. In the Late Bronze Age contact had been essentially with the south, along the Atlantic coast, the so-called Atlantic Bronze Age typified by the depositions of hoards and river finds as well as many shared artefact types – swords, socketed axes, etc. As hoard deposition peters our in the eighth/seventh centuries, contacts become more east-west, with Hallstatt metalwork (Hallstatt C razors and Gündlingen swords, Hallstatt D daggers and brooch types), and later, Early La Tène metalwork and pottery styles. Deposition of metalwork was mainly in river contexts, such as the Late Hallstatt and Early La Tène daggers from the Thames, and only rarely from burials (e.g. the Early La Tène swords from Wetwang in eastern Yorkshire).

The ceramics (largely confined to the south and east of Britain) tell the same story. From about the eighth/seventh centuries fine drinking and eating vessels and even decorated storage jars show general affinities with those of northern and central France, and by the late Hallstatt and Early La Tène, angular cups and bowls resemble contemporary Marnian ceramics. Somewhere around the fourth century the parallel development breaks down, and in the British Middle Iron Age (350–100 BC) there are many local styles few of which can be paralleled in nearby France. Only in the first century BC with the adoption of the potter's wheel does Britain once again join the main stream of continental fashions.

The interpretation implied by the various maps of the expansion of the Celts is based largely on a misidentification by Hawkes and others of the Marzabotto related brooches as La Tène B2 forms rather than La Tène A. The period when the Celts are supposed to arrive, around 250 BC, is actually when contacts with the adjacent continent are at a low ebb. For the same reasons the concept of 'cumulative Celticity' is not only methodologically flawed, it simply does not fit the data. In fact there is no reason why parts of Britain, especially the south-east, should not be included in the area where we see the transition from Hallstatt to La Tène forms (e.g. the daggers from the Thames). Rather than seeing punctuated links with the continent, we can suggest a continuity of contact, sometimes greater, sometimes less, affecting now this, now that, part of the material culture and society's ideology, but certainly not the isolation and lack of movement implied by migrationist theories.

Ireland

The classical authors' knowledge of Ireland was minimal, indeed even its geographical location was ambiguous, with it often being described as lying between Britain and Iberia. The island is referred to as *Ierne* and/or *Hibernia*, but like the Britons, its inhabitants were never considered to be Celts. By the Late Roman period the Irish were known as Scoti. Only Ptolemy gives us greater detail with the names of various tribes, including some known elsewhere, such as the Brigantes.

However, Ireland is the one Celtic-speaking country for which an independent literary tradition has been claimed, in the form of poems, and legal tracts written down in the early Christian era, such as the *Book of Invasions*, or the Ulster cycle of epic poetry. To what extent they are truly independent is a matter of considerable debate at present. The monks who wrote them down seem not to have been simple recorders, but also active participants in what was recorded and the form in which it was recorded. They themselves were highly knowledgeable of the classical sources, and much of what was written, rather than being a 'window on the Iron Age', in fact reflects contemporary political circumstances, material culture and cultural traditions. Their references to the great centres such as Tara and Emain Macha, rather than reflecting a continuous oral tradition, may in fact be an attempt at interpreting the archaeological field monuments, just as modern archaeologists are forced to do. It is difficult, for instance, to understand why the divisions of Ireland into four or five provinces, as it was in the early medieval period, should be the same in the Late Iron Age, when we are given something completely different (a number of distinct tribes) by Ptolemy for the 'Roman' Iron Age.

Ireland's Iron Age archaeology presents in extreme form the problems already encountered in central and western France: a highly fragmented sequence, with little contextual information for the finds that we do have. Most of the data consists of metal objects either from 'watery contexts', or with no information, and for the later phases of the Iron Age outside of Ulster, much of the country is bereft of finds. This problem extends from about the sixth century BC to the fifth/sixth century AD. In the early first millennium BC the extensive hoard evidence belongs with the Atlantic Bronze Age, showing contacts with Brittany and Iberia (the recent dating for the Barbary ape from the Navan Fort suggests these contacts may have continued into the Iron Age). There are also some connections with Scotland and Scandinavia. However, just before the evidence becomes scarce, we can detect a re-orientation towards central and western Europe, in the presence of Hallstatt C metalwork, especially razors and Gündlingen bronze swords.

Hallstatt D and La Tène A are simply blank, but items such as the Lisnacroghera scabbards show that by La Tène B Ireland was following the main decorative traditions in metalwork. The gold torc and other items from Broighter prove that Ireland was not poor, merely lacking in contexts in which material was being deposited. The material is either similar to that found in the rest of Britain (e.g. harness and chariot fittings) or entirely local in character (e.g. the Navan-style brooches), but Barry Raftery has also detected features in the Irish Iron Age which are found on the continent, but not in Britain. Beyond the metalwork, other than items such as querns and stele, timber trackways, some linear earthworks, and the great ceremonial centres of the Navan fort (Emain Macha), Dun Ailinne and presumably Tara, we know nothing of the Iron Age archaeology: no settlements, no pottery, and only a few (late) cremation burials.

The belief promulgated by most authors that Ireland somehow became 'Celtic' in the third/second centuries BC is thus founded on virtually no evidence, or rather a lack of evidence. Though pollen hints that that there may have been some reduction in population between the Late Bronze Age and the Iron Age, the people and their society are almost impossible to detect. It seems most unlikely, as has sometimes been suggested, that the Bronze Age must somehow be extended to fill this gap; there is no evidence that Ireland became isolated from the general European trends, merely there is no evidence, and so we should maintain a neutral stance.

Denmark

The first direct written evidence we have for Denmark and Schleswig-Holstein comes from Tacitus in the late first century AD where he places the Cimbri in the north and the Chauci in the south. It thus seems likely that Jutland was the origin of the Cimbri who ravaged central Europe (113 BC) and southern Gaul in the late second century BC before being defeated by Marius at the battles of *Aquae Sextiae* (Aix-en-Provence) in 102 BC and at *Vercellae* near Milan in 101. Linguistic evidence from later periods show this was a Germanic speaking area, though we should note (sceptically) the claim based on the word *Morimoarusa* that the Cimbri spoke a Gallic language (Pliny *Naturalis Historiae* 4.95). However, the ethnic classification of the Cimbri in the second century BC presents difficulties as this dates to the period before Latin literature was making a distinction between *Galli* and *Germani*, and even as late as by the mid-first century BC Cicero still considered them to be *Galli* (*De provinciis consularibus* 32).

In comparison with the rich finds of the Nordic Bronze Age, to which burial, ritual and hoard deposition all contributed, the finds from the Iron Age 'Jastorf' Culture are poor. The burial rite is cremation in an urn, rarely with any more than one or two personal ornaments such as 'swan's-neck pins'; the hoards disappear as in Atlantic Europe during Hallstatt C when iron and bronze Mindelheim and Gündlingen swords were in circulation. Settlements, while highly informative about house types and farm layout, produce only a limited range of metal and other objects. Ritual deposition continues, and though spectacular in nature, it is limited in comparison to earlier (and subsequent) periods. So, what are we to make of the objects that are deposited? Almost all of them are considered to be imports, some from Italy such as the 'Kjærumsgaard' bronze jugs, but most are labelled as 'Celtic'. One item must be an import, the Gundestrup cauldron, which belongs to a tradition of art totally foreign to Denmark, but its origin on the lower Danube is almost universally agreed; it is worth noting the long tradition of exotic items being imported into Denmark from this area, starting from as early as the Late Mesolithic/Early Neolithic around 4000 BC.

However, we can be less sure of the origin of some of the other items such as the cauldrons from Rynkeby and Brå, or the wagons from Dejbjerg. Because we know so little about local metalworking traditions, we do not know what skills existed and what art styles were being produced, though we must assume that the expertise and skills shown in the Late Bronze Age were not totally lost. These are exotic and high prestige goods, and so are difficult to parallel closely anywhere else, so to assume that because they are in 'Celtic' La Tène style they cannot have been made in 'Germanic' Denmark is obviously false logic. With more prosaic objects we can see that local products were often following the mainstream of central and western artistic traditions. This is true of some of the brooch types, and especially with the class of 'ball torcs' decorated with La Tène motifs not found outside eastern Denmark. It is also true of the shields, swords, and possibly the chain mail found in the Hjortspring deposit (**83**). The ship and other finds are most plausibly interpreted as offerings from a military victory over hostile invaders; present interpretations place the origin somewhere in the Hamburg area, so still in the 'Germanic' area, and dating to around 300 BC.

In the 1930s it was common to refer to the Pre-Roman Iron Age in Scandinavia as 'Celtic' in contrast to the Roman, Germanic and Viking Iron Ages. I have not pursued the literature to find out how much this simply followed the logic of the usage of 'Roman Iron Age' (i.e. though the inhabitants were 'Germanic', they were heavily influenced by the 'Celts' and 'Romans' to the south), or how much it was thought that the inhabitants were indeed Celts, following the views of ancient authors such as Cicero that the Cimbri were Gallic.

In brief, in Denmark we have a group of probably Germanic-speaking people with burial rites and material culture which are considerably different from those living further south, but who were using and manufacturing metalwork with La Tène forms and decoration. I can only agree with Flemming Kaul, who in arguing for a local origin for the Dejbjerg wagons, says 'The carts, ball torques and certain types of brooches demonstrate the areas where "Celtic Art" was executed were not necessarily the areas of Celtic settlement – that Celtic art and Celtic "ethnicity" in this case must be seen as two quite different notions which can be geographically separate.'

Bohemia

The modern name derives from the Boii, one of the groups that participated in the invasion of northern Italy as well as in the migration of the Helvetii in 58 BC. We are also told by Strabo (V 213, 216) that after their defeat at the hands of the Romans at *Mutina* in northern Italy (193 BC), many of the Boii retreated across the Alps. In the mid-first century BC the Boii suffered a further major defeat at the hands of the Dacians under Burebista and abandoned much of their territory, the 'Boian waste'. The name *Boihaemium* appears in Strabo and in Tacitus, referring to territory over-run by the Germanic Marcomanni under their leader Maroboduus, and this does equate to some degree with the modern Bohemia (**54**). Roman place-name evidence locates the Boii in the same general area (*Boiodurum* is identified as Innstadt bei Passau, on the Austrian/Bavarian border). We can thus be fairly confident that the Celtic Boii were present in this area from the second century BC onwards, if not earlier, though we should note that Livy says they entered Italy by the *Poeninus* Pass (Great St Bernard) rather than by one of the more direct routes from central Europe.

Bohemia physically largely divides into two, the highland south rich in minerals and the agriculturally rich loess soils of the north (**78**). This also represents something of a cultural division during the Iron Age, though in terms of material culture both areas show the classic Hallstatt – La Tène sequence of central Europe. After the general conformity of Urnfield cremation cemeteries in the Late Bronze Age, in some areas the cremation tradition continued into Hallstatt C, though some graves had richer grave goods (e.g. the sword burial at Platěnice). Elsewhere, especially in central Bohemia, inhumation under a barrow becomes the dominant rite, with wagons, harness, swords, etc. (the Bylany Culture), with one unusually rich cemetery at Hradenín. Ostentatious burial disappears in Hallstatt D, when simple cremation cemeteries again dominate. This period sees a proliferation of hillforts. One in particular is massive, dominated by an 'Acropolis' with cult buildings, the site of Závist, just south of Prague.

The division between north and south is clearest in the La Tène period. In La Tène A there are cremations under tumuli in the south, the richest with vehicles or harness fittings, and occasional imports such as beaked flagons, in general

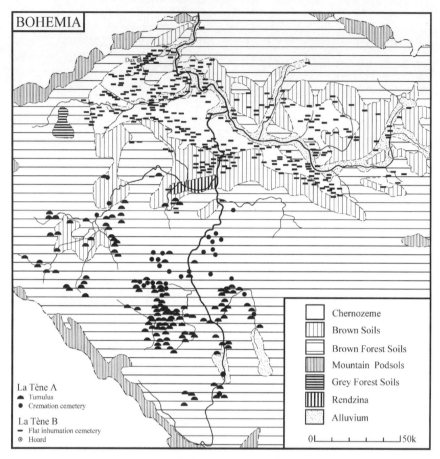

78 *Burial rites in Bohemia in La Tène A and B.* Collis 1984

comparable with the Hunsrück-Eifel. Around Pilsen flat cremation cemeteries predominate, but with La Tène A mask and anthropomorphic brooches. Like other areas with rich La Tène A burials, the south is poorly represented in La Tène B; indeed burials are virtually unknown in this area for the rest of the La Tène period. In contrast, in the north, there are many extended flat inhumation cemeteries, starting in La Tène B1 (the Dux horizon), but disappearing at the end of La Tène C1. After this, burials are also generally unknown in Bohemia until the 'Roman' Iron Age, except a small group of cremation cemeteries in the extreme north. In northern Bohemia open settlements dominate, though they are less well documented for La Tène D. In La Tène A the wealthier settlements may be palisaded, and acquiring imported goods such as Attic Red Figure Ware. Where complete excavations have taken place, e.g. at Radovesice, there is continuity of occupation on or near the same site from Hallstatt D to Late La Tène, and the appearance and disappearance of the inhumation cemetery is not associated with any break in settlement. Oppida are only definitely known in southern Bohemia.

The material culture follows the main trends in central Europe. Brooch types in La Tène A are dominated by various types of mask or anthropomorphic types, and La Tène B by Dux and Münsingen types whose antecedents lie further west (e.g. Baden-Württemberg). Hallstatt D metal types are poorly represented due to the lack of rich burials. The Hallstatt pottery styles include a rich range of painted styles, but these have disappeared by La Tène A when wheel-turned pottery starts to appear, notably the *Linsenflaschen* and Braubach bowls with their rich stamped decoration (**79**). Hand-made vessels, if decorated, have rich burnished geometric patterns. As wheel-turned pottery becomes more dominant in La Tène B and C, decoration tends to disappear, but with corrugation of the profile, and later cordons. Cooking pots made of graphite clays (*Graphittonkeramik*) with vertical combed decoration become common, and, at the end of La Tène C, fine painted wares made on the fast wheel make their appearance.

Up to the 1970s, interpretations were mainly cultural, with a contrast between an indigenous 'Hallstatt' and immigrant 'La Tène' Culture. Thus hand-made pottery from Late La Tène oppida was interpreted as some sort of Hallstatt survival (in fact this is a feature found almost everywhere in the Late La Tène and is not special to Bohemia). It was not helped by some badly recorded finds, e.g. Hallstatt cremations supposedly with Middle La Tène brooches associated with them. The La Tène culture was interpreted as an introduction from the west, though, as we have seen, Déchelette for one considered southern Bohemia as part of the area where La Tène Art had its origin. For Filip the arrival of La Tène was marked by the beginning of the flat inhumation cemeteries (**80**), Braubach bowls, etc., his 'Dux horizon' which he dated to the beginning of La Tène B, though some burials with brooches with 'roof-shaped bows' might just precede them. This he

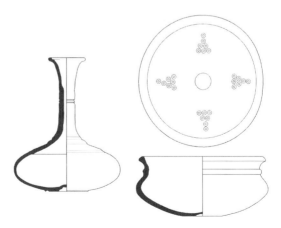

79 *The Braubach bowl and the* Linsenflasche, *La Tène A stamped wares from the Dürrnberg bei Hallein, Austria*

linked in with the arrival of the Celts, but this is problematic given the continuity of settlement patterns and material culture from late Hallstatt to Late La Tène. Waldhauser has proposed a limited immigration of people from the west to account for the introduction of the inhumation burial rite which was then adopted by the native population along with the new styles of La Tène ornament and weaponry. However, this does not explain the equally sudden disappearance of the burial rite, and in fact there is plenty of evidence for La Tène A metalwork, not only in the south of Bohemia. In his review of the Libenice 'sanctuary' Kimmig suggested a substantial re-dating of the pottery in central Europe, basically suggesting that the metalwork should be used to date the pottery rather than vice versa (using the Hunsrück-Eifel chronology). Thus instead of La Tène A metalwork dating to the fourth century as proposed by authors such as Pittioni, it is now dated to the fifth, and with it the ceramics such as the *Linsenflaschen* and Braubach bowls are also pushed back into the fifth century, but the latter was only adopted on the central Rhine in the fourth century. For the pottery the direction of influence was thus the reverse of that claimed by the invasionist theories.

So simplistic interpretations based on Livy's story of a migration from central France certainly do not fit the archaeology if we date this to around 600, and even the revised interpretation dating it to around 400 BC and with an origin in eastern France and western Germany equally presents problems. Rather, we see a mutual exchange, metal types and burial rite spreading from the west, and ceramic types spreading from the east to west where the Braubach bowl was not only adopted on the central Rhine, but as far west as Brittany. Also, we can see no greater break between Hallstatt and La Tène than in those areas where there is supposed continuity.

The apparent absence of Late La Tène in northern Bohemia was interpreted as a buffer zone between the 'Celtic' oppida in the south and Germanic groups beginning to infiltrate from the north, represented by the appearance of cremation burials. Because the pottery types in the burials were standard Late La Tène wheel-turned wares, the population was seen a mixture of Germanic and Celtic. The abandonment, or, in some cases, violent end of the oppida was seen to mark the arrival of the Germanic Marcomanni who introduced the cremation burial rite, and an entirely new range of hand-made ceramic and metal types to northern and central Bohemia, comparable to those found on the lower Elbe. While the archaeological and historical evidence points to some major changes in population at the beginning of the Roman Iron Age, the picture has become less simple, with increasing evidence that northern Bohemia was not so empty in Late La Tène, and also perhaps a slightly earlier end to the oppida in the south.

Austria

The evidence for Celts in Austria is ambiguous. We can start by dismissing the identification of the sixth-century Celtic town of *Nyrax*, mentioned by Hecataeus,

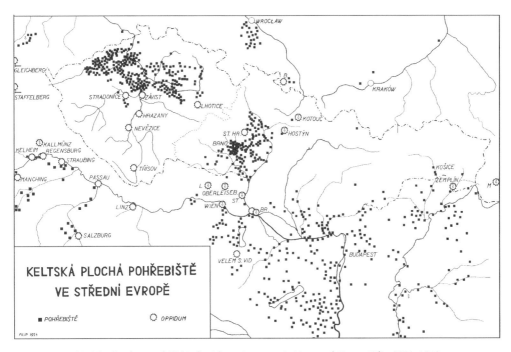

80 *The distribution of 'Celtic flat inhumation cemeteries' in central Europe.* Filip 1956, 1960

with the ancient *Noreia*. The most likely identification of *Noreia* is the Magdalensberg near Klagenfurt (claims by Kruta (2000, 337) and others that the site already bore the name of *Virunum*, the name of the Roman town at Zollfeld which succeeds it are unlikely; I know of no example where a Roman town took the name of its pre-Roman predecessor when the site changed, except perhaps *Narbo*). Historically *Noreia* was in existence by 112 BC when it was attacked by the Cimbri, but the main occupation of the Magdalensberg dates to the late first century BC. Excavation has concentrated on the Roman merchant area, and we know little about the foundation date of the indigenous oppidum, but it is probably second century to judge from the earliest finds and from the foundation dates of other oppida in central Europe.

The archaeology of Austria is complex and varied. In Hallstatt C there are major centres surrounded by tumuli on the borders of Hungary and Slovenia; Sopron and Klein Glein resemble the proto-urban sites of Slovenia and northern Italy. Scattered across Lower Austria there are massive tumuli which produce rich finds of painted pottery and metal goods. In the central Alps there is the eponymous site of Hallstatt itself, with its wide contacts based on the trade of its salt. Typologically the daggers and pottery types are not ancestral to those of Early La Tène, which, as in Bohemia, sees the disappearance of the painted wares and the dominance of the stamped wares of the Braubach tradition. The La Tène metalwork of the fifth century is distinctive and exotic compared with that from the west, and includes items decorated in Situla Art, like the scabbard from Hallstatt and the situla from Kuffarn. Mask brooches dominate.

In La Tène A inhumation burial under a tumulus dominates in northern Austria, and at the Dürrnberg bei Hallein which takes over from Hallstatt as the main salt producing area, there is an Attic dish, chariots, helmets, swords and local bronze vessels including a local imitation of an Etruscan beaked flagon. Unlike the areas further west and north, there is no displacement in the area where the burials occur between La Tène A and B; indeed there is a continuity of burial on cemeteries such as the Dürrnberg and Kuffarn. The Alpine valleys have a very different cultural sequence, with different styles of ceramics and few or no burials. Votive offerings with inscriptions suggest a non-Indo-European language ('Raetic'). But even in these areas some metal objects in La Tène style occur such as the La Tène A pierced belt plate from Hölzelsau in the Tyrol. By the Late La Tène southern Austria was the focus of the kingdom of Noricum whose component tribes included the Taurisci who were considered Celtic by various ancient authors.

Hungary and Slovakia

The western parts of Hungary and Slovakia present much the same sequence as eastern Austria, with a characteristic central European Hallstatt culture, with two sites with concentrations of wealthy burials at Sopron and Pécs, but this is replaced by a La Tène material culture. Recent work has shown that this is not in La Tène B as the traditional interpretation would suggest, but that it was already happening in La Tène A in the fifth century, with its own version of La Tène Art. In eastern Hungary, and eastern Slovakia, however, the pattern is somewhat different. In the sixth century this area seems to be culturally closer to the Steppes, and there are even finds of Scythian style art, and burials with horses, something that is rare in central Europe, but common on the Steppes. This changes in the fourth/third century when La Tène cemeteries, metalwork and ceramics appear. Recent work on settlements in eastern Hungary have shown that the native styles of ceramics continued in use alongside the now wheel-turned pottery, and in this area at least, it would seem that the adoption of La Tène culture is associated with an immigrant population, though with some local continuity.

Northern Slovakia, in the Liptov valley, is another case of apparent cultural assimilation, with the local population adopting La Tène style pottery including Late La Tène painted wares (c.f. figure 73), brooches, coinage, and this Puchov group continues into the first century AD when surrounding areas are adopting more northern styles of ceramics and metalwork, linked apparently with immigration of German speakers. The Puchov group seem to be the Cotini of Tacitus who he remarked spoke Gallic.

Turkey

So far there is little information on the settlements of the Galatai in Galatia. There is a light scatter of La Tène objects, mainly brooches, across Asia Minor, but not showing any special concentration in the areas settled by the Galatians. On the other hand the booty illustrated in the stone panels at the temple of Athene Nikephoros at Pergamum carved around 160 BC show typical La Tène swords, shields and other equipment.

Northern Italy

The historical sequence in northern Italy is quite simple. It was occupied in the seventh century by local Ligurians, possibly Gauls such as the Lepontii (who were labelled Gallic by Cato) and Italic speaking groups such as the Veneti; in the fifth century part of the Po valley was colonised by the Etruscans. In the very late fifth or fourth century (if we ignore Livy's date of 600) various Gauls arrived from across the Alps in a series of waves, and colonised, starting in the western part of the Po valley, but later groups, as they found the territory already occupied by earlier arrivals, moved further and further east until the latest arrivals, the Senones settled on the Adriatic coast, having first sacked Rome around 387 BC. Some areas were not colonised, such as the territory of the Veneti. Though some new arrivals came over during the next couple of centuries, there was a succession of wars during which this territory was slowly claimed by Rome, with some of the Gauls remaining, but others, such as the Boii in 193, retreating back over the Alps.

The archaeological evidence is nothing like so simple! Firstly, we have a certain amount of epigraphic evidence, from funeral stele, and from graffiti inscribed on pots and bronze objects. These show that the Lepontii in fact spoke a Celtic language from at least the sixth century, and presumably earlier, as there is a continuity of culture going back to the Late Bronze Age, perhaps as early as 1300 BC. The graffiti also allow us to suggest the ethnic identity of individuals, and so we find people with Etruscan names married to others with Celtic names, or outsiders turning up in settlements or cemeteries used by other ethnic groups. It is the sort of complexity we might expect if we assume that, though migrations may have taken place, earlier populations survived and were either integrated into the immigrant population, or continued to live alongside them.

If we also then add the evidence of material culture, the situation becomes further complicated. In fact throughout the earlier part of the first millennium BC there is evidence of extensive contacts across the Alps, and so the groups living in the Po valley, indeed even those living in central Italy, can, in cultural terms, be claimed as just regional versions of the 'Urnfield Cultures' north of the Alps, with similar styles of pottery, bronze artefacts and burial rites. On this scenario, we can suggest continuous contact going on throughout the first millennium, not the concept of the impenetrable Alps depicted by the classical authors in the context of the first invasion by the Gauls or of Hannibal crossing with his army. Only with Greek colonisation of southern Italy and the 'orientalising' of central Italy in the seventh century which was to lead on to the Etruscan and Roman civilisations, was there much of a divide between Italy and central Europe, and even then northern Italy was relatively unaffected until the fifth century with the Etruscan expansion, and especially the foundation of the port of Spina near the mouth of the Po which, for the first time, allowed classical Greek and Etruscan goods to become widely available in the north.

Thus, the cultural development north and south of the Alps can be seen as running in parallel, for instance in the increasing wealth of the richer burials, with four-wheeled vehicles, weapons, imported Greek and Etruscan metalwork, pottery for feasting, and personal ornaments. Northern Italy was itself a major exporter of metal goods, such as the ribbed buckets and bronze situlae dating to the sixth and fifth centuries which reached as far as Sweden and Britain. More diagnostic are the buckets decorated with scenes of fighting and partying, the so-called Situla Art (**85**) which occurs at sites such as Bologna and Este, but were exported, or inspired local versions, throughout the eastern Alps, as far north as the Danube. Some specific types of brooches have distributions on either side of the Alps, suggesting similar modes of dress, if not actual individuals moving, for instance with intermarriage. Against this general background, the claims of Livy of a Gallic presence before 400 BC does not seem so fanciful, even if, as I would suggest, we do not see the presence of a Celtic language as necessarily indicating people who considered themselves Celts.

One wonders what we would have made of the presence of La Tène style metalwork and burials in northern Italy without the historical record. Many of the finest objects belong to the fourth century and later; indeed, some scholars suggest that the Waldalgesheim style of art was developed in Italy. There are some cemeteries such as Casalecchio di Reno near Bologna, which look like normal central European flat inhumation cemeteries. In contrast the settlement and cemetery of Monte-Bibele south of Bologna seems to have had a largely Etruscan population, with standard rock-cut chamber tombs and personal names recorded as graffiti. However, a percentage of the burials contain rich La Tène grave goods, and the excavator has suggested a small Gallic component. The Monte Bibele burials contain many Etruscan goods, as well as rich items such as helmets, and this is common in northern Italy, including female burials with gold torcs. Such rich burials are virtually unknown north of the Alps (Waldalgesheim is one of the obvious exceptions), but isolated finds such as the helmets from Agris and Amfreville show that some individuals outside Italy possessed such items even if they did not find their ways into graves (the helmet with a bronze bird sitting on it from Ciumesti in Romania is another exception). Less is known about the settlements; Polybius paints a picture of a dispersed settlement pattern of small villages and farms, with a simple lifestyle, but recent work on urban sites such as Bologna show they were far from deserted – indeed, several such as Milan bear Celtic names.

In summary, the archaeological evidence shows considerable support for the historical sources for an invasion in the early fourth century, as there is certainly an upsurge in the quantities of central European style objects, though there is evidence of continuity as well. Indeed, in the areas such as the Veneto which were not colonised, La Tène goods were finding their way into graves, and the ancient authors commented on the similarities between the Veneti and the Gauls, despite the language difference. However, there are differences in the burial rite between Italy and central Europe in such aspects as the access to Etruscan and Greek goods, and in the wealth of the local items such as swords, helmets and gold torcs.

Conclusions

A number of points emerge from this brief overview. The first is to underline again the patchy nature of the archaeological record, both spatially and chronologically. Though some of this is due to a relative lack of research, much is due to the nature of the archaeological record itself; there is no way a concentration of burials such as we have in Champagne could have been missed in western France or southern Britain. The second is the large degree of 'continuity' which we see in local sequences, even in areas such as northern Italy where we know there was an incursion of population; where breaks are claimed, it is usually because the archaeological record has given up rather than that there are necessarily changes in population or material culture. However, breaks can be detected, and great play has been made between that of the 'Hallstatt' and 'La Tène' cultures, for instance in the nature of pottery and art styles, but this is not necessarily something which need be interpreted in ethnic terms. They are, however, somewhat accentuated in the way in which archaeologists study and present their material; the Bronze Age and the Iron Age, or the Hallstatt and La Tène periods, or prehistoric and classical archaeology, tend to be seen as different specialisms, so the interface can fall in the gap between, especially where one is seen as 'Celtic' and the other not.

A related matter is that of 'origins' and the concept of some sort of La Tène 'Culture' which originated on the central Rhine and northern France. In part this is because of the disparity of the record, especially of burials, but also it is due to preconceived ideas about the interpretation; it is much better to discard ideas of expansion from a specific area, and recognise that different aspects of the material culture can have different origins, indeed if we want to think in terms of a 'culture' it is likely to be multi-centred, with different patterns of dispersal, very much like the 'wave' model in linguistics. It can most clearly be demonstrated for the origin of the stamp-decorated wheel-turned pottery such as the Braubach bowl. This means that we may be looking at a much wider area for the origin of items labelled as 'La Tène', from western France to Hungary, from southern Britain to northern Italy. Across this area we can see considerable regional variation, and the ways in which scholars will be defining the 'La Tène Culture'. But, at the same time we can see considerable similarities, in items such as brooch types, or the 'dragon'/opposing lyre decoration on scabbards which are found from Britain to Hungary and Spain. How do we interpret this? In part we have to see individuals and groups as much more mobile in prehistory than is implied by 'invasion' or 'migration' models. Or rather, we may not necessarily be looking at movements of large populations travelling in one direction, but a continuous coming and going of individuals and small groups. This would explain better the similarities, say, between women's ornaments on the Hungarian Plain and those on the central Rhine. But we can only go so far simply studying obvious aspects such as the typology of artefacts or the details of burial rite. If we are to understand similarities of artefacts types we need first to study production and exchange; who is making a pot, and what is the mode of production and exchange? There are also new techniques which are appearing to define individuals who have moved from their homes, such as isotope analysis of the teeth, or anatomical features, or DNA. The archaeological record still has much potential, but we need to get away from the limited range of traditional interpretations.

9

THE CELTS AND POLITICS

The word 'Celt' defines a group, and thus implies inclusion or exclusion within that group. Whether membership is a good or a bad thing, or whether it is viewed from within or without, has social implications, and so is political in the widest sense of the word. Thus, from the original meaning of the word, something concerning citizens, 'Celt' was political. In this chapter I wish to explore briefly its usage both in the ancient and the modern world, both for groups which were already called Celts when we first hear of them, and for those which were formed under another name and only subsequently took the name over or had it applied to them.

The ancient world

We know virtually nothing of the internal implications of being a Celt or a Gaul in the ancient world. It was, at least seen internally, not necessarily a source of opprobrium as Chapman has implied, as both Trogus Pompeius and Martial seemed happy to trumpet their origins, and even Sidonius Apollinaris' apparent shame of the 'Celtic tongue' is somewhat contrived; if the Arverni had a problem, then so too did his Arvernian brother-in-law Ecdicius to whom he was writing, and his Arvernian father-in-law, Avitus, the Roman emperor.

If Caesar is right in saying that the people of central Gaul called themselves Celtae, in contrast to their neighbours the Aquitani, Belgae and Germani, then this must have had some implications, perhaps in terms of relationships of clientship or of wider political relationships such as those he describes between the aristocracy of the Helvetii and the Aedui. We can also suggest some sort of 'nested' hierarchy: as a Celt or Gaul in the widest European sense; as a Celt rather than a Gaul ('not all Celts are Gauls'); as a member of a specific tribe or state; and presumably at lower levels as well, as the member of a '*pagus*', a clan, or a family group, though by the time Gauls and others start describing their ethnic affiliations (e.g. on tombstones) the tribe or *civitas* seems to be the most relevant. Also, contrary to what some recent authors have suggested, there is likely to have been some feeling of common identity across Europe, at the level of a shared language, difficult though mutual comprehension may have been (see the quote from St Jerome), and probably other aspects of culture may have been shared in common (e.g. religious practices). In the pre-Roman world encounters between the two extremes of the Celtic distribution may have been rare, but in the context of the classical world they would have become increasingly common as individuals were brought together as slaves, as mercenaries, as soldiers in the Roman army, or as Roman citizens; Martial moved to Rome, and Sidonius Apollinaris travelled extensively, including visits to Rome and Ravenna.

Seen from outside, most of the comments we have from the Greek and Roman world are negative, and deal with racial stereotypes: war-like, uncontrolled, child-like, cruel, drunken, and generally 'barbarian'. As late as the Byzantine period, as Chapman has noted, 'Celtic' could be used almost as a synonym for barbarian. Politicians like Caesar could play on the Italian fear of the *terror Gallicus* in excusing his own barbarous and self-seeking activities in Gaul. The conservatives in Rome, such as Cicero, caricatured the new senators from Cisalpine Gaul for their supposed outlandish dress and accents. Real though the basis for some of these differences may have been, we can also see that they are contrived, and the same individuals could have very different reactions in different contexts. Caesar employed Gallic troops, especially cavalry, and the fighting qualities of the Celts had been recognised from at least the fourth century BC when we find Dionysius of Syracuse employing them (Diodorus 15.70), and at a much later date Cleopatra, Herod Phillipus and Herod the Great employed them as well (Josephus 15.7.3; 17.8.3). Caesar also had Gallic advisors on his staff, of whom the father of Trogus Pompeius was one. Leading politicians such as Pompey and Caesar were happy to adopt aristocratic Gauls into their *gens*, and it was Caesar who introduced them into the Senate. Cicero thought his philosophical discussions with the Aeduan Diviciacus worth recording (*De divinatione* I 90).

The extant texts from the classical world thus show a considerable bias in their statements attacking the 'barbarian' and it is these over-blown caricatures which are repeated time and time again in the modern books on the Celts. The reality is somewhat different, a profound respect for Celtic soldiers, their technology (e.g. Pliny's comparison of Norican iron technology with that of the Chinese), druid philosophers, poets, Gallic senators, and, ultimately, a Celtic emperor.

The Atlantic Celts

The early history of the British Isles following the collapse of centralised Roman control is generally written in terms of conflict between 'Celts' and Germanic 'Anglo-Saxons'. However, the use of the term 'Celtic' is, as we have seen, an anachronism, a term which was not to appear in this context for another thousand years. Both the indigenous population and the immigrant Anglo-Saxons could, initially at least, claim Roman legitimacy; the Roman Empire, from Stilicho onwards, was increasingly under Germanic military control, something often over-looked in the story of Hengist and Horsa which has often been taken to imply that Vortigern's invitation of Germanic outsiders was something of a foolhardy innovation in the mid-fifth century AD; it had a history dating back to the fourth century, and the employment of German mercenaries by the Romans extends back even further, to people like Arminius in the period of Augustus.

For Gildas, the distinction is not ethnic; it is between the civilised Romano-Britons and the barbarians from whichever quarter they came. It is with Bede that we begin to see the distinction between the groups which we now call 'English' (Angles, Saxons and Jutes), and those now labelled 'Celts' (Britons, Picts and Irish Scots). His major complaint is against the Britons' failure to convert his Anglo-Saxon forebears to Christianity, though he is more favourable towards the Irish church, despite its failure to hold Easter at the 'right' time or its monks to sport the right tonsure. Warfare and alliances were between individual kings, and were based upon political expediency rather than ethnicity. As the larger kingdoms began to form towards the end of the millennium, they tended to be multi-ethnic; Scotland, for instance, comprised Picts, Irish Scots, Anglians and Norse. The one time that a major alliance was formed against the English, the *armes prydein*, in the tenth century, it may have comprised all the 'Celtic' states, but it also included the Vikings.

Though Buchanan in the sixteenth century was doubtless aware of the political implications of what he was writing, it is from the viewpoint of the Scottish state, not as some group which stood in opposition to the English; England was, after all, ruled by a dynasty of Welsh origin, the Tudors. Simon James, in his book *The Atlantic Celts*, has suggested that Edward Lhuyd was writing from a Welsh nation-alist point of view, though the comment from one of his letters quoted by James is one of amusement at the extreme views of Pezron in promoting Breton nation-alism, rather than Lhuyd promoting the Welsh. I personally see the popularity of the concept of the Celts in the eighteenth century as rooted in the Romantic movement (e.g. the popularity of the Druids in writers such as Rowlands and Stukeley) or the poetry of Thomas Gray (*The Bard*) rather than in any political movement caused by the Act of Union between England and Scotland in 1707. Equally the Irish conflicts, though provoked by the imperialism and conquests of the English State, can be better characterised as a religious conflict between Scottish Presbyterianism and Irish Catholicism rather than anything ethnic. In fact national identity as a basis on which to build a state was a largely a new phenom-enon in the eighteenth century on the continent; the Treaty of Westphalia which brought the Thirty Years War to an end in 1648 is often seen as the watershed which saw the rise of the modern national state, though, as Ferguson has pointed out, a strong case can be made for a Scottish 'nation state' much earlier, in the medieval period.

Celticity as a political phenomenon in Britain and Ireland, I would therefore suggest, is nineteenth-, indeed late nineteenth-, century, and one which incorpo-rated not only the languages but also art and material culture. The Celtic languages at this time were still very much in retreat, as Malcolm Chapman has suggested, not entirely due to oppression by the British state (though, as I have said in chapter 5, it was a major player). The speaking of Irish at school may have been officially suppressed by the use of the cane, the *bata scóir*, it was, however, the Irish themselves who were doing this as the mastery of the English language was the way to economic and social advancement, and as interviews have shown with those who remembered the system, sometimes the parents assisted the school by reporting lapses at home. Welsh was similarly suppressed as late as the 1950s, but this was not only happening in Britain and Ireland, but also in countries such as Canada where the writ of the British state did not run.

The art that appeared on Irish manuscripts and artefacts became increasingly popular in the late nineteenth century as the copying of wheel-crosses for tombstones demonstrates. The intertwining patterns had obvious resonance with the Art Nouveau movement of the 1890s, but it was perhaps not until the publication of Romilly Allen's book in 1905 that Irish Art started to be defined, and its association with 'Celtic Art' became appreciated by a wider audience. However, anyone who has made even a cursory study of the monumental and commercial architecture of a town like Cork at this period cannot fail to appreciate its role in defining Irish culture and it was to appear on the coins and postage stamps of the Irish State.

Celticity was thus a potent component in Irish nationalism; it was less so in a Scottish and Welsh context. Each country was defining its identity through its own specific past and institutions; the Welsh Eisteddfod has no Irish or Scottish counterpart, and the common bonds which are now seen to unite the 'Celtic' countries were only just beginning to receive academic recognition, for instance in the establishment of the Board of Celtic Studies. It is interesting to reflect on what the difference is between being, say, 'Welsh' or 'Irish', and being 'Celtic'. Generally the two terms are assumed to be the same, when in fact the local term is really the one that gives the sense of local identity; the 'Celtic' gives both the international aspect (a group of ethnicities that have a common cause in resisting the encroaching English and French ethnicities), and also a much wider and deeper sense of history in linking in with the Ancient Celts.

France

Writings (and illustrations) of the ancient Gauls in France in the eighteenth and nineteenth centuries were very much within the Romantic tradition, from La Tour d'Auvergne's descriptions of the Druids to Bellini's opera *Norma*, the story of the tragic love of a Druidic priestess for a Roman general. But there are also strong political elements as well. Most obvious was Pezron's promotion of the Breton language as one of the original languages of the Tower of Babel, as the last survivor of the language of the ancient Celts.

In 1789 Sieyès published a pamphlet characterising the French revolution as the indigenous Gauls throwing off the control of their Frankish aristocrats. Though this did not become the accepted interpretation, the idea of a Gallic origin has remained a continuing factor in the mythology of the French democratic state. At the time of the revolution it was even proposed that towns should revert to their pre-Roman Gallic names; so Autun would become *Bibracte*, and Paris *Lutetia*. In 1804 the Académie Celtique was founded under the patronage of the Empress Josephine. Amédée Thierry's book *Les Gaulois*, first published in 1828, and revised several times throughout the nineteenth century, remained the academic textbook used in all the schools until the publication of Camille Jullian's *Histoire des Gaulois* in 1906 (Jullian himself recalled being inspired to study the Gauls through receiving Thierry's book as a school prize). Under the influence of the more general historical works of Jules Michelet and Henri Martin, 'Nos ancêtres les Gaulois' became part of the history curriculum in schools, indeed, I had a Vietnamese teacher working for me in France who had been educated in a French colonial school, and was much amused that he had finally returned to dig up his 'ancestors'!

Under Napoleon III the archaeology of the Roman conquest became a national research project, with major excavations at the supposed sites of the battle of the Aisne, *Gergovia*, *Alesia* and *Uxellodunum*, mainly directed by le commandant Eugène Stoffel, and the plans of the sites and the siegeworks have continued to be reproduced in all books on Caesar's conquest. Recent work at Gergovie, Alise-Ste-Reine and the Puy d'Issolud have all shown how trustworthy Stoffel's work generally was. New roads were constructed and commemorative monuments built to mark the emperor's visits, even if this involved the demolition of part of the Gallic defences at *Alesia* and *Gergovia*; the statue of Vercingetorix at Alesia even has the facial features of the emperor. Encouragement was also given to researchers to investigate major sites, most notably Gabriel Bulliot who worked at Mont Beuvray/*Bibracte* for some 30 years before handing over to his nephew Joseph Déchelette. The latter's *Manuel d'Archéologie*, and more general works on the Celts by authors such as Henri Hubert ensured a continuing interest throughout the early twentieth century.

With the collapse of France in 1940, the Vichy government again promoted Vercingetorix and his glorious defeat. Defeat at the hands of the Romans had led to nearly 500 years of relative peace with Gallo-Roman culture producing great monuments in art and architecture based on unprecedented agricultural and industrial growth, a model which the Vichy government proposed to emulate, this time with German collaboration. Pétain himself visited Gergovie for nationalistic celebrations and the excavations which had been started on the site in the 1930s continued throughout the war years under the exiled University of Strasbourg. New laws protecting archaeological sites and controlling archaeological excavations were passed, and these remained in force for the rest of the twentieth century. Yet, surprisingly, this nationalistic fervour had little effect on the teaching of

81 *François Mitterrand at Mont Beuvray.* Centre archéologique européen du Mont Beuvray

Protohistory in French universities, unlike Germany where many chairs in Classical Archaeology were converted into Pre- and Protohistory (Vor- und Frühgeschichte), and so reflecting Germanic origins. In France archaeology is still generally taught as a subsidiary of History, Art History, Ancient History, or, for the Palaeolithic, Geology, and Iron Age studies have not until recently received the attention given to Palaeolithic or Gallo-Roman studies.

The 1980s saw a revival of Iron Age studies, in part due to internal develop-ments of the subject itself in France with the founding of the internationally important Association Française pour l'Étude de l'Âge du Fer which has provided a focus for both students, senior administrators and academics. But there was also official encouragement. In 1983 the new socialist government under François Mitterrand was looking for national scientific projects to promote. One, put forward by Christian Goudineau and Jean-Paul Guillaumet, was renewed investi-gation of the oppidum of Mont Beuvray, the ancient *Bibracte*. A large research centre and a museum have been constructed near the site, both opened by Mitterrand himself (**81**). Politically the project operates at three levels:

1. Mont Beuvray lies close to Château-Chinon where Mitterrand was mayor (he went to Mont Beuvray to pick mushrooms!). The large expenditure on infra-structure of the centre and the accompanying tourism have provided a stimulus to

the local economy, though the centre was built at Glux-en-Glenne in the socialist Nièvre rather than the larger St Leger-sous-Beuvray in the Gaullist Saône-et-Loire. It is, however, now supported by both left and right, and the museum has been built across the departmental boundary!

2. *Bibracte* saw the gathering of representatives of the Gallic states to decide on a joint policy to combat Caesar, leading to the election of Vercingetorix as supreme commander. It is thus seen as the first attempt at national unity, a major symbolic act for the French state. Mitterrand twice attempted to address the French nation from the hilltop (one occasion was disrupted by striking farmers!), and expressed an (unfulfilled) wish to be buried on the site.

3. By emphasising the 'Celtic' (i.e. international) rather than the 'Gallic' (i.e. French) orientation of the research, the 'Centre européen' aims to encourage international collaboration in Iron Age research. The French state provides funding for the Centre, some of which is used to support the international teams working on the site, and also for French scholars to work in other countries (Hungary is a major recipient of this collaboration). In the last 20 years teams have taken part from many countries: Austria, Belgium, England, France, Germany, Hungary, Italy, Scotland, Slovenia, Spain, and Switzerland, and it has become a thriving centre for training projects (at the time of writing including a joint one with English Heritage!), conferences and research for scholars and students from the whole of the European Union.

Spain

Though it is difficult to define the areas of the Iberian peninsula occupied by the Celts from the classical sources, popular opinion divides it into three: the east coast and the south occupied by the Iberians; the north by the Basques; and the west and centre by the Celts and Celtiberians. Only the latter spoke Indo-European languages, and, as the dominant groups in modern Spain, with the one exception of the Basques, also speak Indo-European languages, the arrival of Indo-European languages has always been a matter of interest to Spanish prehistorians. Despite the lack of evidence, Galicia has made the greatest claims to a Celtic origin (including probably some immigration from Britain in the fifth century AD), and in recent years has aligned itself with the Celtic speaking countries, e.g. through the Lorient festival, though modern Galician is a Romance language closely related to Portuguese. At the end of the Franco period, when Spanish scholars were trying to break out of the restrictions imposed by the fascist dictatorship, Galicia offered to host the International Celtic Congress, an offer rejected by the linguists on the grounds that it was not Celtic speaking (attitudes are now more relaxed, and should be so if one takes into account the role played by *Brigantia* in the founding myths of the Irish!).

Ruiz Zapatero has suggested that nationalist politics have influenced the inter-pretations of the protohistory of Spain; when a Mediterranean orientation has been dominant, the Iberians have figured large, with their obvious links with the Phoenicians, Greeks, and later, the Romans. When links have been to the north, especially in the 1930s and 1940s when Franco was relying on Nazi Germany's funding and technology, it was the common Celtic connection which was empha-sised. In part this was done through the funding of research at an academic level, but it was also reflected in school textbooks, and especially through Museum displays. At the time of writing the finds from Numantia are still prominently displayed in the National Museum in Madrid, with special emphasis on the last stand of the Celtiberians against the Roman army under Scipio in 134 BC which was ideally suited to the ideal of heroic military self-sacrifice for the state. The plaque accom-panying the display, and placed prominently on the wall, gives the flavour:

Among the valiant peoples of the world are to be numbered the people of Numantia. They belong because of the heroism that they showed, even to their own annihilation, in defence of their fatherland. Against the might of Rome, the heroic battle of Numantia is an everlasting example of the many generations which have fought for their freedom. Finds like the pottery counters show the love of games that occupied their periods of leisure. The occurrence of pottery trumpets, which can also be seen in the exhibition case, and the motives which decorate their distinctive pots show the Numantians to have been a happy and indus-trious people.

Translation, author.

In more recent times the Celtic past has been promoted in a range of popular images, such as names of football teams, selling milk or cigarettes (Celtas Cortos, also the name of a well-known pop group). Though, in the same way Viscaya and Catalonia use the Basques and Catalans, Galicia uses the Celts to underline its regional identity in a reaction to the Castilian domination of the Franco period, the Castilian areas are also eager the promote their Celtic past, especially for tourism. The historic site of Numantia near Soria, like its French counterpart at Alesia, is becoming the focus of reconstructions and re-enactments, supported by museum displays on or near the site. At Ávila a recent exhibition on the Celts, held for only three months in the autumn of 2001, and so outside the main tourist period, still attracted some 100,000 visitors, with the town putting on special events (e.g. 'Celtic' menus at restaurants).

At a European level, Spain and Portugal tend to be under-represented in general books on the Celts, despite the extensive work and conferences on the subject in the last decade or so. In part it is because central European archaeo-logists generally have difficulty coming to terms with the archaeology, as the cultural sequence is very different from that of Hallstatt and La Tène, and all attempts in the twentieth century to use such nomenclature clearly did not work in Spain. On the other side, the collapse of the fascist regimes is something that many Spanish and Portuguese archaeologists still remember, and that, followed by joining the European Union, has provided a major stimulus for developing international connections, and the Celts provide one obvious link.

Switzerland

Though Switzerland has been one of the major centres of research on the Iron Age, indeed, the location of the eponymous site of La Tène (now a holiday camp at the northern end of Lake Neuchâtel), the Celts have not played any overt role in the internal politics, other than the obvious choice of a neutral name for the country, Helvetia, after the Celtic people, the Helvetii, something which will offend none of the four linguistic groups, even though this name would not have encompassed all the ancient peoples of the modern state (the non-Indo-Germanic Raeti, the Lepontii, etc.).

Italy

Recent politics in Italy have seen the separatist Northern League emphasising the contrast between 'European' industrialised north and backward corrupt 'Mediterranean' south. The international exhibition in Venice (the largest and most prestigious of the whole of the twentieth century) very much emphasised the historic connections between the Po valley and areas the other side of the Alps (even if Venice lies outside the area occupied by the Celts).

The European Union

The structure of the European Union is such that it would have difficulty in using the Celts in the overtly political way which a nation state can, though the Council of Europe, which has a wider membership, has attempted to include the Celts in the 'routes' which it has set up on various historical themes which unite countries and allow the development of cross-boundary tourism: the pilgrimage routes to Santiago de Compostela; Baroque Architecture; Mozart; the Vikings. The project for the Celts (which I chaired) collapsed due to a lack of understanding between officials and the academics (I failed to meet a deadline, and was immediately dropped, but my colleagues were unwilling to proceed without me), a lack of funding, and concerns that we would end up with racial stereotyping, which has been one of the failures with the Viking routes, and was certainly a problem with the original drafting of the *Celtic Routes*.

However, as we have seen in the case of the research centre at Mont Beuvray, in pushing the concept of the Celts rather than the more nationalistic Gauls, it is the European links which are promoted rather than narrower state interests; individual countries have been happy to use archaeology to enhance their European image, and this is even more true of individual archaeologists or groups of archaeologists (grant applications which link various countries stand a higher chance of funding, indeed, for European funding, have to be international even to be considered by Brussels). The same can be claimed for the international exhibition at Venice already mentioned. Here the links with the then European Economic Union were made clear in the video in which a map of Europe was shown with stars marking the location of the museums which had loaned material for the exhibition. This then coalesced to form the circle of stars which has been used to symbolise European unity under the various versions of political union of the last thirty years. However, it has mainly been archaeologists themselves who have been promoting the European dimension rather than the politicians; the title of a volume accompanying an exhibition in 1980 in Steyr in Austria referred to the Hallstatt period as an 'early form of European unity'. Asking for funding and sponsors for conferences and exhibitions is easier with such an approach, and it is apocryphal that to have the name of the Celts in the title of a book will increase sales five-fold – we all do it!

10

PRESENT CONTROVERSIES

In this chapter I wish to discuss my own attitudes in the light of the analysis I have so far presented, to areas of study such as linguistics, religion, social organisation and genetics which scholars in the past, and still in the present day, use to characterise the Celts, and to suggest that there is something distinctive of people considered to be 'Celts'.

Languages

As already discussed in chapter 6, there are two distinct schools of thought about the origin and spread of the Indo-European languages, one of which suggests an early arrival several thousand years ago and the evolution of the Celtic languages *in situ*, a view most recently advocated by Colin Renfrew who links it with the spread of farming. Thus, a dialect or close descendant of an 'original' Indo-European language arrived with the early farmers in western and central Europe and evolved into the Celtic language groups in that area, at the same time as the other major family groups were evolving elsewhere: Indo-Aryan, Iranian, Slavic, Baltic, Greek, Italic, Germanic. The alternative is to make the time-scale much shorter, from the Early Bronze Age at the earliest, on the evidence of shared vocabulary such as the word for copper, a view promoted by Mallory, and accepted by most linguists. Celtic might thus arrive in central and western Europe in the Bronze Age if not the Iron Age; either the language would arrive fully developed, or the evolutionary process is more accelerated than implied by the Renfrew model, perhaps due to modifications as it is adopted by non-Indo-European speakers.

This is not a unique phenomenon to Europe and western Asia; it has parallels in other continents, such as the Semitic languages of the Near East, the Bantu languages of western, central and southern Africa, the Athabaskan languages of North America, or the Polynesian languages of the Pacific. But alongside these areas dominated by a single language group, there are other areas where there is no dominant group, and there is a plethora of small language groups, or unique languages, for instance in Papua New Guinea. Also there is the problem of small enclaves in the areas dominated by a major language group of peoples who speak totally different languages which are either explained as late arrivals (e.g. Hungarian which was introduced by the Magyars from central Asia in the medieval period), or as survivals of an earlier population, for instance the Basques, or, in the ancient world, the Etruscans, Iberians, and the inhabitants of some of the Alpine valleys.

This starts raising more questions. What was the pattern of language groups like in Europe before the arrival of Indo-European? Was there a previous dominant language group (and if so what?), or a plethora of small groups which included Proto-Indo-European. How big was the area where Indo-European developed; was it a small area from which it then spread by migration, or was there a large area of related languages which evolved in parallel due to continuous interaction as suggested by the 'wave' model? In the nineteenth century when language and race were considered closely interlinked, language change was seen in terms of population replacement, with earlier peoples driven out or massacred, as was, and still is, suggested for the Celtic speakers of eastern England who were 'pushed' into the highland fringes of western and northern Britain. Equally, Raetic might survive in the Alpine valleys, or Basque in the Pyrenees. But if we look at cases of language change in Europe in more recent times where we know more about the historical circumstances, we can see that it can happen in situations where there is considerable continuity of population, and that, where other languages do survive alongside a dominant one, it is often connected with some form of resistance. Thus, in Britain, the Gypsies can be seen as a persecuted group. So, it is useful for them when dealing with the police to have a specific language of their own which cannot be understood, in this case Romany which is itself an Indo-European language, apparently of Indian origin.

In Europe the modern 'nation states' have been fairly (or over?) successful in suppressing alternative languages and dialects, for instance in France where Alsatian, the southern French dialects, Basque and Breton have all but disappeared or are in severe retreat. In contrast, in Spain the survival of Basque, Catalan and Galician represent political resistance to the fascism of the Franco era, and a reaction against the dominant Castilian dialect spoken in Madrid, and to one of Franco's policies which was to prevent these regional languages being used in the schools. In Ireland independence from Britain and the promotion of Irish as a national language did not prevent its decline as the first language spoken in everyday contexts, perhaps because resistance was no longer necessary, whereas the resuscitation of Hebrew by the beleaguered Israeli state has been a success. Welsh, despite the continuing English political and cultural dominance, has proved fairly resistant, and important in emphasising a separate Welsh cultural identity. The point is, in all these cases, it is not what has happened in terms of promotion or repression of a language that decides its fate but whether the language has a continued importance to its speakers.

There are no simple rules about how languages will influence one another. It is often claimed that the indigenous Romano-British population in southern and eastern England must have been driven out or exterminated by the in-coming Anglo-Saxons in the fifth/sixth centuries AD because very few words of Celtic origin were adopted into the Anglo-Saxon vocabulary. However, the same is true for French (Lambert only lists some 120 possible cases of Gallic words surviving in modern French), but in that case we know that a largely Celtic-speaking population had simply adopted Latin with no huge change in population. The Frankish elite, when it arrived, also had little linguistic impact. English, in contrast, absorbed a huge amount of French from its Norman invaders, as major cultural and literary developments demanded a wider and more subtle vocabulary.

The linkage between population migration and language classification has been present from the original studies by Buchanan, Pezron and Lhuyd, with the latter introducing the concept of an earlier invasion by 'Q-Celtic'-speaking 'Goidels' and a subsequent invasion by 'P-Celtic'-speaking 'Brythons'; subsequent studies, especially of 'continental' Celtic, have shown that the reality may not be so simple. The 'wave' model of Schmidt makes it possible for linguistic innovation to crosscut the simple unilinear patterns of the 'Stammbaum' and migrationist models; we must also beware of looking at the past through the viewpoint of the 'nation-state'. Firstly, we must not assume sharp boundaries between linguistic groups when the reality may be a cline between one language and another, for instance between early Celtic languages and Italic languages such as Venetic. Equally boundaries can be blurred if much of the population is bilingual; Luxemburg is a good modern example of a population which is largely trilingual, speaking French and German as well as the local Luxemburgish patois. In fact most Indo-European linguists would prefer the 'wave' model for explaining language change, even for the initial adoption of an Indo-European language; as one might expect from this model, the nearest relatives to a given language are usually the languages geographically closest to it. The exceptions are rare; Tocharian, for instance, has characteristics which relate it more to the western than the eastern dialects, and the same (in reverse) is perhaps true for Romany. In these cases a migrationist model might be more relevant.

However, a similar effect might be produced by the rapid expansion of a single language, with different dialects being formed due to the different linguistic backgrounds of those who were adopting it. Latin is a good example with, in northern Italy, the new language being adopted by speakers of Etruscan, Celtic and Italic languages; in other words, the variations were there from the start, and are not due to an original 'pure' language splitting into regional dialects. Thus there are many interacting factors going on together, like the innovations implied by the wave model, with changes emanating out of areas and groups with special influence (as demonstrated by linguists in modern situations), and also crossing language boundaries (e.g. between, say, Celtic and Italic speaking areas); we should therefore view the simplistic Q/P dichotomy in the Celtic languages with considerable scepticism, especially the chronological interpretation that 'Q' is always older than 'P'. We should also reject oft-repeated concepts such as 'Basque is the oldest language

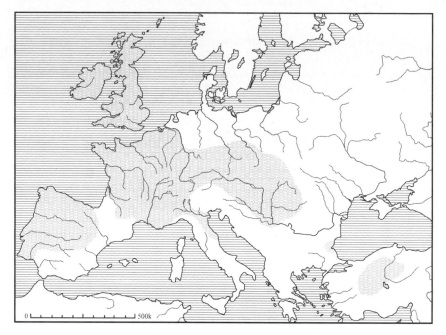

82 *Probable maximum extent of the distribution of Celtic languages in the second to first century BC.* Author

in Europe' or 'Welsh is older than English'. All these languages have equally long histories; the difference is merely that English was introduced into Britain more recently, and Basque probably has a longer history in western Europe than the Indo-European languages.

Where no literary evidence survives, place-name evidence is the only means of documenting earlier languages and language change, but here too interpretation is not straightforward. The best analogy is a flood; a major flood may wipe out all that went before, but more usually subsequent floods will leave major landmarks untouched, or will not reach the same height as the previous one, leaving evidence surviving on the fringes. This is what Pliny had noticed when he talked about looking at the 'eternal names' of rivers and cities. However, we need to look carefully at the context of change; are new areas being colonised because of new technologies or land pressure (e.g. the take-up of marginal land); or are new types of settlement being founded which will need new names (planned villages, Roman towns, medieval castles); is the area under study at the epicentre of change or is it marginal (e.g. the difference in the Saxon colonisation of south-eastern as against south-western England)?

Unfortunately the study of place names is unequally developed across Europe. Britain has a large number of studies based on individual counties coupled with in-depth historical study based on early manuscripts; lists are available for France, but lacking this historical depth; some areas lack any modern survey. This is material ripe for modern analysis (e.g. using Geographical Information Systems), but even for Britain this has yet to be done. When looking at overall patterns we have progressed little beyond the informed speculations of nineteenth-century scholars such as d'Arbois de Jubainville. However, this evidence does allow us to make an informed guess about the areas over which Celtic languages were being spoken at the time of their greatest extent, covering much of the area from Portugal to the Czech Republic and from Ireland to Ankara (**82**).

I am highly sceptical how much archaeology can contribute to the debate. We cannot measure a skull and say what language the man spoke, or usually what language the blacksmith spoke who made a sword, or the warrior who wielded it, unless we have independent information. There are exceptions: when first published the shield from the Fayum in Egypt was identified as a La Tène type; we have evidence of Celtic mercenaries in Egypt from the third to the first century BC, though it has since been re-dated as Roman (the curvature of the shield is not found on the La Tène examples). Similar problems surround the 'Celtic' shields from Hjortsprung in Denmark (**84**). The probability is that the people who carried them and brought the boat that was buried with them came from the Hamburg region, and so probably they spoke a Germanic language, though there is a certain ambiguity about which language the Cimbri spoke. Likewise the warriors who were depicted on the Arnoaldi situla from Bologna dated to the late fifth century BC (**85**); were they Celtic or Italic speakers? At

83 *A shield from the Fayum in Egypt. Despite its similarity to 'Celtic' types the curvature suggests that it is Roman rather than La Tène in date.* Military Museum, Cairo

84 (Left) *Shields from Hjortspring, Denmark.* National Museum of Denmark

85 (Below) *The Arnoaldi situla from a burial dated to c.425 BC from Bologna, with warriors carrying 'Celtic' shields.* After Kromer 1962

best we may be able to pin down periods when linguistic change may have been taking place, or when trading systems may have encouraged a *lingua franca* comparable with Swahili, for instance along the Atlantic coast in the Middle and Late Bronze Age, the so-called 'Atlantic Bronze Age' which extended from Portugal to Scotland. But we must assume that the spread of the Celtic languages was not a uniform process, and that it was both patchy and piecemeal.

Celtic society

> Comparative Philology [= Linguistics] of itself is not in a position to reconstruct the primitive culture of the Indo-Europeans, and if we are to secure our advance step by step over this difficult ground, we can only do so on the condition that the three sisters, Linguistic Research, Prehistoric Research and History, unite in the common work.
>
> Schrader 1890, 149, quoted in Lehmann 1993, 260.

The above quotation reminds us of the close relationship that existed between Archaeology and Linguistics in the late nineteenth century, indeed the questions posed and the methodology of the 'Culture-History' paradigm which dominated archaeological research for much of the twentieth century were essentially established by a German philologist, Gustaf Kossinna, who turned to archaeology as the major means of answering some of his questions. As previously discussed, it was the prehistorian Gordon Childe who picked up on his methodology in the English-speaking world, and it is worth recalling that his first major book was entitled *The Aryans: a study of Indo-European origins* (1926). For linguists such as Lehmann, Schrader's statement is still essentially true, whereas Archaeology has increasingly divorced itself from Linguistics during the course of the twentieth century. As a prehistorian, the triad of subjects I studied for my first degree was Archaeology, Social Anthropology and Physical Anthropology, and, as I continued my research, I found myself closer to Human Geography and the Natural Sciences. In part this was due to the revolution in the 1960s of the 'New Archaeology'; 'Archaeology is Anthropology, or it is nothing', as Lewis Binford so famously put it. Yet, despite the traditional link in American universities between Archaeology, Anthropology and Linguistics, Indo-European studies have not followed Archaeology down the Anthropology route; indeed much of the writing on society and social reconstructions in Linguistics seems largely to ignore the advances made in the twentieth century in Anthropology.

The basic problem lies in a continued tacit acceptance of racial stereotyping in Linguistics. Thus, the speakers of Indo-European languages, especially Proto-Indo-European, become reified into a 'people' who are then assumed to have cultural traits such as a specific social structure (priests, warriors, common people), or specific types of religious belief (a pantheon dominated by a male deity which contrasts with the 'Mother Goddess' of pre-Indo-European Neolithic societies or the monotheistic male dominated religions of Semitic societies). Linguists believe they can reconstruct this society by studying the common denominators of the societies of Indo-European speaking societies and see what they have in common, very much as is done in linguistic reconstruction. The earliest writings in Sanskrit, Greek, High German, and Old Irish talk of heroes who belong to a warrior class (Achilles, Cúchulainn, Siegfried); a priestly caste (Brahmins, druids); and, put simply, these then become assumed features of earlier Pre-Indo-European society. To this are added other features, such as the use of bronze, the importance of a horse as a major means of transport and warfare, and ostentatious burial of male warriors under a tumulus (cf. Patroclus in the Aeneid). Pre-Indo-European linguists then look to archaeologists to find the archaeological correlates with such a society which can be dated to the right period (fourth millennium BC) and area (most commonly seen as the Steppes north of the Black Sea).

Archaeologists, in contrast, have tended to think in terms of social evolution, from the 'Savagery', 'Barbarism' and 'Civilisation' of L.H. Morgan in the late nineteenth century (espoused by Childe), the 'band', 'tribe' 'chiefdom' and 'state' of Elman R. Service (followed by Renfrew and other New Archaeologists), or the 'egalitarian', 'ranked' and 'stratified' society of Morton Fried, likewise popular with New Archaeologists. Though no archaeologists would accept that societies run through simple linear developments, and would agree that simply classifying a society as a 'chiefdom' or 'state' is in itself a pointless task, nonetheless, all would agree that the general trend has been from simple to more complex societies, and the debate has produced some knowledge of the key features and processes to investigate, say, in 'state formation' (e.g. the basis of power of the ruling elite). So to a large extent methodologies have been developed for investigating aspects such as site hierarchies, the roles and function of production and trade, the structure of cores and peripheries, the potential of burial evidence for reconstructing social status, or the role of ideology. The trend has been to avoid generalisations (e.g. general 'laws'), and to investigate how these various factors interacted in specific contexts.

To take the example of burials, what does a burial with rich grave goods signify? Someone who was rich? Someone who was considered saintly (St Cuthbert)? Someone who had lots of friends and relatives each of whom brought something to place in the grave? What do the grave goods mean? A belief in an after-world? Is it a deliberate and ostentatious destruction of wealth by the heirs by which to signify their ability in terms of wealth and status to claim succession? Or were personal possessions taboo, and therefore had to be destroyed? Do they signify the status of the dead person, and if it was status, what sort of status: father, mother, old, young, married, unmarried, warrior, craftsman, witch, foreigner, killed in battle, murdered, struck by lightning? Why construct a visible burial mound? Obviously as some sort of memorial, but commonly archaeologists interpret these ostentatious burials as indicating a newly-established elite still trying to impose its control. If so, why are there no such burials in the Auvergne in the second century BC when the written sources tell us that Luernios was trying to establish himself as king? Why do some areas have visible burials and others not? Why, in most societies in the Iron Age, do we find burials of only part of the society, and those not always with grave goods? Too often we encounter simplistic and probably wrong interpretations.

Instead of going from simplistic interpretations we must work on the principle that a single problem may produce different outcomes in different societies, and equally something that may look similar may have different causes in different societies. In our own society we are shifting over to cremation as the dominant burial rite, replacing extended inhumation, but why? A change in Christian beliefs (no longer believing in the physical resurrection of the dead); a shift away from Christianity because of new immigrant groups who practice cremation (e.g. Hindus); or the indigenous people becoming atheists, agonistics or taking up other religions; the need for hygiene; lack of space for cemeteries; influence of the classical civilisations of Greece and Rome (the poet Shelley); emulation of the ancient druid burial rite as revealed by archaeology (Dr William Price of Llantrisant, in 1893 the first person 'legally' cremated in Britain in modern times); cheaper than inhumation, and encouraged by the state. All these are factors in the adoption of cremation in Britain in the last century and a half! How do modern societies deal with the increasing pressure on space for burial: cremation cemeteries allowing greater density of burial (Britain, Scandinavia); scattered cremation in non-consecrated ground (Britain); family vaults, ossuaries and charnel pits (France); multi-storey tombs for inhumations (Italy). We can only hope to pick our way through some aspects of what is going on by a careful analysis of the cultural and religious background.

But when we turn to interpretations of the Celts all these problems are forgotten. Areas without burials are simply ignored or it is claimed that further research will produce finds (central and western France); areas with recognisable burials are interpreted purely in ethnic terms (central European flat inhumation cemeteries); areas with rich burials are assumed to represent the richest and most important societies, if not the 'origin' of the Celts (Baden-Württemberg, Hunsrück-Eifel, Champagne). Graves containing weapons are almost automatically labelled as of 'warriors', but they could merely signify a freeman who had the right to bear arms; or someone who had died in battle; or, by changing the combination of weapons, signify the position in some sort of military hierarchy to which all males in the society belonged (cases are known with only part of a weapon, or a miniature weapon which could never be used, for instance in the cemetery of Gross Romstedt in Germany). What are we to make of the rich Late Iron Age burials of south-eastern Britain where men are buried with defensive weapons (chain mail, shields), but no offensive weapons (sword, spear, bow and arrow)? Iron Age societies in Gaul which have 'burials with weapons', as I prefer to call them, have been labelled as 'warrior societies', but why are there so few burials (two at present!) among the Arverni who, according to written sources, were the most powerful military force in Gaul in the second century BC?

Worse still, we find societies reconstructed on the basis of the literary evidence, and assuming the racial stereotypes that we encounter in the nineteenth century. These reconstructions take the description of the Gauls given us by Caesar:

> In the whole of Gaul there are two classes of people who are of some account and dignity. For the ordinary people have virtually the status of slaves, who dare do nothing themselves, and are consulted on no matters. . . . Of the two classes mentioned above, one is the druids and the other is the knights.
>
> *De Bello Gallico* 6.13.

These are societies which are states, with elected magistrates, meetings of 'senates', and possessing state funds. In comparison, the societies described in the Irish sources such as the *Táin Bó Cuailnge* several hundred years later are much simpler with 'kings' or 'chiefs'. Nor can we assume they were independent sources, as the Irish monks who wrote these stories down were certainly reading the classical texts. Yet the two are coalesced to produce an idealised 'Celtic' society on the grounds that they spoke related Celtic languages, with priests, bards, a warrior elite, and an oppressed common people. This then is imposed on the interpretation of hillforts in southern Britain such as Danebury, even though it has no support in the archaeological record. This is the vision of the 'timeless Celt' peddled in most of the general books on the Celts, even those written by archaeologists, and yet it is a totally false methodology. From both the written and the archaeological sources it should be obvious that peoples who spoke Celtic languages varied enormously in time and space. It was not their language which places them in an ethnic group which then dictates their social constructions, but their technology, their relationship to core-periphery structures, their settlement patterns, power structures, and ideology; they were societies that were continuously changing and adapting. It is a construct based on colonialist and imperialist attitudes of the unchanging native populations envisaged by our predecessors, as typified by the earlier quote from Worsaae. His views were typical of his time, and can be found, for instance, in Lubbock's *Prehistoric Times*. Nowadays we know they are factually wrong; indeed they would simply be rejected as 'racist'. So, why do we perpetuate them, albeit in disguised and tacit form, in our descriptions of the Celts?

Religion

As I have already indicated, I am equally sceptical that there is anything we can label as 'Celtic religion'. At the time of Caesar's conquest of Gaul, the religious practices, at least in the Celtic and Belgic areas, were very similar to those of the Greeks and Romans, with many local male and female gods, though a few were more widely worshipped. After the Roman conquest these gods were easily incorporated into the Graeco-Roman system, and though attributes might vary, Roman equivalents were relatively easily found. But this is not 'Celtic religion', it was religion as practiced by the Celts of that period, and later speakers of Celtic languages readily changed to monotheistic male-dominated mystery religions of Near Eastern origin, such as Mithraism and Christianity; indeed one form of Christianity was itself to acquire the epithet 'Celtic'.

Though it is often suggested that the Church in Ireland incorporated the poly-theistic prehistoric religion by turning the gods and goddesses into saints such as Bridget, the development of religious practice among Celtic-speaking peoples demonstrates that in this sphere too change was normal. Despite the biased and sensationalist nature of classical descriptions of religious practice such as human sacrifice, or the atmospheric description of a religious site in Lucan's *Pharsalia*, much of the religious activity was so familiar as to excite no comment from classical authors. From the third century BC onwards rural temples were being constructed, with wooden shrines inside ditched and palisaded enclosures at which weapons, ornaments, animals and humans would be sacrificed. Recent finds from Ribemont-sur-Ancre, Acy-Romance and Gondole near Clermont-Ferrand suggest that the reports of human sacrifice were not exaggerated; many of these Iron Age religious sites in Gaul and south-east Britain were to develop into Roman temples. Possible shrines and temples are now also being tentatively identified on urban *oppida* from the second century BC onwards, much as on Mediterranean urban sites. The appearance of these formal areas for religious practice seems to be connected with the process of state formation, just as it had in Greece and Italy in the seventh and sixth centuries BC. For the preceding millennium there had been virtually no such formal sites in much of temperate Europe. The small square enclosure next to the rich burial at Vix dating to the sixth century is one of the rare exceptions, its unusual nature marked by the stone figures of a woman and a male warrior whose smashed remains were found in the ditch fill on either side of the entrance; the complex of sites at Vix shared much in common with contemporary southern sites, and so it is perhaps more typical of Mediterranean practices than those of temperate Europe. However, in Germany, Ireland and northern and western parts of Britain, the adoption of religious centres took much longer, indeed in some areas Christian churches are perhaps the earliest such structures.

The one institution which excited Greek and Roman interest was Druidism, partly because it had no strict equivalent in the classical world. Druids do not seem to have been involved in the day-to-day routines in the temples; in the Roman period we hear of *gutuateres* who seem to be the priests. Nor, because of their special training, were druids simply high-ranking members of the political establishment who were elected to high religious office as in the Roman world (e.g. the *pontifex maximus*), though the one druid we know by name, the Aeduan Diviciacus, was also a major political figure. However, we only have evidence of druids in Gaul and Britain, and later in Ireland, and not throughout the Celtic-speaking world.

One supposed aspect of Celtic religion which has attracted wide-ranging literature is the supposed head cult. It is a mish-mash of information taken from various times and places, and much of the quoted evidence in fact comes from secular contexts with no religious connotations. Using the skull-cap of an enemy as a drinking bowl, and the display of a human head outsides one's house, something which initially disgusted Poseidonius, is connected rather with social display and insulting one's enemies, and it is something which receives confirmation in the archaeological record, like the mounted warrior scratched on to a pot from Aulnat near Clermont-Ferrand, with a human head dangling from in front of the horse (**86**). However, we should not immediately assume that display

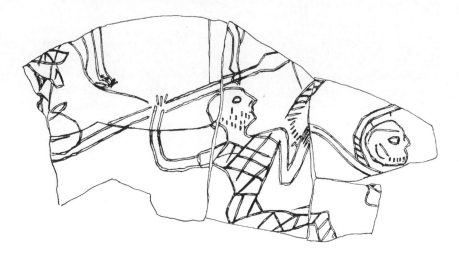

86 *A warrior incised on a pottery vessel from Clermont-Ferrand, France, showing a human head hanging from the front of the horse.* Périchon 1987

of skulls is necessarily connected with insult; from around Clermont-Ferrand we have cases from both Late Iron Age and the Early Roman contexts of the skulls of children being buried with offerings on cemeteries and on domestic sites. One is reminded, in a more recent context, of the nineteenth-century skulls from around Hallstatt which are richly incised with decorated and coloured foliage and the name and the dates of the deceased. Interest in the skull and the head are worldwide phenomena; it is, after all, the main means by which we recognise one another.

Human skulls do indeed occasionally turn up on cult sites as part of religious activity. The examples most commonly illustrated in books on the Celts are the niches for skulls on the site of Roquepertuse near Marseille which has recently been re-dated to the third century BC, and also the nearby town of Entremont which has produced both skulls which were nailed to walls, and carved stone heads; these are presumably enemies who are being insulted. However, these sites are not Celtic, but Ligurian. We should also remind ourselves that Christian religion also displayed human remains as objects of veneration; the New Minster at Winchester possessed the head of St Valentine. So, again, we need to study these phenomena in their local context rather than envisage some sort of universal 'Celtic' cult practice. In contrast, for instance, to the Ligurian sites, at the Belgic site of Ribemont-sur-Ancre human heads are noted by their absence despite the remains of several hundred individuals being found on the site; the skulls were removed for use elsewhere. We should also not assume a religious interpretation for human heads or 'masks' found on La Tène Art any more than we should for the common use of carved heads as decoration in Romanesque churches.

Art and archaeology

What can archaeology contribute to the debates on the Celts? Obviously the documentary sources are limited as they only give us short and ambiguous snapshots of what is happening outside the literate Mediterranean world, and then through the distorting lenses of classical authors who either did not know, or did not understand, what was really happening. We are given little snippets of information which it is not possible to bring together in a coherent picture or narrative. Unfortunately historians, and even archaeologists, then expect archaeology to fill in the gaps that the written record has failed to supply. This approach thus sees Archaeology as an adjunct to the historical sources, the 'handmaiden of history' syndrome which forces archaeology to work with an agenda laid down by another discipline, History, rather than setting its own agenda. It is an argument which has waged in Britain for the last three or four decades for the periods where we have good historical documents, usually more adequate than those we have for the Celts.

This domination of History is perhaps not surprising in the Mediterranean countries (Spain, France, Italy) where in the universities Archaeology is thought of as a speciality, as a sub-discipline, of History or Art History, and where it is not possible to do a first degree in the subject. In contrast, especially in the German-speaking countries, Archaeology is a discipline in its own right, with not only first degrees but also thriving post-graduate schools. In Britain Archaeology departments have typically 12–20 lecturers, in Germany only 3–5, while in France archaeology departments hardly exist. This is perhaps why Britain has in the last half century been the leading exponent of new method-ologies and new theoretical approaches, with the development of the New Archaeology and the Post-Processual critique. Archaeological research should concentrate on doing what Archaeology does best, such as dealing with social, economic and environmental questions.

This does not mean that Archaeology has nothing to contribute on difficult matters like ethnicity. The important point, however, is that Archaeology needs to be using its own techniques and methodologies to produce its results independently of the historical and linguistic sources. Once this had been carried out, the results can be compared and contrasted with those from other disciplines, and from this a synthesis can be achieved, as I have already suggested in the domains of social reconstruction and religion; in both cases we get a very different picture from what Caesar tells us about Gaul, but occasionally striking concurrence (e.g. on human sacrifice). But problems inevitably arise where the two sets of data are mixed indiscriminately as in the case of the reconstruction of the social organisation at Danebury (the archaeological evidence was ignored in favour of a literary based reconstruction), or in the case of 'warrior' burials and 'warrior' societies. Other examples include a failure to look at change as a continuous process; in central Europe the Hallstatt and La Tène periods are treated as discrete entities as La Tène is supposed to mark a break with the 'arrival' or the Celts, very much in Britain as the Roman and Anglo-Saxon periods are treated as discrete entities with their own academic specialisms and methodologies. What does actually happen in this 'transition' period? We may see changes in burial rites, but is this also reflected in settlement patterns, production methods or agriculture? Modes of dress may change, but does this mean a change of population? Do changes in ceramic style indicate a change of lifestyle (ways of eating, cooking methods and menus), or is it merely a superficial change of fashion?

It is clear that there are periods and places where a burial rite, or a style of dress, or even the decoration of a pot, may be an indicator of ethnicity; the problem for the archaeologist is to know when this may be happening, which may be the relevant attribute, and how one can be sure that it is ethnicity which is being signalled, and not, say, social status. Rather than assume an ethnic interpretation (which very commonly happens in the case of the Celts), we need to compare with other variables and categories of evidence. So, one can investigate the nature of putative boundaries (are they sharp or fluid?) as has been done, for instance, with distributions of pre-Roman coinage in Britain. Are there special features marking boundaries such as temples or defended sites? Though we can draw on generalised methodologies and concepts, every case study is likely to be unique in the ways in which ethnicity is expressed, and so needs to be studied in its unique context. These techniques are more likely to pick up distinctions between one Celtic people and another, and certainly not produce some universal indicator which will allow us to tell, say, a Celt from a German.

I have already indicated that I do not subscribe to the assumption that La Tène art necessarily reflects religious beliefs, even less so that one step further advocated by the Megaws that claims that therefore the art represents ideology, and so can be used as an indicator of Celticity. A much more useful approach is to treat language, art and ethnicity as independent variables, and then to study to what extent art (and other material culture) transgressed ethnic and linguistic boundaries (or where they do actually coincide). Why do Germanic speakers in Denmark, and Iberian speakers in Languedoc and Catalonia, adopt La Tène art and artefacts types when the Celtic-speaking Celtiberians did not? Thus, by rejecting historical preconceptions, we shift the nature of the enquiry and the debate.

Genetics

Various people, including physical anthropologists, have suggested to me that the 'problem of the Celts' can most easily be resolved by recent advances in DNA. I am, however, reminded of the claims made for the analysis of copper and bronze objects in the 1960s to reconstruct early trade patterns. Highly sophisticated methods of physical analysis were used to identify trace elements, and complex statistical techniques, but the results produced were clearly rubbish. Ireland, a copper producing country, seemed to be importing much of its metal from central Europe! In fact the theoretical and methodological basis of what was being done had not been thought out, and the wrong statistical techniques were being employed. As the writings of some geneticists and recent discussion in the pages of recent issues of *British Archaeology* (68–70) demonstrate, we have not yet sorted out what the potential and limitations of genetic analysis are.

The debate in *British Archaeology* discussed to what extent the native British population at the end of the Roman period was replaced by an incoming Anglo-Saxon population. It is claimed that the genetic make-up of the 'recent' population of south-east Britain (that is, present inhabitants whose families have been long established in the area) is closer to the population in the Low Countries than to that of western Britain and Ireland. This is then interpreted as 'proof' that the earlier population had been largely 'exterminated' or 'displaced' by the new immigrants. It is an example of geneticists finding a pattern, and then seeking an historical context to explain it. But is it the right context? The original population of Mesolithic immigrants came from the Low Countries as did some of the Neolithic immigrants, and this original genetic pattern was reinforced by continuity of contact across the North Sea (Beaker pottery, Hilversum urns, and Late Iron Age, Roman and Middle Saxon trade with the Rhineland), so the Anglo-Saxon immigration can be seen as merely one phase and one type of contact between populations which were probably already very similar genetically.

A second example is a recent television programme, which tried to deal with the question of whether the Scots, Irish and Welsh are really Celts. The DNA of a bone of a 'Celt' from an Iron Age cemetery from central Europe was compared with results obtained from modern populations in Britain and Ireland; the conclusion was that the modern population did not resemble that of the ancient Celts closely. But was this bone typical of the 'Celts' of Europe? Would this person have considered himself to be a 'Celt'? Can we equate physical characteristics with language and ethnicity, the question that Prichard was grappling with in the early nineteenth century? The problem with both these examples is that, behind them, there lurk the nineteenth-century stereotypes of race, that is the speakers of Celtic languages are 'Celts' who have recognisable physical characteristics. So it is assumed that there should be differences between the populations in the east and west of Britain because one group is 'Germanic' and the other 'Celtic', and that the British 'Celts' are not real Celts when compared to those on the continent because of genetic differences.

So we need to be clear about what it is we are trying to do and how we might legitimately do it. First we need to set up clear models of what may be going on. Genetic change will happen mainly in three ways:

1. There is a gradual natural drift; some genes may become dominant in a given population, others may disappear for no other reason than chance.

2. Genetic mutations may happen, advantageous or disadvantageous for the individual, but often neutral. These may then become disseminated through inheritance to the rest of the population.

3. Specific genes may give individuals who possess them advantages in certain environmental situations; sickle cells in the blood which provide resistance against malaria is a classic example.

There are also other basic rules:

4. Populations are more likely to become genetically distinct when they are small and have a relatively small gene pool; rare genetic variations are more likely to survive in large populations with a large gene pool, though, conversely, they can become dominant in small gene pools.

5. Normally a population will continue to exchange genes with neighbouring populations through intermarriage and patterns of localised migration (e.g. moving to the next town or village). Deviation between populations is only likely to happen where there is some physical boundary such as a long or difficult sea crossing or high mountains which restricts contact, or where there is a cultural boundary (e.g. groups like the Amish or the Jews who tend to marry within the group). However we should not assume that this will be the case; in the case of the Jews, the modern populations superficially tend to resemble their neighbours implying that they are part of the local gene pool, indeed one wonders whether the modern Palestinians are genetically closer to the ancient Jews than the modern Israeli population.

Yet, despite these tendencies towards homogenisation, regional populations do tend to have local genetic characteristics. Tacitus noted that the Caledonians had reddish hair which he put down to a Germanic origin (*Agricola* 11); more scientific analysis of the modern Scottish population shows the highest incidence of reddish or ginger hair anywhere in the world, suggesting that this is a characteristic which goes back a very long way and despite continuous evidence of immigration into Scotland. Using the principles already discussed, the Scottish population is most likely to have become differentiated from surrounding groups when population sizes were small, very possibly in the early phases of colonisation after the last glaciation, so either in the Mesolithic or the early Neolithic. Subsequent increase in population is likely to have mainly been due to natural internal expansion, and though immigration may have been considerable, it was not enough to overturn the basic genetic pattern. That early Mesolithic populations in Britain may have left some genetic legacy is supported by the genetic characteristics of an early post-glacial skeleton from Somerset, 'Cheddar Man', characteristics which still occur in some of the local modern population.

So our general model would suggest genetic continuity rather than the cataclysmic replacements favoured by our nineteenth-century predecessors. But their interpretation was not entirely without foundation, as sources like the Anglo-Saxon Chronicle sometimes talk of slaughter of native populations. The colonialist view that change could only come about from external intervention was based on attempts to explain why there was such variation in technological achievement across the world. Also the experience of European colonisation has often been associated with the demise of indigenous populations overwhelmed by the immigrants. I would suggest four situations in which this might happen:

1. Where the native population is small in comparison to the number of immigrants.

2. Where the immigrants introduce virulent diseases such as smallpox and measles with which the immune system of the natives cannot cope; this had been the major cause of the collapse of native populations in recent times.

3. Where insecurity produces a 'systems' collapse, leading to famine and disease.

4. Where there is a large gap in the technological and organisational expertise of the immigrants (most obvious in military terms in the Spanish conquest of central and southern America), but where there is a conflict for resources which leads to the dominant immigrant group physically exterminating the natives or their habitats (Australian Aborigines, Plains Indians, Amazonian Indians).

Most of these factors are unlikely for the ancient world where there was not a huge disparity in technologies (though there might be in organisational skill), and where large-scale immigration was only likely to come from relatively nearby populations.

From the point of view of genetics, where major change is postulated, the only way to recognise this is to compare reasonably large samples of the populations from either side of the event, especially as the genetic difference between populations is likely to be small. But, as we have seen, large numbers of burials covering long periods of time are not easily obtainable from the archaeological record, and this will be further hampered where the burial rite is cremation or where environmental factors such as acidic soils are not conducive to the preservation of human remains. DNA may be more suitable for looking at relationships between individuals in a cemetery, or, in conjunction with isotope analysis, to identify individuals who have come from outside the immediate community. Comparisons of samples of former populations and the modern population and measuring the degree of genetic distance may be one way forward, but suitable techniques of statistical comparison need to be employed. Should one, for instance, be looking at the occurrence of individual marker genes (in the same way that an physical anthropologists may look at specific anatomical features such as Wormian bones in the skull), or should the whole genetic pattern be compared, and if so, using what form of statistical method? However, one must remain sceptical about the value of DNA for identifying mass migration and population change of the sort implied by theories of invasion, and again one returns to the 'wave' model in linguistics as a possible way of modelling genetic change.

11

IMPLICATIONS

This book represents a radical reinterpretation of the Celts, and in this final chapter I wish to summarise the main conclusions and to explore the implications of the new interpretations. The major impact will be for archaeologists and historians, but there are also implications for modern society and the role that 'Celticity' plays in the new formulations of ethnic identity within Britain and Europe. The main points that I wish to make are:

1. We do not know how Celts were defined in the past, but it varies from one classical author to another, and we need to understand the context and viewpoint of each individual author.

2. Related terms like Celt and Gaul were commonly used for groups of people from Spain in the west to Asia Minor in the east, not only by Greeks and Romans but also by the people themselves; it was never used for the inhabitants of the British Isles except in the most general way for all the inhabitants of western Europe including non-Indo-European speakers such as Basques.

3. The term 'Celtic' to describe the language group is an eighteenth-century innovation, and was due to a misconception that modern Breton was a survival of the language of the ancient Celts who lived in Gaul rather than a more recent introduction from Britain.

4. The definition of a Celt as someone who speaks, or whose recent ancestors spoke, a Celtic language is also an eighteenth-century innovation, and it was wrongly applied to the inhabitants of Britain and Ireland.

5. 'Celtic Art' was first defined in Ireland in the mid-nineteenth century and called 'Late Keltic' on the misapprehension that the ancient inhabitants of Britain and Ireland were Celts.

6. The origin of this art style has been located in northern France, southern Germany and Bohemia, but this takes no account of the bias of distribution (e.g.

the lack of burials in central and western France, and so the lack of finds), and the origin area may have been much larger to include much of France, Germany, the Czech Republic, Switzerland, parts of Austria, and even parts of northern Italy and southern Britain.

7. One interpretation of the historical and linguistic evidence also seeks the origin of the Celts in south-west Germany, but other interpretations of the classical sources are also possible, indeed perhaps more likely, and would include central and western France.

8. In the late nineteenth and early twentieth century it was assumed that archaeological 'cultures' or 'culture groups' can be defined in terms of styles of dress, art, burial rites, house types, pottery, etc., and that these cultures can be correlated with ancient peoples; however, these definitions are often arbitrary, and a correlation with any ancient ethnic group cannot be assumed, indeed it is very often wrong.

9. For the Iron Age two dominant 'cultures' were defined, an earlier 'Hallstatt' and a later 'La Tène'. The latter was correlated with the fifth-century Celts on the upper Danube. As continuity could be demonstrated, especially in western Germany, between the Hallstatt and La Tène burial rites, it was also assumed that the 'Hallstatt Culture' in this area is also Celtic and thus represents the origin of the Celts. However, continuity can be demonstrated or suggested over a much wider area.

10. Using nineteenth-century concepts of race, it is assumed that the Celts were a distinctive racial group whose origin and expansion can be defined by using archaeological data. These ideas were developed by Gustaf Kossinna and adopted by the Nazi party as a foundation of the concept of a German master race. The interpretations of the expansion of the Germans and the Celts use identical methodologies, and are unacceptable.

11. Colonialist theories that progress is usually only initiated by external influences, and, left to themselves, 'natives' will 'degenerate', led to migrationist interpretations of culture change (e.g. in Britain new ideas meant new arrivals from the continent).

12. Races were thought to have characteristic features such as religion, social structure, language, etc. This leads to racial stereotyping and the idea that different sources from different places and different times can be collated to define a 'Celtic Culture' the concept of the 'timeless Celt', an idea that still pervades most general books on the Celts.

As readers of this book will have realised, I reject most of the concepts and methodologies that are found in general books on the Celts, if not in their entirety, at least as general theories and approaches. We need to understand where they come from and what their implications are, and this has been the main aim of this book.

This alternative approach to the Celts has not been without controversy. When *The Atlantic Celts* was first published, Simon James records that he received a number of hostile comments, including one accusing him of 'genocide'! Typical comments from Ruth and Vincent Megaw make strong allegations of right-wing nationalism against us, both quoted in James 1998:

> In the United Kingdom . . . particularly in England, the anti-European mentality seems deeply entrenched; promoting a fear of 'loss of sover-eignty' seems to the Tory Right its main hope of maintaining political control. Celts, ancient or modern, are seen as a possible symbol of internal disintegration and external control; hence, perhaps, the questioning of long-held assumptions as to the existence of such past insular 'peoples' as Celts, Picts or Anglo-Saxons.
>
> Megaw and Megaw 1996, 179.

> The European Union, to which the United Kingdom was a late and reluctant adherent, has often been seen in England as a political threat, not an opportunity. It would indeed be odd if the products of the higher education system did not reflect, however unconsciously, this unease.
>
> Megaw and Megaw 1996, 179.

As almost all of us who have been pursuing these new interpretations tend to be on the liberal left wing of politics, and generally pro-European, one finds this attack somewhat bizarre. Neither Simon James nor myself have any intention of destroying the modern concept of the Celts, or oppose regional diversity (quite the opposite!), nor would we expect the critique of a couple of archaeologists to destroy the way in which millions of people view themselves, and such is not the intention. As I have already stated, my original concerns came purely from problems of archaeological interpretations of sites and areas in which I have been researching.

Europe, as we have known it for the last century or two, is in a major state of flux. The 'nation state', that invention of the seventeenth century, may have run its day. Though it has delivered much to its citizens in terms of health, education, wealth, social and political freedom, and technological advance, it has, in the name of patriotism, destroyed millions of lives. Many of us on the centre and left of politics prefer to look for alternative ways, investing in international co-operation through organisations like the European Union and the United Nations, recognising that our future lies in sharing responsibilities in promoting growth, health, and protecting the environment, indeed the very air we breath.

Yet, even as we join larger and larger political and economic organisations, we are at the same time ever more conscious of our own identities, which generally lie in our historical origins and development. If I consider myself first and foremost as an Englishman, and British only in terms of the citizenship which provides me with protection when I travel around the world, it is not because I am anti-Scottish, Welsh or Irish, indeed the opposite, seeing Britain more as a union of equals. It is a recognition that the partner nations within the British Union have rather different histories, interests and aspirations, a diversity which we can celebrate and enjoy; we will achieve more by mutual respect and by working together than through the domination of the largest ethnic group, the English, something which certain politicians in Westminster have been slow to appreciate. But we must accept that these ethnic identities are fabrications, 'invented traditions', 'imagined communities', as various historians have labelled them. This does not make them any less real, and though names like 'Celts' may be arbitrarily chosen, if we do not use these names, we will only have to invent new ones! Welsh is just a Germanic name for foreigners (interesting given that the Britons were here earlier!), though the internal name is Cymry, the 'fellow inhabitants'. Scotland was named after the Scots who were invaders from Ireland who eventually dominated a coalition of indigenous Picts and Britons, invading Norse, and lowland speakers of an English dialect, Lallans. And England took its name from the Angles, even though the state was established by the West Saxons, and incorporated Jutes, Britons, Danes and Normans. And we have all adopted the term *Pretannoi* that Pytheas encountered in the third century BC for the inhabitants of these islands.

Similar processes are underway in other parts of Europe, sometimes peacefully like the parting of the Czechs and Slovaks, sometimes with a certain amount of civil conflict, as in Spain between the Basques, the Catalans, the Galicians, and the Castilians; and sometimes with all-out war as in the Balkans. The message must surely be that new entities should be allowed to evolve peacefully; in civil conflict everyone loses, even the dominant group, as the Serbs found out as Yugoslavia disintegrated. We are thus walking a tightrope between, on the one hand, regional ethnic identities to which we can subscribe with pride and self-respect; and on the other rampant nationalism which only respects physical force and will not respect the traditions of other groups. The divisions between ethnic groups are often largely arbitrary; usually it is language (e.g. Catalans versus Castilians), but in the case of the Serbs and Croats, it was mainly between two different brands of Christianity. But history is one of the major factors defining ethnicity; indeed, it is often the prime mover, which is why there is an onus on historians and archaeologists to deal honestly and logically with their data, and recognise the ambiguity of the information with which we deal, especially with ethnic interpretations.

There is one question which epitomises many of our problems; is it possible to have a black Celt? Two apocryphal stories, both probably true, illustrate the point. The first, reported in *The Guardian* newspaper, in an inquiry into racism in Ireland, described the case of a woman bearing a normal Irish name who applied for a post

The British Academy — Equal Opportunities

As part of the British Academy's commitment to equal opportunities, the ethnic origin of people who apply to the Academy is monitored. We should therefore be grateful if you would tick one of the boxes below, which reflect the categories employed by the Registrar General in the Census, and in all university student records. Any information you give will remain confidential. The form will be detached from your application, and the information will be used for monitoring purposes only.

Please do not sign the form, or give your name

Please show which group best describes your ethnic origin or descent by ticking ONE of the boxes below:

Bangladeshi		Black African	
Chinese		Black Caribbean	
Indian		Black Other	
Pakistani		White	
Asian Other		Other	

If you do not wish to complete this form, your decision will not affect your application in any way.

87 *Form used by the British Academy to monitor racial and ethnic bias in grant applications*

with the Irish Tourist Board to work in their office at Dublin airport. It was only when she turned up for interview that she was immediately rejected; she was black, a woman of African origin married to an Irishman. This was not the image the Tourist Board wanted of Ireland as a Celtic country; would her children have been similarly rejected, despite their father being Irish? The second story was related to me by Barry Raftery, of a big family union. It included the son of one of the men who had migrated to the Caribbean and married a local black wife; in this case the man was immediately welcomed in as a member of the family, and colour of skin was irrelevant. The contrast here is not only between the official and the private reactions to skin colour, but also the different definitions of Irishness. The official one was backward-looking using outdated stereotypes, while the other is dynamic accepting change, and looking to the future.

It is usually institutions such as governments which are the worst offenders in perpetuating outdated theories. On figure **87** I reproduce the document sent out by the British Academy to monitor any racial or ethnic bias; it is similar to many of the official monitoring schemes used by official institutions such as hospitals, indeed in not so blatant form, also in the national census, though that was altered somewhat after public pressure. I personally have no problems about filling in such forms if they can be used to fight against bigotry, but this one I object to strongly as it confuses two different concepts: skin colour and ethnicity. I usually enter myself under 'other' and 'English', since 'white' is not an ethnicity, it is a skin colour, and is immediately making a distinction between groups considered indigenous (though many may be of European ancestry), and I point out that the form is itself basically racist. It is based upon the nineteenth-century concepts of race which I discussed in a previous chapter (p.59), and it assumes that there is indeed something we can label as 'race' which can be defined objectively.

But, as many black people of Caribbean origin are finding out, their genetic make-up may include genes which are most likely to have come from Europe, especially through their male descent. Children who have one 'white' parent and one 'black' are usually classified as 'black' because the genes which give black or brown pigment to hair, eyes and skin tend to be dominant, whereas those that give fair skin, blonde hair and blue eyes tend to be recessive. What forms such as the British Academy's are doing is denying dark-skinned people the existence of their 'white' genes, and forcing them into the 'black' category; it is perpetuating the concept of 'purity of race' that bedevilled the first half of the twentieth century, and that people from 'mixed' marriages are somehow of 'mixed race', someone made up of two halves rather than a whole human being.

Though we can all recognise the genetic 'extremes' in the world population, and label them as 'Caucasoid', 'Negroid' or 'Mongoloid', much, perhaps most, of the world's population is not so easily classifiable, even when we introduce intermediate terms like 'Mediterranean' or 'Amer-Indian'; with the present interchange of populations on a world-wide level, and increasing intermarriage, this will become increasingly the case. So, I would suggest, the concept of race is something which should be dropped into the dustbin of history, and I would suggest that the term 'racist' be redefined to include anyone who considers race is a valid concept which can be used to categorise and classify people. As such I would suggest that, with its nomenclature of 'Race Relations Act' and 'Race Relations Board', the British Government, like many other British organisations, is institutionally racist.

If we need to monitor colour and ethnic bias, as, sadly, I feel we do, we should keep the two phenomena strictly separate. Skin colour is one way in which we instantly classify one another, independent of what our ethnicity and genetic background may be. Thus a young man in my wife's home town in Norway was beaten up in a racist attack; even though his genetic background was entirely Nordic, he lay at the darker end of the indigenous spectrum and so was perceived as 'foreign' by his attackers. Skin colour is something which can be measured objectively, but splitting it up into specific categories is of necessity arbitrary as we have a continuous spectrum from 'black' to 'white' with a few 'yellows', 'browns' and 'pinks' thrown in; perhaps we should agree some general categories and be allowed to define our own colour.

Self-definition is, when we come to ethnicity, the best means of definition; 'we are what we think we are', though sadly a more common definition is 'we are what others think we are'. Also, we all have multiple identities which can change according to context; towns like Sheffield and Glasgow are divided between the supporters of the two different football clubs, and this has regularly in the past led to violence and even murder. Though the stage on which I personally operate is essentially European, when I travel around Europe I perceive myself (as do my friends and colleagues across Europe) very much as an Englishman, but merely as marking a difference in terms of my attitudes and beliefs. This recognition of 'difference' may include a certain amount of pride in one's home and origins, and one's country, but the essential difference between myself and, say, a member of the British National Party lies not only in our different understanding of the concept of 'race' but also in our attitudes to history as the means of defining Englishness or Britishness. For a member of the British National Party it is something which is defined in a past which has remained static and will do so in the future, whereas I see ethnicity as something which is continuously changing, being 'renegotiated' and redefined by individuals in each succeeding generation. Extreme nationalism is akin to religious fundamentalism which believes that old books (the Bible, the Torah, the Koran) can provide a blueprint of how we should live in the present, especially if the people who wrote it down claim that 'it is the word of God' (a dubious means of claiming one's views are right); as I write these words, the Anglican and Catholic churches are tearing themselves apart over homosexual priests, between those who believe in the spirit of Christianity and those who believe in the written dogma, the 'scriptural tradition'. As an agnostic, I of course reject such attitudes, but as someone who deals with history, I would consider the wisdom and the experience of our ancestors as important in developing the ideals and mores of our own society, but that we should add on the knowledge and experience that we have acquired in the intervening years since the texts were written down. So, I would not take the racial stereotypes of ancient authors such as Caesar and Cicero as a useful guide with which to describe 'Celtic' populations in general, especially modern peoples.

If, as I am suggesting, the past does have such a great influence on the present, 'The strength of the past and its great might' as Kristian Kristiansen quoted in the title of one of his articles, then it is incumbent on historians and archaeologists to question and understand the theoretical basis and the methodology of what we write. I continuously argue that, though I do not see the concept of the Celt as likely to be used in the way in which the prehistory of Germany was used by the Nazis (e.g. armies of Welshmen descending on southern Germany or Ankara to claim back their lost territory), nonetheless we cannot use false methodology in contexts where it does not matter, as it will then be used in situations where is does, in the Balkans, in the Caucasus, in the Near East, where archaeology is being used in modern propaganda battles. It is here that I deviate from the majority of authors who have written on the Celts as they are, usually tacitly, perpetuating methodologies and interpretations which are grounded in the racism and stereo-typing of our nineteenth-century predecessors which, I suspect, most of the authors would themselves reject, if they knew where they came from. Thus we continuously get the view of the Celts as an endangered species, pushed ever further to the fringes of Europe. The guided tour of 'Celtica' at Machynlleth, after taking the visitor though an overview of the continental Celts, a reconstruction of an Iron Age village, and a mystic view of the present as seen from the past, then asks the visitors what happened to the Celts. To a background of a Welsh choir one is told 'we are still here' (to be fair, the exhibition discusses some of the problems of defining Celticity). But what we are talking about as being threatened is not the Celts, but the Celtic languages. The real genetic descendants of the Celts are alive and thriving, but they now speak Galician, Castilian, French, Italian, German, Hungarian, various Slav languages, and Turkish; except, possibly, the Bretons (if they were not all immigrants from Britain), none of them speaks a Celtic language.

The response of Rhodri Morgan, leader of the Welsh Assembly, when asked to comment on Simon James' suggestion that the early Welsh may not have been Celts was:

> Celtic and proud of it! It's just English jealousy. We were civilised first. The earliest poem composed in a post-Classical language was Welsh. The Celts were here when Caesar landed. It's modern Anglo-Saxon propaganda.
>
> Reported in *The Independent*, 27 February 1999.

One suspects he had not read the book, but we see here the claim that the Celts lived in Britain, and had been here longer than the English. As an Englishman from the south of England (though with a bit of Irish input in the eighteenth century!), I suspect I am possibly genetically closer than Mr Morgan to the Britons who stood on the cliffs when Caesar arrived!

But rather than suggesting that modern Celticity is something suspect, we need to see it as something different from the past, though having its roots in an interesting historical process which links it with the ancient Celts. New ideas about what may be 'Celtic' are continually appearing: we had the 'Celtic Church' in the nineteenth century; the term 'Celtic fields' was coined in the 1920s; and in more recent times we have seen trends in music labelled as 'Celtic'. But how are we to define a modern Celt? I have suggested that recently it has been language which has been the key, and on the instigation of the linguists the International Celtic Conference turned down overtures from the Galicians to hold the conference in northern Spain as they did not consider non-Celtic-speaking Galicia to be 'Celtic'. The annual festival at Lorient in Brittany, however, has been more open, welcoming folk culture from areas such as Galicia and the Auvergne, but would that extend to central Turkey? Could participation in Lorient become the arbiter of Celticity, just as participation in the Olympic Games was for being Greek in the ancient world? Perhaps we should have a Celtic football cup, with Glasgow Celtic, Celta Vigo, and Galatasaray, or even cities with Celtic names (Milan, Bologna); anything to make people understand their origins and to bring them together!

In fact when in the past I have expressed in talks the views in this book, I have generally met with interest and a large degree of acceptance, even when I have lectured in Cardiff, Lampeter, Edinburgh and Cork, indeed I am often invited back! If I have received a mauling, it has not been from the local 'Celts' but from fellow archaeologists such as Ruth and Vincent Megaw. After all, some of the original scepticism about the Celts came from the pens of Irish scholars rather than English, such as MacNeill's article 'The re-discovery of the Celts' written nearly a century ago, but nowadays seemingly little read and quoted. What I have written in this book would be accepted by the majority of archaeologists in Britain, and some in Ireland and Spain; colleagues in France, Austria and Germany are beginning to enter the debate, as are some linguists such as Patrick Sims-Williams. However, the major conflict has still been between British archaeologists, as the quote from the Megaws above has demonstrated, and I will finish with a further quote, this time from Barry Cunliffe, who has questioned the quality and validity of scholarship of people such as myself who query traditional interpretations of the Celts:

> The most challenging work on the whole question of validity of the concept of the 'Celtic' is M. Chapman, *The Celts: construction of a myth*. It deserves careful reading as an essential preliminary. Other writers have been quick to espouse a politically correct disdain for the use of 'Celt' though usually without Chapman's depth of scholarship.
>
> Cunliffe 1997, 276.

I hope this book has answered that, and I now pass the debate back to my opponents.

Addendum

Figure **88** shows the areas occupied by the Ancient Celts, and, in Iberia, the Celtiberians and the Celtici; unlike other maps purporting to show areas occupied by Celts, I have distinguished those areas which were occupied by people who spoke Celtic languages, but for whom there is no clear evdidence that they were considered as Celts; this includes groups such as the Britons and the Irish, in Iberia the Vettones and the Vaccei, and in southern France and northern Italy, peoples who were included among the Ligurians. Inevitably there have to be judgement values; so I have, for instance, ignored Tacitus' statement that the Aestiones spoke *Britannice*, but accepted his description of the Cotini, and it is impossible to produce a map that everyone would accept.

In contrast, figure **89** shows the distribution of groups who have considered themselves to be Celtic from the eighteenth century. As can be seen there is virtually no geographical overlap between them and the Ancient Celts. It includes some problematic groups such as the Lowland Scots who have spoken an English dialect for some 1500 years, and so strictly do not fall under the definition of the modern Celt: that is, someone whose recent ancestors spoke a Celtic language. The same is true for the Galicians of northern Spain, but under the other criterion, that is someone who believes themselves to be Celtic, they would qualify, but this is not generally accepted by other Celtic groups.

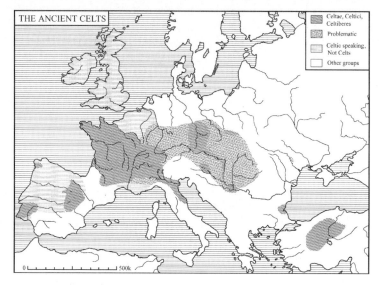

88 *Distribution of the Ancient Celts, Celtici and Celtiberians, and areas where Celtic languages were spoken.* Author

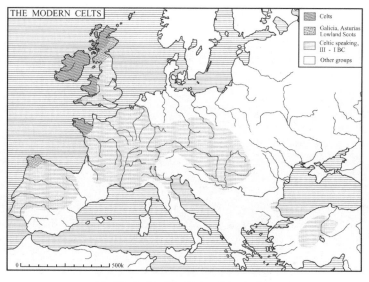

89 *Distribution of the Modern Celts.* Author

NOTES AND BIBLIOGRAPHY

Introduction

I do not pretend to have a definitive list of recent publications, but the following list incorporates the main publications. It includes the books which have accompanied a series of very successful exhibitions: in 1980 at Salzburg (Pauli 1980); 1990 in Venice (Kruta *et al.* 1991); Rosenheim in 1993 (Dannheimer and Gebhard 1993); and in 2002 at Ávila (Diputación Provincial de Ávila 2002). There have also been several exhibitions accompanying the annual meetings of the Association française pour l'Etude de l'Age du Fer, the major forum for discussion of western European Iron Age archaeology; a list of the catalogues for these usually regional exhibitions can be found in Collis 2001 along with the volumes of the proceedings of the conferences. Since that time five more volumes have appeared: Chausserie-Laprée (2000), Méniel and Lambot (2002), Maranski and Guichard (2002), Plouin and Jud (2003) and Buchsenschutz *et al.* (2003). New work is also published by the Centre archéologique européen du Mont Beuvray (Guichard *et al.* 2000; Guichard and Perrin 2002). The best general overviews in English on the Celts are James (1993), Cunliffe (1997) and Ó hÓgáin (2003), though all represent the traditional attitudes which are attacked in this volume, and the last mentioned is weak on the archaeology. James (1997) is the only monograph which deals with more recent ideas. There are also a couple of recent volumes offering dictionaries on Celtic topics (Maier 1997; Kruta 2000), but two major lexicons are underway, one of which will be published under the editorship of John Koch, and the other by the Austrian Academy of Sciences.

Recent books on the Celts

Almagro-Gorbea, M. ed. 1993. *Los Celtas: Hispania y Europa*. Madrid, Universidad Complutense.

Arenas Esteban, J.A. and Palacios Tamayo, V. eds 1999. *El Origen del Mundo Celtibérico: actos de los encuentros sobre el origen del mundo Celtibérico, Molina de Aragón, 1–3 de octubre de 1998*. Molina de Aragón, Ayuntamiento de Molina de Aragón.

Armit, I. 1997. *Celtic Scotland*. London, Batsford/Historic Scotland.

Black, R., Gillies, W. and Ó Maolalaigh, R. eds 1999. *Celtic Connections*, Vol. 1. Proceedings of the Tenth International Congress of Celtic Studies, Tuckwell Press.

Buchsenschutz, O., Bulard, A., Chardenoux, M.-B. and Ginoux, N. eds 2003. *Décors, images et signes de l'âge du Fer européen. Actes du XXVIe Colloque de l'AFEAF, Paris et St. Denis, mai 2002*. Revue Archéologique du Centre de la France, supplément 24.

Brown, T. ed. 1996. *Celtism*. Amsterdam and Atlanta, Studia Imagologica.

Carr, G. and Stoddart, S. eds 2002. *Celts from Antiquity*. Antiquity Papers 2. Cambridge, Antiquity Publications.

Chapman, M. 1992. *The Celts: the construction of a myth*. Basingstoke, Macmillan Press.

Charpy, J.-J. ed. 1995. *L'Europe celtique du Ve au IIIe siècle avant J.-C.: contact, échanges et mouvements de populations*. Sceaux, B.Y. Kronos Editions.

Charpentier, V. ed. 1995. *Les Éclats du Passé: redécouverte des Gaulois*. Paris, Editions Errance.

Chausserie-Laprée, J. ed. 2000. *Les Temps des Gaulois en Provence*. Musée Ziem, Martigues.

Collis, J. 1984. *The European Iron Age*. London, Batsford (reprinted 1997, London, Routledge).

Collis, J. ed. 2001. *Society and Settlement in Iron Age Europe. L'Habitat et l'Occupation du Sol en Europe. Actes du XVIIIe Colloque de l'AFEAF Winchester, Avril 1994*. Sheffield, J.R. Collis publications.

Cunliffe, B.W. 1997. *The Ancient Celts*. Oxford, Oxford University Press.

Dannheimer, H. and Gebhard, R. eds 1993. *Das keltische Jahrtausend*. Mainz am Rhein, Philipp von Zabern.

Davies, J. 2000. *The Celts: prehistory to the present day*. London, Cassel & Co.

Diepeveen-Jansen, M. 2001. *People, Ideas and Goods: new perspectives on the 'Celtic Barbarians' in western and central Europe (500–250 BC)*. Amsterdam Archaeological Studies 7, Amsterdam University Press.

Diputación Provincial de Ávila, 2002. *Celtas y Vettones*. Ávila, Excma. Diputación Provincial de Ávila.

Ellis, P. Berresford 1990. *The Celtic Empire: the first millennium of Celtic History, c.1000 BC – 51 AD*. London, Guild Publishing.

Eluère, C. 1992. T*he Celts: first masters of Europe*. London, Thames and Hudson.

Ferguson W. 1998. *The Identity of the Scottish Nation*. Edinburgh, Edinburgh University Press.

García Castro, J.A. ed. 1990. *Los Celtas en la Península Iberica*. Revista de Arqueología.

Green, M.J. 1986. *The Gods of the Celts*. Stroud, Alan Sutton.

Green, M.J. 1995. *Celtic Goddesses: warriors, virgins and mothers*. London, British Museum Press.

Green, M.J. ed. 1995. *The Celtic World*. London, Routledge.

Green, M.J. 1996. *Celtic Art*. London, Weidenfeld and Nicholson, Everyman Art Library.

Guichard, V. and Perrin, F. eds 2002. *L'aristocratie celte à la fin de l'âge du Fer*. Glux-en-Glenne, Centre archéologique européen du Mont Beuvray. Bibracte 4.

Guichard, V., Sievers, S., and Urban, O.H. eds 2000. *Les processus d'urbanisation à l'âge du Fer. Eisenzeitliche Urbanisationsprozesse*. Glux-en-Glenne, Centre archéologique européen du Mont Beuvray. Bibracte 5.

Haywood, J. 2001. *The Historical Atlas of the Celtic World*. London, Thames and Hudson.

James, S. 1993. *Exploring the World of the Celts*. London, Thames and Hudson.

James, S. 1999. *The Atlantic Celts*. London, British Museum Press.

James, S. and Rigby, V. 1997. *Britain and the Celtic Iron Age*. London, British Museum Press.

Koch, J. ed. 1995. *The Celtic Heroic Age: literary sources for ancient Celtic Europe and early Ireland and Wales*. Malden, Massachusetts, Celtic Studies Publications.

Koch, J. ed. forthcoming. *Encyclopaedia of Celtic History and Culture*.

Kruta, V. 2000. *Les Celtes: histoire et dictionnaire*. Manchecourt, Robert Laffont.

Kruta, V., Frey, O.H., Raftery, B. and Szabó, M. eds 1991. *The Celts*. London, Thames and Hudson.

Lorrio, A.J. 1997. *Los Celtíberos*. Alicante, Universidad de Alicante/Universidad Complutense de Madrid.

Maier, B. 1997. *Dictionary of Celtic Religion and Culture*. Woodbridge, Boydell and Brewer.

Maranski, D. and Guichard, V. eds 2002. *Les Âges du Fer en Nivernais, Bourbonais et Berry oriental. Regards Européens sur les Âges du Fer en France. Actes du XVIIe Colloque de l'AFEAF, Nevers; mai 1993*. Collection Bibracte 6. Glux-en-Glenne, Centre archéologique européen du Mont Beuvray.

Megaw, R. and V. 1989. *Celtic Art, from its Beginnings to the Book of Kells*. London, Thames and Hudson.

Méniel, P. and Lambot, B. 2002. *Découvertes récentes de l'âge du Fer dans les massifs des Ardennes et ses marges. Repas des vivants pour les morts en Gaule*. Reims, Mémoire de la Société Champenoise, No. 16, Supplément au Bulletin, no. 1.

Ó hÓgáin, D. 2003. *The Celts: a history*. Woodbridge, Boydell and Brewer.

Pauli, L. ed. 1980. *Die Kelten in Mitteleuropa: Kultur, Kunst, Wirtschaft*. Salzburger Landesaustellung 1 Mai - 30 Sept. 1980 im Keltenmuseum Hallein, Österreich.

Plouin, S. and Jud, P. eds 2003. *Habitats, mobiliers et groupes régionaux à l'âge du Fer. Actes du XXe Colloque de l'AFEAF Colmar-Mittelwihr, mai 1996*. Revue Archéologique del'Est, supplément 20.

Py, M. 1993. *Les Gaulois du Midi*. Paris, Hachette.

Raftery, B. 1984. *La Tène in Ireland: problems of origin and chronology*. Marburg, Vorgeschichtliches Seminar Marburg.

Raftery, B. ed. 1990. *Celtic Art*. UNESCO, Flammarion.

Raftery, B. 1994. *Pagan Celtic Ireland: the enigma of the Irish Iron Age*. London, Thames and Hudson.

Rankin, D. 1987. *Celts and the Classical World*. London, Routledge.

Rieckhoff, S. and Biel, J. 2001. *Die Kelten in Deutschland*. Stuttgart, Theiss.

Roymans, N. 1990. *Tribal Societies in Northern Gaul: an anthropological perspective*. University of Amsterdam, Cingula 12.

Unión Cultural Arqueólogica, 1996. *Celtas y Celtíberos; realidad o leyenda. Actas de las jornadas celebradas en la Universidad Complutense de Madrid del 27 febrero al 8 de marzo de 1996*. Madrid, Unión Cultural Arqueólogica.

1 Classical sources

The best, though still incomplete, list of relevant authors is to be found in d'Arbois de Jubainville (1902), and Duval (1971) provides comprehensive summaries in note form of the main sources for pre-Roman and Roman Gaul. Most of the main classical Greek and Latin authors can be found in English translation with the accompanying original text in the Loeb Classical Library series, produced by Harvard University Press. Fragments of texts of other Greek authors were gathered together in Müller (1878, 1883, 1887), though the commentary and translation are in Latin. Dinan publishes many early Greek and Latin texts with English translations, but stops in the first century BC; the classic compilation of the sources for Poseidonius is that of Tierney (1960). Rankin (1987) discusses the classical texts, though there are mistakes like transposing the story of Luernios from France to Asia Minor.

d'Arbois de Jubainville, H. 1902. *Principaux auteurs à consulter pour l'histoire des Celtes*. Cours de Littérature Celtique 12.

Dinan, W. 1911. *Monumenta Historica Celtica. Notices of the Celts in the writings of the Greek and Latin authors from the tenth century BC to the fifth century AD, arranged chronologically with translations, commentary, indices and a glossary of the Celtic names and words occurring in these authors*. London, David Nutt.

Duval, P.-M. 1971. *La Gaule jusqu'au milieu du Ve s*. Les sources de l'histoire de France des origines à la fin du XVe s. Paris, Éditions A. et J. Picard.

Justinus, 1902. *Epitoma Historiarum Philippicarum Pompei Trogi: Justin, Cornelius Nepos and Eutropius, literally translated with notes and a general index by John Selby Watson*. Bohn's Libraries. London, Bell.

Müller, C. 1878. *Fragmenta Historicorum Graecorum*, Vol II. Paris, Firmin-Didot.

Müller, C. 1883. *Fragmenta Historicorum Graecorum*, Vol III. Paris, Firmin-Didot.

Müller, C. and Müller T. 1885. *Fragmenta Historicorum Graecorum*, Vol I. Paris, Firmin-Didot.

Rankin, D. 1987. *Celts and the Classical World*. London, Routledge.

Tierney, J.J. 1960. 'The Celtic ethnography of Posidonius', *Proceedings of the Royal Irish Academy* 60c, 189-275.

2 Peopling the West

Asher (1993) deals with the supposed Trojan origin of the Franks, as well as Annius of Viterbo, and Goudineau with the claims to Trojan origin of the Aedui and Arverni (Goudineau and Peyre 1993, 171–4). The Brutus story is still most comprehensively related by Kendrick (1950), but the more direct impact on the relations between Scotland and England are summarised in Mason (1987) and Merriman (1987); Ferguson (1998) gives the wider political context, indeed is essential reading as he also deals with the impact of authors such as Fordun, Buchanan, Lhuyd and Pezron. Morris (1980) provides a useful source for Nennius, and the most accessible source for Geoffrey of Monmouth is in the translation by Thorpe (1966). A translation of the *Lebor Gabála*, the *Book of Invasions*, can be found in Koch 1995, and an earlier one in Macalister (1938–56). Byrne (1974) discusses the problems of *Book of Invasions* as a historical source, and Dillon and Chadwick (1967) discuss the gods of the *Tuath Dé Donnan*. Archer (1889) gives a summary of the life of Fordun, Sprott (1893) of Mair, and Mackay (1886a) of Boece. Fordun's works were translated by Skene (1872) along with a summary of the problems with the Scottish royal genealogies. The Annius forgery is discussed by Kendrick (1950), and Piggott (1967). There are several biographies of Buchanan: MacMillan (1906), Morton (1906) and especially McFarlane (1981), and a summary in Mackay (1886b); Ferguson (1998) defends him and Boece from more recent critics. The English translation is Aikman (1827). However, none of these deals adequately with the first book of the *Historia*, but a good summary on the Celts can be found in MacNeill (1913–14), and Collis (1999) attempts to analyse the text and its importance. A useful little overview of concepts of chronology can be found in Hanson's booklet (2002).

Aikman, J. 1827. *The History of Scotland, translated from the Latin of George Buchanan, with Notes and a Continuation to the Union in the Reign of Queen Anne.* Glasgow, Blackie, Fullerton & Co., and Edinburgh, Archibald Fullerton & Co.

Archer, T.A. 1889. 'John Fordun' in L. Stephen (ed.) 1889, 430–1.

Asher R.E. 1993. *National Myths of Renaissance France; Francus, Samothes and the Druids.* Edinburgh, Edinburgh University Press.

Black, R., Gillies, W. and Ó Maolalaigh, R. eds 1999. *Celtic Connections*, Vol. 1. Proceedings of the Tenth International Congress of Celtic Studies, Tuckwell Press.

Buchanan, G. 1582. *Rerum Scoticarum Historia.* Edinburgh, Alexander Arbuthnet.

Byrne, F.J. 1974. '*Senchas*: the nature of Gaelic historical tradition', *Historical Studies* 9, 137–59.

Camden, W. 1586. *Britannia. Sive florentissimorum regnorum Angliae, Scotiae, Hiberniae, et Insularum adiacentium ex intima antiquitate Chorographica descriptio, etc.* London, Radulphus Newbery.

Camden, W. 1610. *Britannia: or a chorographicall description of the flourishing Kingdomes of England, Scotland and Ireland and the islands adjacent. Written first in Latine by W. Camden, translated newly into English by Philemon Holland.* London, George Bishop and John Norton.

Collis, J.R. 1999. 'George Buchanan and the Celts of Britain' in R. Black *et al.* eds 1999, 91–107.

Dillon, M. and Chadwick, N. 1967. *The Celtic Realms.* London, Weidenfeld and Nicolson.

Ferguson, W. 1998. *The Identity of the Scottish Nation.* Edinburgh, Edinburgh University Press.

Goudineau, C. and Peyre, C. 1993. *Bibracte et les Eduens: à la découverte d'un peuple gaulois.* Paris, Editions Errance.

Hansen, M.H. 2002. *The Triumph of Time: reflections of a Historian on time in History.* Copenhagen, Museum Tusculanum Press.

Holder, A. 1896. *Alt-Celtischer Sprachschatze I: A – H.* Teubner, Leipzig.

Kendrick, T.D. 1950. *British Antiquity.* London, Methuen.

Koch, J. ed. 1995. *The Celtic Heroic Age: literary sources for ancient Celtic Europe and early Ireland and Wales.* Malden, Massachusetts, Celtic Studies Publications.

Latham, R.E. 1965. *Revised Medieval Latin Word List from British and Irish Sources.* London, Oxford University Press.

Latham, R.E. 1981. *Dictionary of Medieval Latin from British Sources.* London, Oxford University Press.

Lee, S. (ed.) 1893. *Dictionary of National Bibliography: Vol. 35.* London, Smith, Elder and Co.

Lhuyd, E. 1707. *Archaeologia Britannica, giving some account additional to what has been hitherto publish'd of the Languages, Histories and Customs of the Original Inhabitants of Great Britain, from Collections and Observations in Travels through Wales, Cornwal, Bas-Bretagne, Ireland and Scotland.* Oxford, Oxford Theatre.

Macalister, R.A. 1938–56. *Lebor Gabála Érenn, the Book of the Taking of Ireland.* Dublin, Irish Text Society 34, 35, 39, 41, 44.

McFarlane, I.D. 1981. *Buchanan.* London, Duckworth.

Mackay, A. 1886a. 'Hector Boece or Boethius' in L. Stephen (ed.) 1886a, 297–300.

Mackay, A. 1886b. 'George Buchanan' in L. Stephen (ed.) 1886b, 186–93.

MacMillan, D. 1906. *George Buchanan: a bibliography.* Edinburgh, George A. Morton.

MacNeill, E. 1913–14. 'The re-discovery of the Celts', *The Irish Review* 522–32.

Mason, R. 1987. 'Scotching the Brut: politics, history and national myth in sixteenth-century Britain' in R. Mason (ed.) 1987, 60–84.

Mason, R. (ed.) 1987. *Scotland and England 1286–1815.* Edinburgh, John Donald Publishers Ltd.

Merriman, M. 1987. 'James Henrisoun and "Great Britain": British union and the Scottish commonweal' in Mason R. (ed.) 1987, 85–112.

Morris, J. 1980. *Nennius: British History and the Welsh Annals, edited and translated by John Morris.* London and Chichester, Phillimore; and Totown, Rowman and Littlefield.

Morton, G.A. 1906. *George Buchanan: a biography.* Edinburgh.

Piggott, S. 1967. *Celts, Saxons and the Early Antiquaries. The O'Donnell Lecture, 1967.* Edinburgh, Edinburgh University Press.

Sammes, A. 1676. *Britannia Antiqua Illustrata.* London.

Sherely-Price, L. 1955. *Bede: a history of the English Church and People.* Penguin Books, Harmondsworth.

Skene, W.F. (ed.) 1872. *John of Fordun's Chronicle of the Scottish Nation* (translated from the Latin text by Felix J.H. Skene). Edinburgh, Edmonston and Douglas.

Sprott, G.W. 1893. 'John Major' in S. Lee (ed.) 1893, 386–8.

Stephen, L. (ed.) 1886a. *Dictionary of National Bibliography: Vol. 5.* London, Smith, Elder and Co.

Stephen, L. (ed.) 1886b. *Dictionary of National Bibliography: Vol. 6.* London, Smith, Elder and Co.

Stephen, L. (ed.) 1889. *Dictionary of National Bibliography: Vol. 19.* London, Smith, Elder and Co.

Thorpe, L. 1966. *Geoffrey of Monmouth: the History of the Kings of England.* Penguin Books, Harmondsworth.

3 People and languages

The general history of linguistics is given in Robins (1979), and of the Celtic languages by Poppe (1992) and Tristram (1996), though none mentions Buchanan and only Poppe mentions Prichard; in the case of Buchanan I have attempted to describe his contribution to linguistics (Collis 1999). Early work, including lists of words, can be found in Boxhorn (1658) and Pezron (1703); English translations of Pezron are Jones (1705) and Pezron (1809), the latter with a brief history of his life. Lhuyd contributed to the 1695 Gibson version of Camden, and his *Glossography* was published in 1707; Emery (1971) gives a survey of his life, as does Gunther (1945) in the discussion of his correspondence; James (1999) discusses his role in Celtic studies. Scaliger (1610), Parsons (1767) and Jones (1786) provide early studies leading up to the recognition of the Indo-European languages; Parson's life is outlined by Wroth (1895). Bopp (1823), Grimm (1822), Schleicher (1863) and Schmidt (1872) represent the major developments in the nineteenth century, and Prichard (1831), Bopp (1938), Zeuss (1853) and Holder (1896, 1904, 1907) are the major milestones in the study of the Celtic languages. Renfrew (1991) and Mallory (1989) represent two major reviews of the Indo-European languages with very opposing viewpoints, and Ball and Fife (1993) and Macaulay (1992) contain recent papers on the Celtic languages.

Ball, M. and Fife, J. (eds) 1993. *The Celtic Languages.* London, Routledge.

Black, R., Gillies, W. and Ó Maolalaigh, R. (eds) 1999. *Celtic Connections*, Vol. 1. Proceedings of the Tenth International Congress of Celtic Studies, Tuckwell Press.

Bopp, F. 1823. Vergleichenden Zergliederung des Sanskrits und der mit ihm verwandten Sprachen. *Phil hist. Abh der Kgl. Akad. d. Wiss, Berlin* 1823.

Bopp, F. 1838 Über die celtischen Sprachen vom Gesichtspunkt vergleichenden Sprachsformen. *Phil hist. Abh der Kgl. Akad. d. Wiss, Berlin* 1838:187–292.

Boxhorn, M.Z. 1654. *Originum Gallicarum Liber.* Amsterdam, apud Joannem Janssonium (republished in facsimile, Rodopi, Amsterdam, 1970).

Brown, T. (ed.) 1996. *Celtism.* Amsterdam and Atlanta, Studia Imagologica.

Buchanan, G. 1582. *Rerum Scoticarum Historia.* Edinburgh, Alexander Arbuthnet.

Camden W. 1695. *Camden's Britannia, newly translated into English; with large additions and improvements. Publish'd by Edmund Gibson.* London, A. & J. Churchil.

Collis, J.R. 1999. 'George Buchanan and the Celts of Britain' in R. Black *et al.* (eds) 1999, 91–107.

Dante 1973. *De Vulgari Eloquentia.* Translated into English by A.G. Ferrers Howell. London, Rebel Press.

Emery, Frank V. 1971. *Edward Lhuyd FRS 1660–1709*. Caerdydd, Gwasg prfysgol Cymru.

Ferguson, W. 1998. *The Identity of the Scottish Nation*. Edinburgh, Edinburgh University Press.

Grimm, J. 1822 *Deutsche Grammatik*.

Gunther, E.T. 1945. *Early Science in Oxford. Vol. XIV. Life and Letters of Edward Lhwyd, Second Keeper of the Musæum Ashmoleanum*. Oxford, privately printed.

Holder, A. 1896. *Alt-Celtischer Sprachschatze I: A – H*. Teubner, Leipzig.

Holder, A. 1904. *Alt-Celtischer Sprachschatze II: I – T*. Teubner, Leipzig.

Holder, A. 1907. *Alt-Celtischer Sprachschatze III: U – X*. Teubner, Leipzig.

James, S. 1999. *The Atlantic Celts*. London, British Museum Press.

Jones, D. 1705. *The Antiquities of Nations; more particularly of the Celtae or Gauls, taken to be originally the same people as our Ancient Britains, by Monsieur Pezron, englished by Mr. Jones*. London, S. Ballard.

Jones, W. 1786. 'Third anniversary discourse: "On the Hindus"' reprinted in *The Collected Works of Sir William Jones III*. London, John Stockdale, 1807:23–46.

Lhuyd, E. 1707. *Archaeologia Britannica, giving some account additional to what has been hitherto publish'd of the Languages, Histories and Customs of the Original Inhabitants of Great Britain, from Collections and Observations in Travels through Wales, Cornwal, Bas-Bretagne, Ireland and Scotland*. Oxford, Oxford Theatre.

Mallory, J.P. 1989. *In Search of the Indo-Europeans: language, archaeology and myth*. London, Thames and Hudson.

Macaulay, D. (ed.) 1992. *The Celtic Languages*. Cambridge, Cambridge University Press.

Newton, I. 1728. *Chronology of Ancient Kingdoms amended, to which is prefixed a short Chronicle, from the First Memory of Things in Europe to the Conquest of Persia by Alexander the Great*. London, Conduit.

Parsons, J. 1767. *Remains of Japhet: being historical enquiries into the affinity and origin of the European languages*. London, privately printed (reprinted by The Scolar Press, Menston, 1968).

Pezron Paul–Yves, 1703. *Antiquité de la Nation et de la Langue de Celtes autrement appellez Gaulois*. Paris.

Pezron, Paul-Yves, 1809. *The Rise and Fall of States and Empires; or the Antiquity of Nations, more particularly of the Celtae or Gauls*. London, M. Jones.

Poppe, E. 1992. 'Lag es in der Luft? Johann Kaspar Zeuss und die Konstituierung der Keltologie', *Beiträge zur Geschichte de Sprachwissenschaft* 2, 41–56.

Prichard, J.C. 1831. *The Eastern origin of the Celtic Nations*. London, Houlston and Wright, and Bernard Quaritch.

Renfrew A.C. 1991. *Archaeology and Language: the puzzle of Indo-European origins*. Harmondsworth, Penguin Books (first published by Jonathan Cape in 1987).

Robins, R.H. 1979. *A Short History of Linguistics*. London, Longmans.

Scaliger, J. 1610. 'Diatriba de Europaeorum linguis' in *Opuscula Varia antehac non edita*, pp.119–22. Paris.

Schleicher, J. 1863. *Die Darwinsiche Theorie und die Sprachwissenschaft*. Weimar.

Schmidt, J.J. 1872. *Die Verwandschaft der indogermanischen Sprachen* Weimar, Böhlau.

Tristram, H.L.C. 1996. 'Celtic in linguistic taxonomy' in T. Brown (ed.) 1996, 35–60.

Wroth, W. 1895. 'James Parsons' in S. Lee (ed.) 1895. *Dictionary of National Bibliography: Vol. 43*. London, Smith, Elder and Co., pp.403–4.

Zeuss, J.K 1853. *Grammatica Celtica*. Leipzig.

4 Race and time

The importance of Prichard's contribution to physical anthropology is discussed by Symonds (1849) and by Stocking (1973), and in an archaeological context by Morse (1999a, 1999b). Daniel's two books on the history of archaeology (1964, 1967) deal with the events around 1859 and the publication of *The Origin of Species*. I have tried to deal with some of d'Arbois de Jubainville's ideas in Collis (forthcoming). Brief lives of d'Arbois de Jubainville and Bertrand can be found respectively in Ledos (1939) and Prevost (1954), and of Jullian in Goudineau (1998).

Bertrand, A. 1876. *Archéologie Celtique et Gauloise: mémoires et documents relatifs au premiers temps de notre histoire nationale.* Paris, Didier.

Bertrand, A and Reinach, S. 1894. *Les Celtes dans les Vallées du Pô et du Danube.* Paris, Ernest Leroux.

Broca, P. 1864. 'Qu'est-ce que les Celtes', *Bulletin de la Société d'Anthropologie* 5, 557–62.

Collis, J.R. forthcoming. 'D'Amédée Thierry à Joseph Déchelette: hypothèses du XIXᵉ siècle sur l'arrivée des Celtes en Gaule', In B. Mandy and A. de Saulce (eds). *Les Marges de l'Armorique à l'âge du Fer. Archéologie et Histoire; culture materielle et sources écrites. Actes du XXIIIe Colloque de l'AFEAF, Nantes, mai 1999.* Revue Archéologique de l'Ouest, Supplément no. 10.

Collum, V.C.C. 1935. *The Tressé Iron-Age Megalithic Monument.* Oxford.

Daniel, G. 1964. *The Idea of Prehistory.* Penguin Books, Harmondsworth.

Daniel, G. 1967. *Origins and Growth of Archaeology.* Penguin Books, Harmondsworth.

d'Arbois de Jubainville, H. 1877. *Premiers Habitants de l'Europe d'aprés les Auteurs d'Antiquité et les Recherches le plus Récentes de la Linguistique.* Paris. Second edition 1889.

d'Arbois de Jubainville, H. 1875. 'Les Celtes, les Galates, les Gaulois', *Revue Archéologique* 2, 4–18.

d'Arbois de Jubainville, H. 1902. *Principaux Auteurs à consulter pour l'histoire des Celtes.* Cours de Littérature Celtique 12.

d'Arbois de Jubainville, H. 1903. 'Conquéte par les Gaulois de la région située entre le Rhin et l'Atlantique', *Revue Celtique* 1903, 162.

d'Arbois de Jubainville, H. 1904. *Les Celtes depuis le Temps les plus anciens jusqu'au l'An 100 avant notre Ére.* Paris.

Dinan, W. 1911. *Monumenta Historica Celtica. Notices of the Celts in the writings of the Greek and Latin authors from the tenth century BC to the fifth century AD, arranged chronologically with translations, commentary, indices and a glossary of the Celtic names and words occurring in these authors.* London, David Nutt.

Goudineau C. 1998. *Regard sur la Gaule.* Paris, Editions Errance.

Jullian, C. *L'Histoire de la Gaule.*

Ledos, E.-G. 1939. 'Arbois de Jubainville, Henri Marie' in M. Prevost and R. d'Anat (eds) *Dictionnaire de Biographie Française* 3, 281–3.

Morse, M. 1999a. *Redefining the Celts: rival disciplinary traditions and the peopling of the British Isles.* Unpublished doctoral thesis, University of Chicago.

Morse, M. 1999b. 'Craniology and the adoption of the Three-Age system in Britain', *Proceedings of the Prehistoric Society* 65, 1–16.

Niebuhr, B.G. 1827–32. *Römische Geschichte.* 2nd Edition, 3 volumes.

Prevost, M. 1954. 'Bertrand, Alexandre' in M. Barroux and M. Prevost (eds) *Dictionnaire de Biographie Française* 6, 264.

Prichard, J.C. 1813. *Researches into the Physical History of Man.* London, John and Arthur Arch.

Prichard J.C. 1831. *The Eastern Origin of the Celtic Nations.* London, Houlston and Wright, and Bernard Quaritch.

Prichard, J.C. 1973. *Researches into the Physical History of Man, edited and with an introductory essay by George Stocking Jnr.* Chicago and London, University of Chicago Press.

Schiller, F. 1979. *Paul Broca: founder of French Anthropology, Explorer of the Brain.* Berkeley, University of California Press.

Stocking, G. 1973. 'From chronology to ethnology: James Cowles Prichard and British Anthropology 1800–1850' in J.C. Prichard 1973, iv–cxliv.

Symonds, J.A. 1849. *Some Account of the Life, Writings and Character of the Late James Cowles Prichard.* Bristol, Evans and Abbott.

Thierry, A. 1828/1857 *Histoire des Gaulois.* Paris.

Davis, J.B. and Thurnam, J. 1865. *Crania Britannica.* London.

Wilde, W.R. 1861. *A Descriptive Catalogue of the Antiquities of Animal Materials and Bronze in the Museum of the Royal Irish Academy.* Dublin, Hodges, Smith and Co.

5 Art and archaeology

The most useful books on eighteenth-century antiquarianism, and especially on Stukeley, are those by Piggott (1985 and 1989), and Smiles (1994) produces some excellent illustrations in the arts and discusses the interaction of art and archaeology in the Romantic period, though I am confused by his use of the term 'Celtic'. There are several versions of Boswell's *Journal of a Tour to the Hebrides*; I have used the text prepared by Pottle and Bennett (1936). The best overview of the Druids is still Owen's book, *The Famous Druids* (1962), but Piggott's 1968 book has useful additional information. Discussion of Toland can be found in Huddleston (1814) and Fergusson (1997). The Society of Antiquaries, London, Hallstatt *Protokoll* is published by Hodson (1991); The Ornavasso cemeteries which had long been a key site for late Iron Age chronologies finally received full publication from Graue in 1974. For German readers Eggers (1959) gives an excellent overview of the early developments in the construction of archaeological chronologies in the nineteenth century, as well as a major critique of Kossinna; the latest study of Kossinna is Grünert (2002). Reinecke's papers have been usefully assembled as *Mainzer Aufsätze* (1963). An appreciation of Franks can be found in Wilson (1984), and of Virchow in Ottaway (1973). Déchelette has received considerable renewed attention since the opening of the Mont Beuvray centre, and information on his life can be found in Limouzin-Lamothe (1965), F. Déchelette (1962) and Gran-Aymerich (1983), though none really place him in his academic context.

Allen, J. Romilly 1904. *Celtic Art in Pagan and Christian Times.* London, Methuen and Co. First edition (facsimile reprinted by Bracken Books, Studio Editions, London 1993). First book on 'Celtic' art.

Childe, V.G. 1929. *The Danube in Prehistory.* Oxford, Clarendon Press.

Cuming, H.S. 1857. 'On the discovery of Celtic crania in the vicinity of London', *Journal of the British Association* 13, 237–9.

Cuming, H.S. 1858. 'On further discoveries of Celtic and Roman remains in the Thames off Battersea', *Journal of the British Association* 14, 326–30.

Déchelette, F. 1962. *Livre d'Or de Joseph Déchelette: centenaire 1862–1962.* Roanne, Sully.

Déchelette, J. 1910. *Manuel d'Archéologie Préhistorique, Celtique et Gallo-Romaine. II–1: Age du Bronze.* Paris, Librairie Alphonse Picard et fils.

Déchelette, J. 1913. *Manuel d'Archéologie Préhistorique, Celtique et Gallo-Romaine. II-2: Second Age du Fer ou Époque de Hallstatt.* Paris, Librairie Alphonse Picard et fils.

Déchelette, J. 1914. *Manuel d'Archéologie Préhistorique, Celtique et Gallo-Romaine. II-3: Deuxième Age du Fer ou Époque de La Tène.* Paris, Librairie Alphonse Picard et fils.

de Mortillet, G. 1870–1. 'Les Gaulois de Marzabotto dans l'Apennin', *Revue Archéologique* 22, 288–90, Pl. 22.

de Navarro, J.M. 1972. *The Finds from the Site of La Tène, I: scabbards and the swords found in them.* London, Oxford University Press.

Eggers, H.-J. 1959. *Einführung in die Vorgeschichte.* Munich, Piper Verlag.

Evans, J. 1849. 'On the date of British coins', *Numismatic Chronicle* 12, 127.

Evans, J. 1885. 'The coinage of the Ancient Britons and Natural Selection', *Transactions of the Hertfordshire Natural History Society* 3-4, 1–15.

Evans, A.J. 1890. 'On a late Celtic urnfield at Aylesford, Kent', *Archaeologia* 52, 315–88.

Evans, A.J. 1897. 'The Greek elements in ancient British Art', *Transactions of the Liverpool Welsh Society* 1896-7, 24–38.

Ferguson, W. 1998. *The Identity of the Scottish Nation.* Edinburgh, Edinburgh University Press.

Genthe, H. 1874 *Über etruskischen Tauschhandel nach dem Norden.*

Gran-Aymerich, E. and J. 1983. 'Les grands archéologues: Joseph Déchelette', *Archéologia* 185, 71–3.

Graue, J. 1974. *Die Gräberfelder von Ornavasso: eine Studie zur Chronologie der späten Latène- und frühen Kaizerzeit.* Hamburger Beiträge zur Archäologie, Beiheft 1.

Grünert, H. 2002. *Gustaf Kossinna (1858–1931). Vom Germanisten zum Prähistoriker. Ein Wissenschaftler im Kaiserreich und in der Weimarer Republik.* Rahden, VML.

Hodson, F.R. 1991 *Hallstatt: the Ramsauer graves*. Bonn, Habelt.

Hildebrand, H. 1874. 'Sur les commencements de l'âge du fer en Europe', *Congrés Internationale d'Anthropologie et d'Archéologie Préhistorique, Stockholm*, 592–601.

Huddleston, R. (ed.) 1814. *A New Edition of Toland's* History of the Druids *with an Abstract of his Life and Writings*. Montrose.

James, S. 1999. *The Atlantic Celts*. London, British Museum Press.

Kemble, J.M., Franks, A.W., and Latham, R.G. 1863. *Horae Ferales. Studies in the Archaeology of the Northern Nations*. London, Lovell Read and Co.

Kossinna, G. 1911. Zur Herkunft der Germanen. Zur Methode der Siedlungsarchäologie. *Mannus-Bibliothek* 6.

La Tour d'Auvergne, T. Correy de 1796. *Origines Gauloises, celles de plus anciens peuples de l'Europe*.

Limouzin-Lamothe, R. 1965. 'Déchelette, Joseph' in R. Limouzin-Lamothe and R. d'Anat eds *Dictionnaire de Bibliographie Française* 10, 482.

Lindenschmidt, L. 1858–81. *Alterthümern unserer heidnischen Vorzeit*.

Montelius, O. 1903. *Die typologische Methode: die älteren Kulturperioden im Orient und Europa*. Vol. 1. Stockholm, privately printed.

Ottaway, J.H. 1973. 'Rudolph Virchow: an appreciation', *Antiquity* 47, 101–8.

Owen, A.L. 1962. *The Famous Druids; a survey of three centuries of English literature on the druids*. Oxford, Oxford University Press (republished by Sandpiper Press, 1997).

Piggott, S. 1968. *The Druids*. London, Thames and Hudson.

Piggott, S. 1985. *William Stukeley: an eighteenth-century antiquarian.*. London, Thames and Hudson.

Piggott, S. 1989. *Ancient Britons and the Antiquarian Imagination: ideas from the Renaissance to the Regency*. London, Thames and Hudson.

Pottle, F.A. and Bennett, C.H. 1936. *Boswell's Journal of a Tour to the Hebrides with Samuel Johnson LL.D., now first published from the Original Manuscript*. London, William Heinemann.

Reinecke, P. 1963. *Mainzer Aufsätze zur Chronologie der Bronze- und Eisenzeit*. Bonn, Habelt (reprint of papers 1903–9).

Roessler, C. 1908. *L'Art Celtique avant et après Colomban*. Paris, Librairie Charles Foulard.

Smiles, S. 1994. *The Image of Antiquity: Ancient Britain and the Romantic imagination*. New Haven, Yale University Press.

Stead, I.M. 1985. *The Battersea Shield*. London, British Museum.

Stead, I.M. and Rigby, V. 1999. *Iron Age Antiquities from Champagne: the Morel collection*. London, British Museum.

Stukeley, W. 1740. *Stonehenge: a temple restored to the British Druids*. London.

Stukeley, W. 1743. *Abury: a temple of the British Druids*. London.

Thomsen, C. 1837. *Leitfaden zur nordischen Altertumskunde*. Copenhagen.

Tischler, O. 1885. Ueber Gliederung der La-Tène-Periode und über der Dekorierung der Eisenwaffen in dieser Zeit. *Correspondenz-Blatt der Deutschen Gesellschaft für Anthropologie, Ethnologie und Urgeschichte* 14, 157–61, 172.

Wilde, W.R. 1861. *A Descriptive Catalogue of the Antiquities of Animal Materials and Bronze in the Museum of the Royal Irish Academy*. Dublin, Hodges, Smith and Co.

Wilson, D.M. 1984. *The Forgotten Collector: Augustus Wollaston Franks of the British Museum*. London, Thames and Hudson.

6 Locating the Celts

There has not been much discussion of the purely literary evidence for the expansion of the Celts in recent years, so the main discussions still tend to be those of the late nineteenth and early twentieth centuries, e.g. d'Arbois de Jubainville (1875, 1902, 1903) and Bertrand (1889). Vitali and Kaenel (2000) discuss the recent find from Mantua. The problems with Herodotus' text and the location of *Pyrene* are dealt with by Fischer (1972) and Hind (1972). The Celtic languages in Spain are discussed by de Hoz (1990, 1996), Gorrochateui (2002), and Vilar (2002), and those in Italy by Prosdocimi (1991). Lambert (1995) provides the major overview of the finds from France, and Py (1993) an overview of the linguistic complexity of the south of France.

Arenas Esteban, J.A. and Palacios Tamayo, V. (eds) 1999. *El Origen del Mundo Celtibérico: actos de los encuentros sobre el origen del mundo Celtibérico, Molina de Aragón, 1–3 de octubre de 1998.* Molina de Aragón, Ayuntamiento de Molina de Aragón.

Bertrand, A. 1889. *Archéologie Celtique et Gauloise: mémoires et documents relatifs au premiers temps de notre histoire nationale.* Paris, Ernest Leroux.

Chapman, M. 1992. *The Celts: the construction of a myth.* Basingstoke, Macmillan Press.

Cunliffe, B.W. 1997. *The Ancient Celts.* Oxford, Oxford University Press.

Dannheimer, H. and Gebhard, R. (eds) 1993. *Das keltische Jahrtausend.* Mainz am Rhein, Philipp von Zabern.

d'Arbois de Jubainville, H. 1875. 'Les Celtes, les Galates, les Gaulois', *Revue Archéologique* 2, 4.

d'Arbois de Jubainville, H. 1902. *Principaux Auteurs à consulter pour l'histoire des Celtes.* Cours de Littérature Celtique 12.

d'Arbois de Jubainville, H. 1903. 'Conquéte par les Gaulois de la région située entre le Rhin et l'Atlantique', *Revue Celtique* 1903, 162.

de Hoz, J. 1990. 'Las lenguas célticas peninsulares' in J.A. García Castro (ed.) 1990. *Los Celtas en la Peninsula Iberica.* Revista de Arqueología, pp.36–41.

de Hoz, J. 1996. 'Las lenguas célticas de la Antigüedad en su contexto etnohistorico' in Unión Cultural Arqueólogica *Celtas y Celtíberos; realidad o leyenda. Actas de las jornadas celebradas en la Universidad Complutense de Madrid del 27 febrero al 8 de marzo de 1996.* Madrid, Unión Cultural Archeólogica 52–63.

Duval, P.-M. 1977. *Les Celtes.* Paris, Gallimard.

Fischer, F. 1972. 'Die Kelten bei Herodot: Bermerkingen zu einigen geographischen and ethnographischen Problemen', *Madrider Mitteilungen* 13, 109–24.

García Castro, J.A. (ed.) 1990. *Los Celtas en la Peninsula Iberica.* Revista de Arqueología.

Gómez Fraile, J.M. 1999. 'La geographía de Estrabón y el origen de los Celtíberos' in J.A. Arenas Esteban and V. Palacios Tamayo (eds) 1999, 55–67.

Gorrochateui, J. 2002. 'La lengua celtibérica' in Diputación Provincial de Ávila, 2002. *Celtas y Vettones.* Ávila, Excma. Diputación Provincial de Ávila, pp.201–7.

Haywood, J. 2001. *The Historical Atlas of the Celtic World.* London, Thames and Hudson.

Hind, J. 1972. 'Pyrene and the date of the Massiliot sailing manual', *Rivista Storica dell' Antichità* 2, 39–52.

James, S. 1993. *Exploring the World of the Celts.* London, Thames and Hudson.

Lambert, P.-Y. 1995. *La Langue Gauloise.* Paris, Editions Errance.

Megaw, R. and V. 1989. *Celtic Art, from its Beginnings to the Book of Kells.* London, Thames and Hudson.

Moreau, J. 1958. *Die Welt der Kelten. Grosse Kulturen der Frühzeit.* Stuttgart, J.G. Cotta'sche Buchhandlung Nachfolger.

Müller, C. and Müller, T. 1885. *Fragmenta Historicorum Graecorum I.* Paris, Firmin Didot.

Pare, C. 1991. '*Fürstensitze,* Celts and the Mediterranean world: developments in the West Hallstatt Culture in the 6th and 5th centuries B.C.', *Proceedings of the Prehistoric Society* 52(2), 183–202.

Pauli, L. (ed.) 1980. *Die Kelten in Mitteleuropa: Kultur, Kunst, Wirtschaft.* Salzburger Landesaustellung 1 Mai – 30 Sept. 1980 im Keltenmuseum Hallein, Österreich.

Powell, T.G.E. 1958. *The Celts.* London, Thames and Hudson.

Prosdocimi, A. 1991. 'The language and early writing of the Celts' in V. Kruta, O.H. Frey, B. Raftery and M. Szabó, (eds) 1991. *The Celts.* London, Thames and Hudson, pp.51–60.

Py, M. 1993. *Les Gaulois du Midi.* Paris, Hachette.

Raftery, B. 1994. *Pagan Celtic Ireland: the enigma of the Irish Iron Age.* London, Thames and Hudson.

Renfrew, A.C. 1991. *Archaeology and Language: the puzzle of Indo-European origins.* Harmondsworth, Penguin Books.

Stead, I.M. 1991. 'Somme-Bionne' in V. Kruta, O.H. Frey, B. Raftery and M. Szabó, (eds) 1991. *The Celts.* London, Thames and Hudson, pp.174–5.

Unión Cultural Arqueólogica 1996. *Celtas y Celtíberos; realidad o leyenda. Actas de las jornadas celebradas en la Universidad Complutense de Madrid del 27 febrero al 8 de marzo de 1996.* Madrid, Unión Cultural Arqueólogica.

Vilar, F. 2002. 'La lengua de los Celtas y los otros pueblos indoeuropeanos de la Península Ibérica' in Diputación Provincial de Ávila, 2002. *Celtas y Vettones.* Ávila, Excma. Diputación Provincial de Ávila, pp.114–21.

Vitali, D. and Kaenel, G. 2000. 'Un Helvète chez les Etrusques vers 300 av. J.-C.', *Archäologie der Schweiz* 23/3, 115–22.

7 The nature of the archaeological sources

My book *The European Iron Age* (1984), though a bit dated, is probably still the most accessible and comprehensive introduction to the period. Kristiansen (1998) and Cunliffe (1997) provide more recent details. Morris (1987) discusses the difficulties of interpreting the presence (and absence) of burials in a Greek context, with ideas applicable to the rest of Europe. Torbrügge (1971), Bradley (1990) and Bonnamour (2000a, 2000b) deal with river finds. Settlement sites are discussed in Audouze and Buchsenschutz (1991). The debate in Iron Age studies in Britain is covered in the articles by Hawkes (1931, 1958), Hodson (1960, 1962, 1964), and Cunliffe (1991), and Collis (1994) considers the history of Iron Age studies in Britain in the late twentieth century. Though there are several good studies in the Post-Processual paradigm in the Iron Age, there is no general review of the new theoretical approaches as it impinges on the Iron Age; Johnson (1999) provides a good general overview of recent developments, though his review of the 'New Archaeology' does not cover the full range of developments.

Audouze, F. and Buchsenschutz, O. 1991. *Town, Villages and Countryside of Celtic Europe.* London, Batsford.

Bradley, R. 1990. *The Passage of Arms: an archaeological analysis of prehistoric hoards and votive deposits.* Cambridge.

Bonnamour, L. 2000a. *Archéologie de la Saône: le fleuve gardien de la mémoire.* Paris, Errance.

Bonnamour, L. (ed.) 2000b. *Archéologie des fleuves et des rivières.* Paris, Errance.

Childe, V.G. 1929. *The Danube in Prehistory.* Oxford, Clarendon Press.

Clarke, D.L. 1968. *Analytical Archaeology.* London, Methuen.

Collis, J.R. 1977a. 'An approach to the Iron Age' in J.R. Collis (ed.) *The Iron Age in Britain: a review.* Sheffield, Dept of Prehistory and Archaeology, 1977, 1–7.

Collis, J.R. 1977b. 'The proper study of Mankind is pots' in J.R. Collis (ed.) *The Iron Age in Britain: a review.* Sheffield, Dept of Prehistory and Archaeology, 1977, 29–31.

Collis, J. 1984. *The European Iron Age.* London, Batsford (reprinted 1997, London, Routledge).

Collis, J.R. 1994. 'The Iron Age' in B. Vyner (ed.) *Building on the Past: a celebration of 150 years of the Royal Archaeological Institute.* pp.123–48.

Collis, J.R. 1977. 'Pre-Roman burial rites in north-western Europe' in R.M. Reece (ed.) *Burial in the Roman World.* London, Council for British Archaeology Research Report no. 22, 1–12.

Cunliffe, B.W. 1991. *Iron Age Communities in Britain.* Third edition. London, Routledge and Kegan Paul.

Cunliffe, B.W. 1997. *The Ancient Celts.* Oxford, Oxford University Press.

Evans, J. 1885. *The Coinage of the Ancient Britons.* London.

Déchelette, J. 1914. *Manuel d'Archéologie Préhistorique, Celtique et Gallo-Romaine. II-3: Deuxième Age du Fer ou Époque de La Tène.* Paris, Librairie Alphonse Picard et fils.

Díaz-Andreu, M. 1996. 'Constructing identities through culture: the past in the forging of Europe' in P. Graves-Brown, S. Jones and C. Gamble Cultural Identity and Archaeology. London, Routledge. pp.48-61.

Filip, J. 1956. *Keltové ve střední Evropě.* Prague, Československé Akademie Věd.

Filip, J. 1960. *Keltská Civilizace a její Dedictví* (Revised edition 1963). English translation *Celtic Civilisation and its Heritage* (1962). Prague, Akademia.

Frey, O.H. 1991. 'The formation of the La Tène Culture in the fifth century BC' in V. Kruta, O.-H. Frey, B. Raftery and M. Szabó (eds) *The Celts.* London, Thames and Hudson. pp.127–44.

Giessler, R. and Kraft, G. 1942. 'Untersuchungen zur frühen und älteren Latènezeit am Oberrhein und in der Schweiz', *Bericht der Römisch–Germanischen Kommission* 32, 20–116.

Hawkes, C.F.C. 1931. 'Hillforts', *Antiquity* 5, 60–97.

Hawkes, C.F.C. 1960. 'The ABC of the British Iron Age' in S.S. Frere (ed.) 1960. *Problems of the Iron Age in Southern Britain*. London, Institute of Archaeology, Occasional Papers 11. Reprinted 1977 pp.1–16.

Hodson, F.R. 1960. 'Some reflections on the "ABC" of the British Iron Age', *Antiquity* 34, 138–40.

Hodson, F.R. 1962. 'Some pottery from Eastbourne, the "Marnians" and the pre-Roman Iron Age', *Proceedings of the Prehistoric Society* 28, 140–55.

Hodson, F.R. 1964. 'Cultural groupings within the British pre-Roman Iron Age', *Proceedings of the Prehistoric Society* 30, 99–110.

Hodson, F.R. 1968. *The La Tène Cemetery of Münsingen–Rain*. Acta Bernensia 5.

Hodson, F.R. 1970. 'Cluster analysis and archaeology: some new developments and applications', *World Archaeology* 1, no.3, 299–320.

Jimeno Martínez, A. 2002. 'Numancia' in Diputación Provincial de Ávila, 2002, *Celtas y Vettones*, pp.238–47.

Johnson, M. 1999. *Archaeological Theory: an introduction*. Oxford, Blackwell.

Kossinna, G. 1911. 'Zur Herkunft der Germanen. Zur Methode der Siedlungsarchäologie', *Mannus–Bibliothek* 6.

Kristiansen, K. 1998. *Europe before History: the European World in the 1st and 2nd millennium BC*. Cambridge, Cambridge University Press.

Moberg, C.A. 1950. 'When did Late La Tène begin?', *Acta Archaeologia* 21, 83–136.

Morris, I. 1987. *Burial and Ancient Society: the rise of the Greek city-state*. Cambridge, Cambridge University Press.

Rybová A. and Soudský, B. 1962. *Libenice: Keltská svatnevěstředních čechách*. Prague, československé Akademie Věd.

Spindler, K. 1976. *Magdalenenberg IV: der hallstattzeitliche Fürstengrabhügel bei Villingen*. Villingen-Schwenningen, Neckar Verlag. Graves 83-127.

Torbrügge, W. 1971. 'Vor- und frühgeschichtliche Flüssfunde', *Bericht der Römisch–Germanischen Kommission* 51–2, 1–146.

Wahle, E. 1941. 'Zur ethnischen Deutung frühgeschichtlicher Kulturprovinzen; Grenzen der frühgeschichtliche Erkenntnis I', *Sitzungberichte der Heidelberger Akademie der Wissenschaften*. Philosophisch–historische Klasse, Jahrgang 1940/1941, 2 Abhandlung, pp.5–147.

Worsaae, J. 1859/2002. 'Concerning a new division of the Stone and Bronze Ages' translated, and reprinted in A. Fischer and K. Kristiansen (eds) 2002. *The Neolithisation of Denmark: 150 years of debate*. Sheffield, J.R. Collis Publications. pp.47–56.

Wyss, R. 1974. 'Grabrite, Opferplätze und weitere Belege zur geistigen Kultur der Latènezeit' in W. Drack (ed.) *Ur- und Frühgeschichtliche Archäologie der Schweiz*, Band IV, *Die Eisenzeit*, Basel, pp.167–96.

8 The archaeology of the Celts

Many of the sites and areas described here are dealt with in Kruta *et al.* 1991, and there are useful papers in Charpy 1995. There is extensive literature on the Hunsrück-Eifel, especially the metalwork, but Diepeveen-Jansen provides the most recent overview of the richer burials. Krause (1991) discusses burial rites, and Nicholson (1989) ceramic production; the Waldalgesheim burial has recently been published as a monograph by Joachim (1995). Diepeveen-Jansen also provides an overview of the Marne area, and Demoule (1999) a monograph on the chronology of the burials; the site of Acy-Romance is partly published in the volumes by Lambot *et al.* (1992, 1994), but there are updates on this and other finds in Méniel and Lambot (2002). The various chronologies for Baden-Württemberg are developed in Zürn (1970), Pauli (1972) and Gersbach (1976, 19), and reviewed sceptically in Collis (1986), but they are still causing confusion in the specialist literature. The most recent study of Bourges is by Buchsenschutz and Ralston (2001), and of the Auvergne by Jones (2001), though the most recent large-scale excavations will be covered in the proceedings of the AFEAF conference of 2003. The best synthesis of southern France in the Iron Age is provided by Py (1993) and recent work on the Celtiberians is to be found in Lorrio (1997), and in more summary form in Arenas Esteban and Palacios Tamayo (1999) and Diputación Provincial de Ávila (2002). For Hungary, results on some recent work can be found in Guillaumet (2000).

Arenas Esteban, J.A. and Palacios Tamayo, V. (eds) 1999. *El Origen del Mundo Celtibérico: actos de los encuentros sobre el origen del mundo Celtibérico, Molina de Aragón, 1–3 de octubre de 1998*. Molina de Aragón, Ayuntamiento de Molina de Aragón.

Charpy, J.-J. (ed.) 1995. *L'Europe celtique du Vᵉ au IIIᵉ siècle avant J.-C.: contacts, échanges et movements de populations*. Sceaux, Kronos B.Y Editions.

Collis, J. 1986. 'Adieu Hallstatt! Adieu La Tène!' in A. Duval and J. Gomez de Soto (eds) 1986. *Actes du VIIIe Colloque sur les Ages du Fer en France non-Mediterranéenne, Angoulême, 1984*. Aquitania, Supplément 1, 327–30.

Gersbach, E. 1976. 'Das Osttor (Donautor) der Heuneburg bei Hundersingen (Donau)', *Germania* 54, 17–42.

Guichard, V. 1986. 'L'occupation protohistorique du Châtelard de Lijay (Loire)', *Cahiers Archéologique de la Loire* 6, 19–45.

Demoule, J.-P. 1999. *Chronologie et société dans les necropolis celtiques de la culture Aisne-Marne, du VIe au IVe siècle avant J.-C*. Amiens, Revue Archéologique de Picardie.

Diepeveen-Jansen, M. 2001. *People, Ideas and Goods: new perspectives on the 'Celtic Barbarians' in western and Central Europe (500-250 BC)*. Amsterdam Archaeological Studies 7, Amsterdam University Press.

Diputación Provincial de Ávila, 2002. *Celtas y Vettones*. Ávila, Excma. Diputación Provincial de Ávila.

Filip, J. 1956. *Keltové ve střední Evropě*. Československé Akademie Věd.

Filip, J. 1960. *Keltská Civilizace a její Dedictví*. (Revised edition 1963). English translation *Celtic Civilisation and its Heritage* (1962). Prague, Akademia.

Gerdsen, H. 1986. *Studien zu den Schwertgräbern der älteren Hallstattzeit*. Mainz, Philipp von Zabern.

Guillaumet, J.-P. (ed.) 2000. *Dix ans de coopération franco-hongroise en archéologie 1988–1998*. Budapest, Collegium Budapest.

Hodson F.R. 1964. 'Cultural groupings within the British pre-Roman Iron Age', *Proceedings of the Prehistoric Society* 30, 99–110.

Joachim, H.E. 1995. *Waldalgesheim: das Grab einer keltische Fürstin*. Bonn, Rheinsches Landesmuseum.

Jones, S.D. 2001. *Deconstructing the Celts: a skeptic's guide to the archaeology of the Auvergne*. Oxford, BAR International Series 965.

Kaul, F. 1991. 'The Dejbjerg carts' in V. Kruta *et al*. (ed.) 1991, 536–7.

Kimmig, W. 1965. 'Review of A. Rybová and B. Soudský (1962), Libenice: keltská svatněve středních čechách', *Germania* 43, 172–84.

Krause, E.B. 1991. 'Brandgräber type Laufeld' in A. Haffner and A. Miron (eds) *Studien zur Eisenziet in Hunsrück-Nahe-Gebiet*. Treier Zeitschrift, Beiheft 13, 35–52.

Kruta, V., Frey, O.H., Raftery, B. and Szabó, M. (eds) 1991. *The Celts*. London, Thames and Hudson.

Lambot, B. and Méniel, P. 1992. *Le site protohistorique d'Acy-Romance (Ardennes). I: L'habitat gauloise, 1988–1990*. Mémoire de la Société Archéologique Champenoise 7.

Lambot, B., Friboulet, M. and Méniel, P. 1994. *Le site protohistorique d'Acy-Romance (Ardennes). I: Les nécropoles dans leur contexte régional (Thugny-Trugny et tombes aristocratiques, 1986-1988–1989*. Mémoire de la Société Archéologique Champenoise 8.

Lorrio, A.J. 1997. *Los Celtíberos*. Alicante, Universidad de Alicante/Universidad Complutense de Madrid.

Méniel, P. and Lambot, B. 2002. *Découvertes récentes de l'âge du Fer dans les massifs des Ardennes et ses marges. Repas des vivants pour les morts en Gaule*. Reims, Mémoire de la Société Champenoise, No. 16, Supplément au Bulletin, no. 1.

Metzger, R. and Gleischer, P. (eds) 1992. *Die Räter; I Reti*. Bolzano, Casa Editrice Athesia.

THE CELTS: ORIGINS, MYTHS & INVENTIONS

Nicholson, P.T. 1989. *Iron Age Pottery Production in the Hunsrück–Eifel–Kultur of Germany: a World–System perspective.* Oxford, British Archaeological Reports S501.

Pauli, L 1972. *Untersuchungen zur Späthallstattkultur in Nordwürttemberg: Analyse eines Kleinraums im Grenzbereich zweier Kulturen.* Hamburger Beiträge 2.

Py, M. 1993. *Les Gaulois du Midi.* Paris, Hachette.

Raftery, B. 1994. *Pagan Celtic Ireland: the enigma of the Irish Iron Age.* London, Thames and Hudson.

Rieckhoff, S. 1995. *Süddeutschland im Spannungsfeld von Kelten, Germanen und Römern: Studien zur Chronologie det Spätlaténezeit im südlichen Mitteleuropa.* Trier, Rheinisches Landesmuseum.

Rieckhoff, S. and Biel. J. 2001. *Die Kelten in Deutschland.* Stuttgart: Theiss.

Szabó, M. 1971. *Auf den Spuren der Kelten in Ungarn.* Budapest, Corvina.

Szabó, M. 1992. Les Celtes de l'Est: le second âge du Fer dans la cuvette des Karpates. Paris, Errance.

Unión Cultural Arqueólogica, 1996. *Celtas y Celtíberos; realidad o leyenda. Actas de las jornadas celebradas en la Universidad Complutense de Madrid del 27 febrero al 8 de marzo de 1996.* Madrid, Unión Cultural Arqueólogica.

Zürn, H. 1970. *Hallstattforschungen in Nordwürttemberg,* Veröffentlichungen des staatliche Amtes für Denkmalpflege, Reihe A.H. 16.

9 The Celts and politics

General books on nationalism and ethnicity are those by Anderson (1983) and by Hobsbawn and Ranger (1983). The use of archaeology in this context has been explored by Jones (1997) and in the essays in Atkinson *et al.* (1996) and Graves-Brown *et al.* (1995). Studies of ethnicity and Celtism include Chapman (1993) (though I disagree with his basic premise that Celt was a word imposed from outside), James (1997), Megaw and Megaw (1995) and Morse (1997). Snyder (2003) looks at the Britons, including the evidence for colonisation in the fifth century AD along the Atlantic coast, and Giot *et al.* (2003) look in detail at Brittany. Chapman also discusses the reasons for the demise of Gaelic as a primary spoken language, and the *bata scóir* and its use is described by Ó Súilleabháin (1940), though only part of the text is in English, showing the policy was not completely successful! Dumville (1983) deals with the *armes prydein*. France in the late eighteenth and early nineteenth century is discussed by Jourdan (1996) and by Rigney (1996), and more recent times by Ilett (1996) and by Olivier (1997, 1998). In Spain, the traditional approaches are represented especially by the younger Almagro (Gorbea), including the exhibition held in Ávila in 2002 (Diputación Provincial de Ávila, 2002), whereas Ruiz Zapatero puts forward a more radical approach similar to that presented in this book. The English version of the volume which accompanied the Venice exhibition was edited by Kruta *et al.* (1991).

Anderson, B. 1983. *Imagined Communities: reflections on the origin and spread of nationalism.* London, Verso Editions and NLB.

Atkinson, J.A., Banks, I. and O'Sullivan, J. (eds) 1996 *Nationalism and Archaeology.* Glasgow, Cruithne Press.

Chapman, M. 1992. *The Celts: the construction of a myth.* Basingstoke, Macmillan Press.

Dumville, D.N. 1983. 'Brittany and the *Armes Prydein Vawr'*. *Etudes Celtiques* 20, 145–89.

Fleury-Ilett, B. 1995. 'The identity of France: archetypes in Iron Age Studies' in P. Graves Brown, S. Jones, and C. Gamble (eds) *Cultural Identity and Archaeology: the construction of European communities.* London, Routledge, pp.197–208.

Giot, P.-R., Guignon, P. and Merdrignac, B. 2003. *The British Settlement of Brittany: the first Bretons in Armorica.* Stroud, Tempus Publishing.

Graves Brown, P., Jones, S. and Gamble, C. (eds) 1995. *Cultural Identity and Archaeology: the construction of European communities.* London, Routledge.

Hobsbawn, E.J. and Ranger, T. (eds) 1983. *The Invention of Tradition.* Cambridge, Cambridge University Press.

James, S. 1999. Th*e Atlantic Celts.* London, British Museum Press.

Jones, S. 1997. *The Archaeology of Ethnicity: constructing identities in the past and present*. London, Routledge.

Jourdan, A. 1996. 'The image of Gaul during the French Revolution; between Charlemagne and Ossian' in T. Brown (ed.) 1996. *Celtism*. Amsterdam and Atlanta, Studia Imagologica, pp.183–206.

Kruta, V., Frey, O.H., Raftery, B. and Szabó, M. (eds) 1991. *The Celts*. London, Thames and Hudson.

Megaw, R. and V. 1995. 'The Prehistoric Celts: identity and contextuality' in M. Kuna and N. Venclová (eds) 1995 *Whither Archaeology? Papers in Honour of Ev̌en Neustupný* . Prague, Institute of Archaeology, pp.230–45.

Megaw, R. and V. 1996. 'Ancient Celts and modern ethnicity', *Antiquity* 70, 175–81.

Morse, M.A. 1997. 'What's in a name? The "Celts" in presentations of Prehistory in Ireland, Scotland and Wales', *Journal of European Archaeology* 305–28.

Olivier, L. 1997. 'Bibracte ou l'invention des origines nationales', *Journal of European Archaeology* 5 no. 2, 173–88.

Olivier, L. 1998. 'L'archéologie française et le régime de Vichy (1940–1944)', *European Journal of Archaeology* 1 no. 2, 241–64.

Ó Súilleabháin, S. 1940. '*Bata scóir*' in J. Ryan (ed.) *Féil–sgíbhinn Eóin Mic Néill, Essays and Studies presented to Professor Eoin MacNeill*. Dublin, Three Candles. pp.551–66.

Rigney, A. 1996. 'Immemorial routines: the Celts and their resistance to history' in T. Brown (ed.) 1996. *Celtism*. Amsterdam and Atlanta, Studia Imagologica, pp.159–81.

Ruiz Zapatero, G. 1995. 'Celts and Iberians: ideological manipulation in Spanish archaeology' in P. Graves Brown, S. Jones, and C. Gamble (eds) *Cultural Identity and Archaeology: the construction of European communities*. London, Routledge, pp.179–96.

Snyder, C.A. 2003. *The Britons*. Oxford, Blackwell Publishing.

Steyr, 1980. *Die Hallstattkultur: Frühform europäischer Einheit*. Schloss Lamberg, Steyr, Exhibition Catalogue.

10 Present controversies

The recent books on Indo-European languages are Lehmann (1993), Mallory (1989) and Renfrew (1987/1991); Greller (1998) takes a sceptical view of recent attempts to link archaeology and linguistics. Critiques of reconstructions of 'Celtic Society' are given by Collis (1994) and Webster (1996). The seminal study of La Tène Art is that by Paul Jacobsthal (1944) in which he demonstrates the process of 'orientalising' and defines the major developments of 'Early', 'Waldalgesheim', 'Plastic' and 'Sword' styles. In addition to the books by Miranda Green listed in the notes to the Introduction, the most useful on recent finds, especially from France, is Haffner (1995), with many illustrations; Webster (1995a, 1995b) gives a rather different view of Celtic religion. Hjortspring is discussed by Randsborg (1995), and the classic studies of Situla Art are by Lucke and Frey (1962) and Frey (1969). Bodmer (1992) gives the standard approach to genetics by a geneticist, but Evison (1997, 2000) gives a more considered approach; Barham *et al.* (1999) discuss the case of 'Cheddar Man'.

Barham, L., Priestley, P. and Targett, A. 1999. *In Search of Cheddar Man*. Stroud, Tempus Publishing.

Binford, L.R. 1962. 'Archaeology as anthropology', *American Antiquity* 11, 217–25.

Bodmer, W.F. 1992. 'The genetics of Celtic populations', *Proceedings of the British Academy* 82, 37–57.

Childe, V.G. 1926. *The Aryans: a study of Indo-European origins*. London, Kegan Paul.

Collis, J.R. 1994. 'Reconstructing Iron Age Society' in K. Kristiansen and J. Jørgensen (eds) *Europe in the First Millennium B.C.* 1994, 31–9. Sheffield, J.R. Collis Publications.

Evison, M. 1997. 'Lo, the conquering hero comes (or not)', *British Archaeology* 23, April 1997, 8–9.

Evison, M. 2000. 'All in the Genes? Evaluating the biological evidence of contact and migration' in D.M. Hadley and J.D. Richards (eds) *Cultures in Contact: Scandinavian settlement in England in the ninth and tenth centuries*. Turnhout, Brepols, pp.275–94.

Frey, O.-H. 1969. *Die Enstehung der Situlenkunst: Studien zur figürlich verzierten Toreutik von Este.* Römisch-Germanishe Forschungen 31. Berlin, Verlag Walter de Gruyter.

Fried, M.H. 1967. *The Evolution of Political Society.* New York, Random House.

Greller, W. 1998. 'Getting the record straight: archaeology and language', *European Journal of Archaeology* 1 no. 2, 273–81.

Haffner, A. (ed.) 1995. *Heiligtümer und Opferkulte der Kelten.* Stuttgart, Theiss.

Jacobsthal, P. 1944. *Early Celtic Art.* Oxford, Oxford University Press.

Kromer, K. (ed.) 1962. *Situlenkunst zwischen Po und Donau: Verzierten Bronzearbeiten aus dem ersten Jahrtausend v. Chr. Austellung in Wien 1962.* Vienna, Naturhistorischen Musuem.

Lehmann, W.P. 1993. *Theoretical Bases of Indo-European Linguistics.* London & New York, Routledge.

Lucke, W. and Frey, O.-H. 1962. *Die Situla in Providence (Rhode Island): ein Beitrag zur Situlenkunst des Osthallstattkreises.* Römisch-Germanishe Forschungen 26. Berlin, Verlag Walter de Gruyter.

Mallory, J.P. 1989. *In Search of the Indo-Europeans: language, archaeology and myth.* London, Thames and Hudson.

Périchon, R. 1987. 'L'imagerie celtique d'Aulnat', *Mélanges offerts au Dr. J.-B. Colbert de Beaulieu.* Paris, Le Léopard d'Or, pp.677–95.

Randsborg, K. 1995. *Hjortspring: warfare and sacrifice in early Europe.* Aarhus, Aarhus University Press.

Renfrew, A.C. 1991. *Archaeology and Language: the puzzle of Indo-European origins.* Harmondsworth, Penguin Books (first published by Jonathan Cape in 1987).

Schrader, O. 1890. *Prehistoric Antiquities of the Aryan Peoples: a manual of comparative philology and the earliest cultures.* London, Griffin.

Service, E.R. 1975. *Origins of the State and Civilisation: the Process of Cultural Evolution.* New York, Norton.

Webster, J. 1995a. '*Interpretatio:* Roman word power and the Celtic gods', *Britannia* 26, 153–61.

Webster, J. 1995b. 'Translation and subjection: *interpretatio* and the Celtic gods' in J.D. Hill and C.G. Cumberpatch (eds) *Different Iron Ages: studies on the Iron Age in Temperate Europe.* British Archaeological Reports, International Series 602. Tempus Reperatum, Oxford, pp.175–83.

Webster, J. 1996. 'Ethnographic barbarity: colonial discourse and "Celtic Warrior Societies"' in J. Webster and N. Cooper (eds) *Roman Imperialism: post-colonial perspectives.* Leicester Archaeology Monographs 3. Leicester, pp.111–24.

11 Implications

Chapman (1992) deals specifically with the Celts, though, as I have suggested, his understanding of the classical sources and the early development of concepts of the Celts is limited. I give a separate listing of the recent articles which have been developing the discussion, but a major debate which largely sums the conflict up took place in the pages of *Antiquity*, articles by the Megaws (1996, 1998), Collis (1997), James (1998) and Sims-Williams (1998), though it should be noted that the Megaws do regularly misrepresent the views of their opponents (e.g. 1998, 433 where it is suggested I said the ancient Celts never existed!).

Anderson, B. 1983. *Imagined Communities: reflections on the origin and spread of nationalism.* London, Verso Editions and NLB.

Atkinson, J.A., Banks, I. and O'Sullivan, J. (eds) 1996. *Nationalism and Archaeology.* Glasgow, Cruithne Press.

Chapman, M. 1992. *The Celts: the construction of a myth.* Basingstoke, Macmillan Press.

Cunliffe, B.W. 1997. *The Ancient Celts.* Oxford, Oxford University Press.

Graves Brown, P., Jones, S. and Gamble, C. (eds) 1995. *Cultural Identity and Archaeology: the construction of European communities.* London, Routledge.

Hobsbawn, E.J. and Ranger, T. (eds) 1983. *The Invention of Tradition.* Cambridge, Cambridge University Press.

Jones, S. 1997. *The Archaeology of Ethnicity: constructing identities in the past and present.* London, Routledge.

Kristiansen, K. 1992. '"The strength of the past and its great might": an essay on the use of the past', *Journal of European Archaeology* 1, 3–32.

MacNeill, E. 1913–14. 'The re-discovery of the Celts', *The Irish Review* 522–32.

Recent articles and books dealing with the debate on Celticity

Carr, G. and Stoddart, S. (eds) 2002. *Celts from Antiquity.* Antiquity Papers 2. Cambridge, Antiquity Publications.

Champion, T. 1996. 'The Celt in Archaeology' in T. Brown (ed.) *Celtism,* 1996, 61–78. Amsterdam and Atlanta, Studia Imagologica.

Collis, J.R. 1985. 'Review of B. Cunliffe 1984 (Danebury excavations)', *Proceedings of the Prehistoric Society* 51, 348–9.

Collis, J.R. 1986. 'Adieu Hallstatt! Adieu La Tène!' in A. Duval and J. Gomez de Soto (eds) *Actes du VIIIe Colloque sur les Ages du Fer en France non-Mediterranéenne, Angoulême, 1984,* 1986, 327–30. Aquitania, Supplément 1.

Collis, J.R. 1994. 'Reconstructing Iron Age Society' in K. Kristiansen and J. Jørgensen (eds) *Europe in the First Millennium B.C.* 1994, 31–9. Sheffield, J.R. Collis Publications

Collis, J.R. 1993. 'Los Celtas en Europa' in M. Almagro-Gorbea (ed.) *Los Celtas: Hispania y Europa,* 1993, 63–76. Madrid, Universidad Complutense.

Collis, J.R. 1995. 'Celtes, culture, contacts: confrontation et confusion' in R. Boudet (ed.) *L'Âge du Fer en Europe sud-occidentale,* 1995, 447–56. Actes du XVIe Colloque de l'AFEAF, Agen, 28–31 Mai 1992. *Aquitania,* supplément 7.

Collis, J.R. 1995. 'Celts and politics' in P. Graves Brown, S. Jones and C. Gamble (eds) *Cultural Identity and Archaeology: the construction of European communities,* 1995, 167–78. London, Routledge.

Collis, J.R. 1996. 'The origin and spread of the Celts', *Studia Celtica* 30, 17–34.

Collis, J.R. 1997. 'Celtic Myths', *Antiquity* 71, 195–201.

Collis, J.R. 1999. 'George Buchanan and the Celts of Britain' in R. Black, W. Gillies and R. Ó Maolalaigh (eds) 1999. *Celtic Connections,* Vol. 1. Proceedings of the Tenth International Congress of Celtic Studies, 1999, 91–107. East Linton, Tuckwell Press.

Collis, J. 1999. 'Los Celtas antiguos y modernas' in J.A. Arenas Esteban and V. Palacios Tamayo (eds) *El Origen del Mundo Celtibérico. Actos de los encuentros sobre el origen del mundo Celtibérico, Molina de Aragón, 1–3 de octubre de 1998,* 1999, 13–17. Molina de Aragón, Ayuntamiento de Molina de Aragón.

Collis, J.R. 2000. 'Les tombes à char "Belges"?' in A. Villes and A. Bataille-Melkon (eds) 2000. *Fastes des Celtes entre Champagne et Bourgogne aux VIIe–IIIe Siècles avant notre Ère,* 2000, 411–18. Actes du XIXème Colloque de l'Association Française pour l'Etude de l'Age du Fer, Troyes, mai 1995. Reims, Mémoire de la Société Champenoise, no. 15.

Collis, J. forthcoming. 'D'Amédée Thierry à Joseph Déchelette: hypothèses au XIXe siècle sur l'arrivée des Celtes en Gaule.' Actes du XXIIIème Colloque de l'Association Française pour l'Etude de l'Age du Fer, Nantes, mai 1999.

Dietler, M. 1994. '"Our ancestors the Gauls"': Archaeology, ethnic nationalism, and the manipulation of Celtic identity in modern Europe', *American Anthropologist* 96(3), 584–605.

Evans, D. Ellis 1999. 'Linguistics and Celtic ethnogenesis' in R. Black, W. Gillies and R. Ó Maolalaigh (eds), 1999. *Celtic Connections,* Vol. 1. Proceedings of the Tenth International Congress of Celtic Studies, 1999, 1–18. East Linton, Tuckwell Press.

Fitzpatrick, A.P. 1995. 'Celtic Iron Age Europe: the theoretical basis' in P. Graves Brown, S. Jones and C. Gamble (eds) *Cultural Identity and Archaeology: the construction of European communities,* 1995, 238–53. London, Routledge.

Hill, J.D. 1989. 'Rethinking the Iron Age', *Scottish Archaeological Review* 6, 16–23.

James, S. 1998. 'Celts, politics and motivation in archaeology', *Antiquity* 72, 200–9.

James, S. 1999. *The Atlantic Celts.* London, British Museum Press.

James, S. 1999. 'The tribe that never was', *The Guardian, Saturday review.* Saturday 27 March 1999.

Megaw, R. and V. 1995. 'The Prehistoric Celts: identity and contextuality' in M. Kuna and N. Venclová (eds) *Whither Archaeology? Papers in Honour of Evžen Neustupný*, 1995, 230–45. Prague, Institute of Archaeology.

Megaw, R. and V. 1996. 'Ancient Celts and modern ethnicity', *Antiquity* 70, 175–81.

Megaw, R. and V. 1998. '"The mechanism of (Celtic) dreams": a partial response to our critics', *Antiquity* 70, 432–5.

Megaw, R. and V. 1999. 'Celtic connections past and present' in R. Black, W. Gillies and R. Ó Maolalaigh (eds), 1999. *Celtic Connections*, Vol. 1. Proceedings of the Tenth International Congress of Celtic Studies, 1999, 19–81. East Linton, Tuckwell Press.

Merriman, N. 1987. 'Value and motivation in prehistory: the evidence for "Celtic Spirit"' in I. Hodder (ed.) *The Archaeology of Contextual Meanings,* 1987, 111–16. New Directions in Archaeology, Cambridge, University Press.

Morse, M.A. 1996. 'What's in a name? The "Celts" in presentations of Prehistory in Ireland, Scotland and Wales', *Journal of European Archaeology* 4, 305–28.

Morse, M.A. 1999. 'Craniology and the adoption of the Three-Age System in Britain', *Proceedings of the Prehistoric Society* 65, 1–17.

Piccini, A. 1999. 'Welsh Celts or Celtic Wales? The production and consumption of a (not so) different Iron Age' in W. Bevan, *Northern Exposure: interpretative devolution and the Iron Ages in Britain,* 1999, 51–63. Leicester, Leicester University Press.

Ruiz Zapatero, G. 1990. '¿Quienes eran las Celtas?' in J.A. García Castro (ed.) *Los Celtas en la Peninsula Iberica,* 1990, 6–11 Revista de Arqueología.

Ruiz Zapatero, G. 1993. 'El concepto de Celtas en la prehistoria europea y española' in M. Almagro-Gorbea (ed.) 1993, 23–62. *Los Celtas: Hispania y Europa.* Madrid, Universidad Complutense.

Ruiz Zapatero, G. 1995. 'Celts and Iberians: ideological manipulation in Spanish archaeology' in P. Graves Brown, S. Jones and C. Gamble (eds) *Cultural Identity and Archaeology: the construction of European communities,* 1995, 179–96. London, Routledge.

Ruiz Zapatero, G. 1996. 'La noción de Celtas y su empleo académico y politico' in *Celtas y Celtíberos: realidad o leyenda. Actas de las jornadas celebradas en la Universidad Complutense de Madrid del 27 febrero al 8 de marzo de 1996,* 1996, 23–36. Madrid, Unión Cultural Arqueólogica.

Ruiz Zapatero, G. 2002. '¿Quienes eran las Celtas? Disipando la niebla; mitología de un *collage* histórico' in *Celtas y Vettones* 2002, 23–62. Ávila, Excma. Diputación Provincial de Ávila.

Sims-Williams, P. 1998. 'Celtomania and Celtoscepticism', *Cambrian Medieval Celtic Studies* 36, 1–35.

Sims-Williams, P. 1998. 'Genetics, linguistics and prehistory: thinking big and thinking straight', *Antiquity* 72, 505–27.

Taylor, T. 1991. 'Review of Megaw and Megaw 1989', *Scottish Archaeological Review* 8, 129–32.

Watson-Smith, K. 1999. 'Celts were "really just a Scotch myth"', *The Independent,* Saturday 27 February 1999.

Webster, J. 1995. '*Interpretatio:* Roman word power and the Celtic gods', *Britannia* 26, 153–61.

Webster, J. 1995. 'Translation and subjection: *interpretatio* and the Celtic gods' in J.D. Hill and C.G. Cumberpatch (eds) *Different Iron Ages: studies on the Iron Age in Temperate Europe.* British Archaeological Reports, International Series 602. Tempus Reperatum, Oxford, pp.175–83.

Webster, J. 1996. 'Ethnographic barbarity: colonial discourse and "Celtic Warrior Societies"', in J. Webster and N. Cooper (eds) *Roman Imperialism: post-colonial perspectives.* Leicester Archaeology Monographs 3. Leicester, pp.111–24.

INDEX

Printed in Great Britain
by Amazon

86745483R00147